NO GREATER LOVE

NO GREATER LOVE

Life Stories from the Men
Who Saved Baseball

Todd W. Anton

Jim and Billie—
Thanks for your service!
Todd Anton

ROUNDER BOOKS
Burlington, Massachusetts

Published by Rounder Books

an imprint of
Rounder Records Corp.
One Rounder Way
Burlington, MA 01803

Cover and color insert design by Sara Radawich
Interior design by Jane Tenenbaum

Anton, Todd W., 1964–
No Greater Love
Life Stories from the Men Who Saved Baseball

1. Baseball Players, military history 2. Anton, Todd
First edition
2007924456
796.357'092

ISBN-13: 978-1-57940-144-3
ISBN-10: 1-57940-144-9

Printed in Canada

DAY THE NATIONAL WWII MUSEUM

The National World War II Museum is a national treasure. Founded by the late, renowned historian and author Stephen E. Ambrose and dedicated in 2000 as The National D-Day Museum, the museum has now been honored by the United States Congress with the designation of the country's official World War II Museum.

This remarkable museum illuminates the American experience during the World War II years with moving personal stories, powerful interactive displays and priceless historic artifacts, from massive C-47 aircraft and Higgins boats to the dogtags of fallen heroes. From the Normandy invasion to the sands of Pacific Islands and the Home Front, visitors come to know the American Spirit—the courage, teamwork, optimism and sacrifice—of the men and women who won the war that changed the world. They learn with their minds and their hearts that freedom is not free.

The National W.W. II Museum is dedicated to preserving the history, the lessons and the ideals of World War II, and encouraging the expression of these values by future generations. A visionary expansion is underway to create a six-acre campus of exhibition pavilions and museum experiences telling the entire and profound story of World War II—every service, every campaign, every hero. D-Day was only the beginning as we create a Museum as epic as the war it honors.

I am proud to serve as a Trustee of The National World War II Museum, and hope that you will join with me in supporting the educational mission of this unique and important institution. More than 130,000 members nationwide are helping us pass the torch to future generations. For more information about the museum and how you can help, please visit www.NationalWW2Museum.org or call 1-877-813-3329.

Sincerely,
Todd Anton

Mom and Dad in Yokohama, Japan.

Contents

Acknowledgments

This book is more than a book. It has been a journey. Along the way I have learned that people are decent, helpful, compassionate, and most of all generous. It is proof to me that when we remember the World War II adage: "We are all in this together," great things can happen. Before I list all who have helped, special mentions are in order.

This four-year labor of love could not have happened without the prayerful support of a devoted wife and friend Susan and of my two great kids Jamie and Jason who can tell you everything about the men in this book they have grown to respect and admire. Thank you Sue, Jamie, and Jason for your faith and patience all along this journey. I'll remember your prayers at night when you asked God to "Let daddy's book happen." Well, it did—*finally*!

Thanks to my sister Susan and her husband Jeff Lester and Big Picture Studios; you have been the sounding board of faith, reason, and vision. This would not have happened without you. You not only believed in me, you believed in this story. Somewhere Al Lowman is smiling.

Most importantly, I'd like to thank my co-everything in producing this book, Bill Nowlin and Rounder Books. Bill is my publisher, among many editors, my agent, and my friend. Bill, after my agent Al Lowman died, I turned to you and asked if this is a book Rounder Books would be interested in. You said, "Yes." After the myriad of e-mails, reading, re-reading, and assistance, you and Rounder have shown me the patience of Solomon. Thank you just isn't enough. Also BIG thanks to the editors-reviewers at Rounder Books: Steve Netsky, Terry Kitchen, Brad San Martin, and David Schlichting. Your input and hard work on my behalf is appreciated more than you'll ever know!

My thanks to the best friend in the world, Morgan Reed. Morgan, you have been here from day one, you have been a part of this journey and have understood it. It isn't just the baseball and our endless conversations, writings, etc.... it is your heart. You have the biggest heart of anyone I know. Thanks for making London, Paris, Normandy, Spicheren, and Berlin come true. Go Dodgers!

Thanks to the National World War II Museum (formerly known as the National D-Day Museum) in New Orleans. Not only is this organization the premier WWII museum in the world, it is a family which has welcomed me in and adopted this son of World War II. A special thanks to Dr. Stephen E. Ambrose—you said to write it myself and I did!

Thanks to Hugh Ambrose, Mrs. Stephen E. Ambrose, Dr. Nick Mueller, Governor Pete Wilson, Tom Hanks for your inspirational talk, and my partners on the Board of Trustees at America's premier National World War II Museum.

I could write about everyone who has helped, but that would be longer than the book. However I must mention the support of the following:

Andy Strasberg; Bill Swank, I owe you so very much; The National Baseball Hall of Fame at Cooperstown NY—thanks to Jeff Idelson and John Horne; the Society of American Baseball Research(SABR)—Ted Williams Chapter and Tom Larwin; the San Diego Hall of Champions and Bob Breitbard; the family of Ken Coleman; the family of Bert Shepard; the family of Warren Spahn; Ralph Kiner; Carl Erskine; Fox News Channel's *War Stories with Oliver North* crew—thanks for making my baseball story a TV special; Gail Schultz—for Dutch; Curt Schilling; Katie Leighton; Herb and Beverly Fuhrman; the Los Angeles Dodgers—Vin Scully, Rick Monday, Ross Porter, Mark Langill and Angela Parker; the Los Angeles Angels of Anaheim and Tim Mead, Mickey Hatcher and his wife Patty, Steve Physioc, Rex Hudler, Mike Scioscia, Ron Roenicke; the Detroit Tigers and pitcher Jamie Walker—I remember your dad's service; Julie Harwell; Alan and Holly McKewen; the Eisenhower Center for American Studies—Douglas Brinkley, Kevin Wiley, Michael Edwards; Drs. David and Marti Peck; Debi Whiting; the 70th Infantry Division Association; the 82nd Airborne Association, Stewart Koppel, Jeff Crandall, David Carroll, Wendi and Mario Rodriguez, Dennis Zimmerman; the Tri-Community Kiwanis Club of Phelan and Jim Dauber: thanks, Jim, for Billy

Southworth Jr. and his story; and thanks to my teachers who inspired me to live history rather than read it: Kent Hayden, Dave Braxton of Yucaipa High School, and Dr. Kent Schofield, Dr. Ward MacAfee, and Dr. Robert Blackey of California State University San Bernardino; the Snowline Unified School District and Heritage School; Dr. Art Golden; John Garner; Rick Holtz; David Pearson; Yvonne Barton; Col. and Mrs. Bruce Stewart; Dave and Janet Molina; and most of all my students past, present, and future. May you learn the heritage preserved for you from those have gone on before. I may have been your teacher, but you all taught me something, too. Thanks for that!

—Todd W. Anton
Victorville, California
February 25, 2007

Introduction

The term "Greatest Generation" has been employed time and time again by a host of people to describe the generation of Americans who served, survived, and died during the Second World War. While the term "great" is routinely applied to this generation of men and women, and justifiably so, most writers, historians, and ordinary folks have no true comprehension of *why* this generation was so great.

American author Tom Brokaw and noted World War II historian Stephen E. Ambrose are two among many individuals who have given voice to this "greatest generation" while simultaneously allowing the reader to understand the shared experiences and profound sense of duty and sacrifice that characterizes this generation. Through the magic of their words and dutiful adherence to the facts, authors like Brokaw and Ambrose have made a compelling case to the world for *why* America's World War II generation is the greatest. This book, *No Greater Love*, serves to further validate the claim.

The book you hold in your hands is one of the most extensive and personal accounts you will ever read on what was at stake for America's "greatest generation" and America's pastime, for the Axis Powers not only threatened liberty around the world but our beloved game of baseball at home.

In the late 1930s, Europe and rest of the world held its collective breath as Adolf Hitler's German army steamrolled through Europe. Hitler scoffed at European leaders, and their policy of appeasement, as his mighty army marched into the Sudetenland, Austria, and Czechoslovakia. The world shuddered and gasped as the leaders of Germany and Japan revealed their plans for expansion and domination. The voices in the countries that represented democracy and freedom remained timid, meekly protesting as Hitler's army began an inexorable march through Europe when it invaded an overmatched Poland on September 1, 1939.

Europe's other nations fell before the blitzkrieg as Hitler's forces swathed through opposing armies like grain before the farmer's scythe. France, who at the time was thought to possess one of the world's premier fighting forces, was a mere speed bump on the road to the shores of Dunkirk in 1940. While some of Hitler's forces positioned themselves for the anticipated assault on the Soviet Union in 1941, the rest of the Nazi war machine was preparing to vanquish Europe's one unconquered nation—Great Britain. Britain survived the "Blitz" and gave the world a flicker of hope that democracy could survive.

Then came December 7, 1941. On this day, the shackles of isolation were blown off. On this day, Americans were confronted by the brutal realization that their way of life was now hanging in the balance. The attack on Pearl Harbor served to unite Americans as no event has before or since, including 9/11. The men and women of America began an epic, unifying mobilization as the U.S. prepared to embroil itself in history's biggest war. Among these people were the men whose stories are told through first-hand interviews in this book, men whose common thread is their connection to America's pastime—baseball—and their willingness to shed their major league flannels in order to don the colors of one of the branches of the United States' military.

In the pages of this book, author Todd Anton utilizes his interviews of men who played baseball yet readily and willingly answered the call to arms when their nation faced its greatest threat in order to convey *why* this World War II generation was so great. The men tell their stories; the author is the conduit to you, the reader.

Todd's message resonates with me particularly because his close connection to his own father, a veteran of two wars, mirrors my own relationship with my father. I was raised by a man who proudly served twenty years in the United States Army, and during those years Dad instilled in me a profound sense of appreciation of and respect for the men and women whose core values centered on service to others. I have spent my life in awe of these people who believe in service to others as their ultimate calling. In my mind, no act better embodies that ideal than making the commitment to serve in the armed forces of the United States. These people are the heroes.

"Heroes." "Heroism." I marvel at the casual manner in which these terms are so freely used in the world of sport. During the Red Sox remarkable 2004 American League Championship Series and World Series run, much was made of my "heroic" bloody sock performance, when I pitched on a sutured, damaged ankle for the good of my team. Granted, it took dedication and faith to perform at such a level under such adverse circumstances, but it was, and is, misguided to lionize me as a hero. What I did was not heroic because I was merely playing a game...a game! If you want to see *real* heroes, talk to an American veteran. Or go visit the war-wounded at the Walter Reed Military Hospital. Or talk to a Gold Star Mother. These are the heroes. They have stood up to evil and have sacrificed in the name of humanity and liberty.

The men who played, or aspired to play, major league baseball in these years, but answered their nation's call to arms after Pearl Harbor changed America forever, will always be heroes. Despite having so much to lose, they did not hesitate to volunteer for military service, risking life, limb, and their big league careers for a cause greater than themselves or glory on the diamond. To a man, these ballplayers felt privileged to serve; leaving the ballfield for the battlefield was not a sacrifice.

I have a personal connection with a few of the men in this book. For example, during my stint in the National League, I had the pleasure of meeting Jerry Coleman, a broadcaster for the San Diego Padres and a veteran of both World War II and the Korean War. What first struck me upon meeting Jerry was how much he reminded me of Ted Williams. Neither of these men felt that that their service to their country constituted a sacrifice. No, it was a responsibility, a privilege even, that every American should experience. For the good of the nation and for the liberty of others, men like those you will come to know in the pages that follow will reveal their true greatness not as stars on the diamond but as citizen soldiers who answered the call to serve their nation during its time of greatest peril.

When you read these stories, I hope you gain a greater appreciation for the reasons why I know this to be the greatest country on the face of the Earth. It is a country protected by common citizens, farmers, ballplayers, and yes, even fathers.

—Curt Schilling

NO GREATER LOVE

1

Saving Private Ryan

Son, You Want to Know How the F--- It Was?

Dad answered the phone in his usual singsong way, "Helloooooooo!"

"Hi, Dad," I responded.

"Hey, pal."—his usual reply to me.

"Dad, I went and saw *Saving Private Ryan* tonight."

"What did you think?"

I said, "Dad, you know, I've read all these books, I've seen every movie, I've watched every documentary, I have hundreds of books on World War II in my library at home, even earned a history degree, and all of it was just words and old black and white images. I never felt the emotion of what you went through in the war until now. I'm sorry." I just kept repeating that I was sorry that he had to go through that and several times I said, "I just didn't know...I just didn't know."

Then my dad called me back. "I tell you what. Why don't you and your brother Brent and me go see *Saving Private Ryan* together tomorrow?"

"Absolutely!"

The following day, Dad, Brent, and I went to the Kirkorian Theater in Redlands, California and saw *Saving Private Ryan* together. I remember everything about it. Brent was on my dad's right, and I was on Dad's left. As soon as the movie started, he draped an arm around each of our shoulders—they stayed there during the entire movie. I mean, he held us tight, and he would not let go; he wasn't crying, but he was holding us very tightly. After the movie, we walked out of the theater. Dad and I got in my car. I was going to drive him home. Brent went home in his truck. As I started to back out of the parking space, I started talking to Dad about the movie, and he began to cry. With tears trickling down his face and his voice quivering Dad stridently said, "Son, do you want to know how the f--- it was? That's how the

f--- it was! You know, at the beginning of the movie, that's how it was."
I stopped the car and pulled back into the spot and listened. I never
had heard my dad use the f-word before. I was stunned. Also, I knew
when he called me "Son" he was making a point. Usually he called
me "Pal."

Dad was plagued by the same survivor's guilt displayed by Private
Ryan when he asked his wife to confirm that his life had meaning,
that he had earned the right to survive. Dad felt the weight of this burden too... to the day he died, Dad could not bring himself to watch
that scene ever again. Watching that scene brought up those self-
imposed inadequacies, those feelings that the life he had lived did not
equal the price paid by those who had died.

2

Dreams or Excuses

Tom Hanks the Teacher

Two white shuttle vans pulled up to the curb in front of the Joe Wo-
mack Auditorium. It was a brisk autumn evening in the southern California high desert town of Phelan. On the surface, these buses looked
like the typical shuttle vans you might see at any airport. The difference was in the passengers they conveyed; they were neither tourists
nor travelers. They were war veterans. The residents of Barstow Veterans Home had arrived for dinner, and these men were among the
honored guests. This Veterans Day dinner drew 400 people from
more than a dozen towns scattered around Phelan.

Meeting the vans at the curb were four or five sharply dressed
students from the Heritage School, which is located in Phelan. The
Heritage School has a student population of 500 from kindergarten
through eighth grade. These kids were anxious, nervous, not knowing
what to expect, but all waiting for their moment to serve. As the doors
of the bus abruptly opened with a hydraulic "whoosh," some veterans
emerged, walking on their own while wearing their Veterans of Foreign Wars "overseas" caps, or their black baseball caps displaying their
divisional patch. These were the men able to walk on their own,
though some used canes and some used walkers.

You could hear the clink of their medals hanging from their shirt
pockets. Many other men remained inside the bus, waiting in turn to
be positioned in their wheelchairs and lowered out the back of the bus
on the hydraulic lift, then pushed into the school cafeteria for the meal
in their honor. Many of these men were missing legs, arms, their
hearing, or their eyesight.

These were by no means just older World War II veterans, the kind
of men ravaged by time, slowed by age. Although W.W. II veterans
were well represented among those being honored, many of the men

who arrived on the shuttles were relatively young. Some men were in their 50s or their 60s, and there were men in their 40s. The students welcoming these guests flashed many smiles full of braces, and offered eyes full of hope and innocence.

It was Veterans Day 1997.

It is human nature to notice something different, and some of the students understandably fixed their eyes on the disabilities that war had dealt these men. Many tried to avert their gaze, thinking it impolite. But they had to look. Of course, the veterans noticed—but they were used to it. After an awkward, uncomfortable pause—just a few seconds—these young middle school kids descended upon their guests, engaging them with a passion and humility that brought tears to the eyes of many men who believed they had been forgotten, cast aside or ignored. At this moment, it struck me that my students were going to learn a great lesson. It was the lesson about the price of one of the greatest of all gifts—freedom—and these kids were meeting those who had helped pass on that gift to them. This was the best history lesson they were ever going to get. I should know, I had learned the same lesson.

I am their teacher. This dinner was my idea. There was more than a dinner planned. A history lesson was at work. I had more than one goal in mind. The kids call me Mr. A, but usually I'm known as Todd Anton or Mr. Anton. Sometimes I get called other names, but that is part of the profession.

These veterans are my heroes and at this veterans dinner in 1997, a pageant of history was unfolding around me, and also for a student of mine, a 13-year-old girl named Jill.

History can be the most tedious of subjects in school, especially if taught with the methods familiar to a lot of adults my age and older. "Read the chapter and answer the questions" is a mantra recited by archaic teachers who have done the discipline a disservice. It's pure book learning, by rote, divorced from any accompanying experience. A two-dimensional teacher offers no way for a student to internalize history, no way to truly feel it, no opportunity to emote, and no way to grasp the past in its full significance. To tangibly feel the presence of the past, one must experience it. I wanted my students to experience history.

If a historian like Stephen Ambrose—my favorite—was able to teach me and involve me in history through his words and examples, I ought to be able to try to do the same by using a similar methodology with my students. While I realized my attempts might be at a more basic and elementary level than Ambrose, I thought, "Why not? Let's give it a shot." This Veterans Dinner was one such attempt.

I clearly remember seeing one particular wheelchair-bound veteran who was obviously a quadriplegic. He had a mouthpiece and could guide his chair by manipulating it, but it soon became clear that he was unable to feed himself. He was from the local veterans home in nearby Barstow, and had a nurse attending to him. I was sitting about 20-30 feet away from this quadriplegic veteran. Was I as uncomfortable as the kids? Yes, I was. I occasionally got up to make sure the kids were doing their jobs, or talking to various veterans. All the while I watched the man in the wheelchair out of the corner of my eye. I stopped to talk to one veteran about the food. Since this was a first-time venture, the menu was...well...basic; we were serving fried chicken, hot dogs, potato chips, and other assorted typical all-American delights. The veteran I was talking with looked up at me and sarcastically remarked, "The Germans didn't get me, but your dinner will." I enjoyed the ribbing dished out by the veterans as I walked around and talked with many of them. I warned them that if they kept it up, I'd give them chipped beef on toast the following year. They quickly changed their kidding to compliments to avoid the threat of this standard Army meal commonly known as SOS—"Shit on a Shingle."

Watching the students and veterans interact, I noticed that none of my students were going over to this gentleman, the quadriplegic, in the wheelchair. His nurse had gotten a plate and was feeding him. I thought to myself, "No, I want one of my kids to do that." The nurse does this all the time, I reasoned. I want my kids to feed him, interact with him, and to experience his sacrifice, even if only vicariously.

I was standing beside my table and looked over at a seventh-grade girl named Jill. She seemed to be looking for something to do. I had Jill follow me over to this veteran and I spoke to his nurse. I asked her if it would be okay for Jill to feed the man his dinner. The nurse said, "Absolutely." I told the nurse to go get herself a plate and take a break. I then stood about 20 feet away as Jill began cutting up the food and feeding him.

He was a portly man; in fact, he kind of resembled Santa Claus with his white beard. Jill, being a teenager, possessed the knack that teenagers have for stating the obvious and yet simultaneously ignoring it. I thought that this might get interesting...and it did! Jill stood back and looked at the man and, as only teenagers do, put her hands on her hips, cocked her head to the side, and asked him, "So dude, how did you get crippled?"

I cringed, thinking to myself, "Oh my God! This guy is going to lose it and cuss her out or something." I began to edge over casually, prepared to intervene, when I heard him reply, "Well, honey, I was a Huey chopper pilot, and I evacuated the wounded out of Vietnam. In fact, I would land on the LZ [landing zone], and I would pick up the wounded and fly out. I was shot down and when we crashed, I was paralyzed. And that was how I was wounded." He continued, "In fact, I was shot down eight times in my time in Vietnam."

Jill stood back, eyed the vet in disbelief, and said, waving her hands "Wait, wait, wait. Dude, you were shot down EIGHT times?"

"Yes," he responded. "Eight times."

She looked at him, shook her head, and blurted out, "You must not have been a very good pilot." I was mortified. Calling this brave man "dude" was bad enough, but I thought, "Oh no! Strike two. I'm totally going to watch this guy lose it." I increased my pace, heading over to intervene before it was too late.

As I approached them, from deep inside of this wheelchair-bound quadriplegic, I heard the thunderclap of one of the most resounding laughs I'd ever heard. He laughed hard for a long time. After her initial surprise, Jill began to laugh with him. Jill didn't have a clue what she had done. Some people would have deemed Jill's behavior and questioning as rude—I know I did—but she didn't seem to notice. It was a teenage "duhhh" moment for her. Only kids can get away with that one!

The man continued to laugh so loud and so hard, as if he would never stop. The nurse came over to me, grabbed my arm, planted a kiss on my cheek, and said, "Todd, in my 10 years of working with him, I have never heard him laugh." This demonstrates the power of kids, and their ability to heal and to do great things. Jill had made a man laugh who hadn't laughed in nearly a decade...and all this by making a seemingly impolite remark.

As the dinner was winding down, I was wiping down tables. I went over and asked Jill how it was going, allowing a break in the conversation and the opportunity for her to leave gracefully. She stood up, ready to go, but this veteran in his chair said, "Honey, you are not going anywhere. God is talking to me tonight, and it is through you. So honey, you are not going to go anywhere." He continued, "I want you sit down here for a second." I also sat down to listen, learn, and watch...and then he began.

This vet who hadn't laughed in years proceeded to tell her about what it was like to lie in the spider grass of Vietnam. He described the sensation of feeling your body leave you forever. He continued telling her what it was like to "have the North Vietnamese come around and pick you up, and there is nothing you can do about it and just throw you down like trash and piss on you." He told Jill that he thought he was "done for" and "how totally helpless it feels to be a prisoner in your own body." Then he looked Jill directly in the eyes and said that despite all of the misery he had experienced, he "wouldn't trade his life for anything in the world because he saved some of the greatest men he ever knew." For him it was worth it all, because he had gotten them home: "We all came home!"

The vet then told Jill that while he may not be able to move his arms and legs, he could still move his heart, his mind, and his soul, and nobody could take that away from him. Nobody! He kept repeating, "Do you understand me, girl? Do you understand me, girl?" She kept nodding her head. I was in tears.

Jill stayed with this dear brave man the rest of the evening, riveted to what he was saying. When the event came to its end, she wheeled him out to the shuttle van for his return journey. It was when she came back into the auditorium that I saw the tears rolling down her cheeks. She came up to me and put her arms on my shoulders, speechless. When I asked her if she was okay, Jill looked at me with those innocent eyes overwhelmed by tears and replied, "Mr. Anton, I just didn't know...I just didn't know what these guys did for us."

I said, "That is okay. This is what tonight is all about."

She said, "I hear you when you say freedom isn't free. Now I know why. Now I know what it means."

A few weeks later I got a call from the Barstow Veterans Home and the nurse who was at that dinner that night told me the vet had died. She said for the two weeks after our dinner he was a new man ...he was "born again. He was free." The nurse wanted me to make sure that Jill knew all of this, so that she could appreciate the impact she had on this man in his final days. I wish I knew his name. All I have is a memory. As I hung up the phone, I was struck by a profound insight: "What a tremendous power kids have."

Over the years we have made these dinners an annual event at school. We had one this year and will have one next year, and we will continue the dinners until the day I retire from teaching. I always marvel at how the students come out of those dinners transformed. And now, instead of me breaking the ice and encouraging the students to talk to the vets, they come up to me, grab me by the arm, start pulling me in their direction and exclaim, "Mr. Anton, you've got to talk to this guy (or this woman). They have a great story. Come on."

The dinner has become a vehicle by which the students can interact with veterans and set up interviews with them at school. These kids become emotionally connected to the American past and they realize that, in talking to these veterans, they are a part of something bigger than themselves. They benefit from some of the same values my dad imparted to me.

He always loved hearing about these interactions.

My dad told me, "You are not worth a damn unless you are working for something bigger than yourself, whether it be as a father, an employee, or whatever. Whatever you do, do it as if you are doing it for somebody else. You will find that by serving others, the rewards are much greater than any self-centered motivation that you have for yourself. Life is like being on a baseball team, son. For success, set aside your agenda, play your part, and you'll accomplish a lot. You might not always win, but who says you can't win most of the time?"

My Father's War

My commitment to transmitting the legacy of veterans, when coupled with my job as a U.S. history teacher, gave me a vehicle through which I could educate my students about veterans and the honor it is to be an American citizen, and instill within them the values (duty, honor, service, loyalty) I learned from my father. What resulted was an annual project in which my eighth grade students interviewed anyone who lived through the W.W. II experience. Then they transcribed that taped conversation to paper. The results have been impressive and at times even sublime.

I have sent some of the transcriptions to the Eisenhower Center and The National D-Day Museum, both creations of Stephen Ambrose. The staffs at both research institutions were greatly impressed, nearly incredulous that 13- and 14-year-olds were so skillful at conducting and compiling these interviews. Some of the interviews were rife with tragedy, while others were somewhat humorous. Still others were extraordinarily poignant and inspirational.

Among those Eisenhower Center and D-Day Museum staff members who took notice of my students' work was Stephen Ambrose himself, who, when told about it, responded that it was "a hell of a thing." He then added, "We'll need to have him [me] come out here to New Orleans for the opening of the museum in June [2000]." Stephen even called me himself and wanted me to send him a recent interview. At that moment I hadn't anything recent. So I told him I could interview my dad. All he told me was to "get it right!" So I tried.

Get It Right

The National D-Day Museum, located in New Orleans, is, by act of Congress, America's World War II Museum. I had been interviewing veterans for their oral archives and raising money to preserve the American war experiences for a few years. I felt it important as a historian and as a teacher to be involved actively within my profession. As a result of all my work with the D-Day Museum, I got a few speaking engagements through them. I also began writing the oral history of the Trailblazer Artillery units in W.W. II. Consequently, I was asked to be the Assistant Divisional Historian of Dad's division, the 70th Infantry Division ("The Trailblazers"). The resulting self-published book was titled *Distant Thunder: The 70th Infantry Division Artillery in World War II*. The 70th Infantry Division Association liked what I was doing with the D-Day Museum and wanted a son of their own to tell a part of their World War II saga, so I accepted the position as historian. Stephen Ambrose told me in New Orleans that, at age 37, I must the youngest World War II divisional historian he knew. He said, "They must be hard up for an historian or you must be very good." After reading my artillery book, he said I was pretty damn good and that if I remember one thing as a historian, I would be a great keeper of the veterans' trust. What was that one piece of advice? Simply it was this... "Get it right." So I started by preparing to interview my dad.

Now, as the divisional historian, I had access to service records, phone numbers, and other personal connections that would allow me to see Dad through the new and unfiltered perspective of his comrades who served alongside him. I was going to meet Dad with or without his permission.

As I started to talk to these veterans, they showed me a side of Dad I didn't know and would likely never have seen. There were stories about selfless acts of compassion, trust, and ability that a self-effacing man would never recount about himself. But his friends all told me what they saw. McDougal Helsley, also of the 882 Field Artillery, remembered, "Wallace was a guy who would make sure that hot food, drinks, and equipment made it to us machine gunners stuck

Occupation Duty—70th Infantry Division baseball Team members leaving Spicheren, France for the Army World Series in Germany 1945. Courtesy National Baseball Hall of Fame.

in a fox hole protecting the 105mm cannons at night. He would crawl out in the snow or drive a jeep in pitch black to bring us what we needed. He didn't have to do this. We had rations enough to keep us full, but it was this act of teamwork and fairness that made me love him so much. Also included in these care packages was always a small part of someone's liquor ration. Usually these liquor rations were rather excessive for officers and comparatively nil for us regular guys. In fact, all we usually got was this crappy beer. It made that beer we were drinking back in training camp in Ft. Leonard Wood, Missouri called Greasy Dick sound pretty good. But ol' Wally would not let us go without. We all owed him for it."

As time passed, I started asking Dad about men like McDougal Helsley, Bill Atherton, Isaac Gustin, Bill Clark, and his good friend Sgt. Sigmund Usalis, many of whom I had already interviewed. I started asking about stories these guys mentioned to me and Dad would ask, "How do you know that?" Or he would just smile that smart-aleck smile of his and admit, "Okay, I'll tell you what you want, because you're going find it out anyhow!" Some of his stories were truly humorous but many were tragic.

My dad joined the U.S. Army in 1943 after receiving his draft notice from the President, starting as it always did with the familiar word …"Greetings." He was inducted at Fort MacArthur, California, near San Pedro. Dad was sent to basic training at Camp Roberts, also in California, and applied for flight school as part of the Army Specialized Training Program (ASTP). As a high school kid, he had worked at Cal-Aero Airfield washing planes and even taking some basic ground school, so he easily qualified for flight school and instruction. Staff Sergeant Anton was sent to Washington State University for training. He flew what is commonly known as a Piper Cub. He was in training to become an observation pilot/observer.

He would always tell me, "Flying is the purest form of freedom you can ever have in your life. Up there, Todd, it is just you and God. What happens is all up to you. You control your destiny."

I thought this a very important admission from a person virtually passed off to be raised by his grandparents by a mother more interested in herself than raising her son during the Depression. Dad's own father was killed in a car accident in North Dakota when Dad was young. So freedom and self-sufficiency and belonging were important attributes to Dad. Becoming part of the American "team" was a real thrill for Dad. But very late in his air training the ASTP program for flying staff sergeants was disbanded. As a result, he was sent to Camp Adair, Oregon to join the 70th Infantry Division.

"Todd, upon entering the division they issue you what is called your M.O.S. which is your 'Military Occupation Specialty'—your job. Since I had flight hours under me, I was assigned to Artillery that had many support units to it. Each 'Arty' battalion, son, had its own air reconnaissance with it and that is where I went. I became an air observer and ground forward observer. Basically it was my job to see where the shells were landing and tell them over the radio or phone to correct fire or keep it on the target. You know those ol' grasshopper planes we flew were really kites. No weapons. They were unarmored. In fact, I put a 2-inch-thick piece of metal under my seat cushion. I wanted kids and I wanted the fun of making them. You couldn't do that if your marbles get shot off!

"We all did our training in Oregon, at Camp Adair, and then went to Ft. Leonard Wood, and eventually left for Europe in January 1945 from Camp Myles Standish, Massachusetts aboard the USS *Mariposa,* a converted luxury cruise ship. I think it was formally called the USS *America.* All I really remember was that it was from the Matson family of liners. I remember sailing through the Strait of Gibraltar and landing in southern France at the Port of Marseilles. I saw my first 'naked' lady in France. The thing I remember most about that was that her legs needed a shave, and how totally empty she looked. We all were waiting in town to get haircuts and some food before going to our base camp. She had on this red dress with nothing on underneath. She would go around to groups of GIs and start dancing, hoping for money, food or whatever... I guess this was supposed to be a real treat and a turn-on, but all I remember was the dark hair on her legs and that did it for me and the rest of us. We paid her to stop! *We really did!*

"Then we rode in quarter-ton trucks pulling our guns behind up to the front and went into combat in February where I did my Forward Observation work and some flying. Mostly, I was on the ground scouting."

I was really amazed with the amount of information Dad was telling me. It was coming so easy. He was telling me a good story, but it wasn't anything truly personal, emotional, or as he would put it...

private. So I cut to it, and asked Dad to tell me about his two worst experiences in combat. I asked him to describe them to me so that not only I, but also his grandchildren, would see that war is not glamorous, but really tragic. I gathered myself for a question not every son asks his dad.

"Dad, just this one time. Tell me, did you kill anyone?"

He leaned back and closed his eyes and ran his fingers through his thinning gray hair. I could see his forehead wrinkle and I could only guess where his mind was. For a moment, I was afraid.

"Son, I am sure I killed a lot of people—soldiers and civilians alike. Artillery did most of the destruction. Many times when we went through a recently liberated town, it was a common sight to see the bodies of German soldiers lying alongside civilians on the grass. We usually assumed it was artillery that did that. I only asked this question once when I saw the small black shoes of a little girl sticking out from under a blanket. We were told that artillery had done it. The bad thing was our battalion was the only one that had fired on this section. It really bothered me. I was there to kill Germans. Not kids."

"Dad, did you personally kill a German up close?" I asked.

"Yes."

"Can you describe it for me? I won't ask you again."

"Why is that important to you? What difference does it make?"

I had no real answer, other than… "Dad, it is a question that I am sure I'll be asked someday. I've always wanted to know anyway."

"All right. All right. One day we [observation scouts] went out to find a position where we could just observe German movements across this river called the Saar. We were told that the Germans were across the river and our side was 'secure.' Well, there is nothing ever secure in the Army or on the battlefield. We got into our jeep and drove a few miles to this old farmhouse that bordered this river and had many trees around it as well as small buildings, mostly chicken coops.

"I suggested that we keep our jeep parked behind the farmhouse out of sight of the Germans across the river. Why advertise that we were there? I thought. Also I didn't think that using the house was a good idea. I'm sure it was pre-sighted. So we made our way down to the chicken coops, which were about 100 yards away, and as we came up on these coops, the chickens started to scatter and out walked two Germans, arms full of eggs. It was my first time being this close. It seemed like it took forever, or was it all in slow motion? I'm not sure. They just started to grab for their guns and I just pulled the trigger on my BAR [Browning Automatic Rifle] and pointed. If you don't know what this gun does, let me tell you: its 45-caliber bullets broke them into pieces. My God, those screams, I still hear them."

"All because of eggs."

"We all heard voices and I couldn't tell if they were German or English so we ran to our jeep. Then came the shellfire. I was right. Germans. The farmhouse was pre-sighted and it blew up with a sound I'll never forget. We jumped into our jeep and drove away. I looked back at those two bodies covered in blood and eggs.

"That was the only time I killed anyone up close. But God...those screams. Those sounds just stick with you.

"One last thing, Todd. Near Saarbrucken was this labor camp full of Russian and Polish workers. They were sick, starving, thin and beaten. They wouldn't look at us in the eye. You know, like a beaten dog shaking.

"I got over my killing those two Krauts real fast. I've never felt guilty since."

I was stunned.

Quiet.

"My war ended in late March. That was when we fired our last round. We were assigned to Occupation Duty. I taught some of the local French kids baseball. They picked it up pretty easily. We had a few 'Over the Line' tournaments. I rewarded the winning team with chocolate bars. I then helped to organize an artillery baseball team and we got a league going. Equipment came in and we had German POWs separate the equipment. They didn't know shit about baseball. They would take a glove and throw it down. Pick up another one and throw it down. I told them to hang the gloves up on the nails on the wall. 'Get on with it!' Through a translator, they told us why they were frustrated. They couldn't find the matching left-handed gloves to go with all these right-handed ones. We all laughed.

"I just figured baseball had finally come to Europe in 1945."

This league and many others like them really made a difference for the men in the service. But many guys were leaving to go home, piecemeal. Dad told me many times, "What made going home tough was that we all were shipped out in different units and many of us wore a different patch home. Some of us had been together for years. I remember seeing Boston fade away when we [artillery and Divisional supporting units] left aboard the USS *Mariposa* as a team in January of 1945; now I was coming home alone. That was frustrating. Of course I was happy to be home, but still something was empty. I don't know if others felt this way or not. But I sure wish we came home together."

I then asked him, what was the first thing he did when he got home, back to the USA?

"Well, Son, home at first was Camp Kilmer, New Jersey. It was June 1946. I got a 48-hour pass, hopped on a train and went to Ebbets Field, in Brooklyn, New York."

The Dodgers and baseball have been a part of our family ever since!

Stephen Ambrose loved this story.

I was aware that the Eisenhower Center staff wanted me to come out to New Orleans to visit the museum and the Center, but I assumed that it was just for a tour of the museum sometime after it opened. That is why I was rendered speechless—an unusual thing for me—when I opened the rather large envelope from the National D-Day Museum. The envelope contained VIP passes for me and a guest to attend a number of exclusive functions celebrating the opening of The National D-Day Museum in New Orleans from June 3 through June 6, 2000! I was blown away. VIP treatment and all access to every one of the events! This was heady stuff.

I thought, with trepidation, "Now I am going to be hanging out with the big dogs! Am I ready?" In reality, I was overwhelmed. I had read these historians' books: Ambrose, Douglas Brinkley, Tom Brokaw, etc., and now I would be meeting them face-to-face. Wow. These were my "superstars." I was beset by conflicting emotions at that moment—feeling intimidated yet simultaneously ecstatic that I was going to get the chance to meet these chroniclers of our country's past.

After the initial shock wore off, I settled into the process of making my plans to take the trip. In a perfect world, my father and I would travel together, but Dad was 75 and really just a homebody at this stage of life. His health wasn't the best. His home gave him comfort. His ponds, stocked with trout and catfish, and his Christmas tree ranch were his priorities now, but my heart ached for him to go. To be honest, I knew Dad would say no, but I wanted to ask anyway. The answer was indeed no. Dad also felt that he would be a drag on my big moment since he did not have my stamina, nor keep my late hours. I understood that, but still it was a father and son moment lost and I regretted it. I still do. It would have been perfect. It would have been just the two of us.

The night of June 5 was the Black Tie Gala celebrating the "Major Donors" and corporate sponsors. It was exclusive, to say the least. I couldn't shake the heavy pit in my stomach, the anxious feeling that I didn't belong there. I kept asking myself, "What the hell am I doing here?" The number of dignitaries and celebrities (who donated huge sums of money) in attendance was overwhelming. If I had the money to give, I certainly would, but teachers don't usually have the wealth to justify such elite company. My sense of inadequacy surfaced many times that evening. Because I was wearing a tux like many others, they didn't notice the difference in status, but I was well aware of it and it weighed on me. I drew strength, though, from those I represented. My students. My father.

I walked down to the museum from the Ambassador Hotel in my black tux. It seemed incongruous to me that here I was strolling down these industrial streets in a tuxedo, but—heck—everything seemed out of place for me at this time. I arrived at the museum for the reception and from there all the guests were going to be transported by buses to the elegantly and patriotically decorated banquet room of the Fairmont Hotel.

Upon arriving at the Fairmont, my good friend Lance Villers and I made our way inside. Lance had joined me in place of Dad. We walked up two flights of stairs and strolled over to a table where we checked in. A young woman glanced at our credentials, handed us a gift bag, and escorted us to our table. Lance and I were the first people to arrive at the table. We sat down and chatted and speculated about the others who would be joining us. Eventually people began to trickle into the dining room and take their seats. Others joined us, and we all began to introduce ourselves and explain our connection with Dr. Ambrose. I felt so self-conscious, as if being a public school teacher required me to justify my presence there. While the activity at our table was a little mundane, what was happening at the table behind me was not. As people began to take their seats, I was able to "call the roll" as it were. In the chair directly behind me sat Tom Hanks! Accompanying him were Dr. Ambrose and his wife Moira, Steven Spielberg, Tom Brokaw, and William Cohen, the U.S. Secretary of Defense at that time. Awestruck, I began to gawk at the scene. I kept thinking, "Wow, there sure is a lot of power and influence at that table." Dr. Ambrose leaned back in his chair, caught my eye, and nodded at me in a tacit greeting.

The next thing I knew, Dr. Ambrose was waving me over. "Oh wow, my God," I thought. In a moment of boldness, I became an assertive fan, figuring that if I were getting called over to their table, I ought to make it count. I grabbed the poster of the grand opening of the museum that was part of our gift bag, and made my way over, hoping those at his table would autograph it. They all did. With that distinctively gravel sounding voice, Dr. Ambrose proceeded to introduce me around the table as "the kid who has caught my bug!"

I liked this introduction. Tom Hanks was somewhat preoccupied, signing autographs for others, and he didn't hear Dr. Ambrose's introduction of me as not only as a person who has caught his bug for veterans, but also as a damn fine teacher from California whose students were recording these "unbelievable oral histories for the museum." Dr. Ambrose's praise for my students was very satisfying. Everyone at the table was very complimentary in their remarks.

Just at this moment, Tom Hanks was drawn back into the conversation.

"I'm sorry, what is your name again?" he asked, grabbing my hand in a handshake.

"My name is Todd," I replied.

"I didn't hear everything Steve was saying. What is it that you do?"

I looked around at all these faces knowing who each of them were. Either I had been entertained by them, or read their books, or benefited by their service to our country in politics. I felt totally outclassed and way out of place. Wouldn't you? It felt as if a light was shining just on me as I started to answer Tom Hanks' question. I was nervous and my voice must have contained something less than enthusiasm, for my reply to him was, "Oh, I'm just a public school teacher."

My answer must have seemed as if I was implying I'd rather be doing something else. That is not true.

Chuckling and asking me at the same time, Tom persisted, "OK, Todd, what is it you *want* to do?"

I pointed to Stephen Ambrose and proclaimed, "I want to do what he does. I want to talk to veterans and learn first-hand how they survived and came back and built the freest society in the history of mankind; they did that for me and you."

"OK, Todd, what does that take?" Tom queried.

"I think it takes, most of all, passion, graduate school, a PhD dissertation, and lots of money. But I am a full-time teacher, I'm married, and I have two children and a mortgage. I can't afford that."

He leaned back in his chair, looked me straight in the eye, and with his head tilted to one side and face plastered with that familiar smirk of his, said, "So what you are telling me, Todd, is that you have dreams and you have excuses.... What is it going to be?"

This book is an attempt to answer that question.

3

June 6, D-Day 2002

A Part of Me Died Today

On the morning of June 6, 2002, I went down to Wimbledon Village, a strip mall in Victorville, California, to do radio spots for three local Clear Channel stations: AM 960, KATJ, and Y-102. Since all three stations are located in the same building, I was able to move easily from show to show, in order to plug the upcoming local D-Day program I was organizing to raise money to support the National D-Day Museum. Not only did I encourage people to come hear the veterans speak, but I also emphasized that people would be able to see the Steven Spielberg/Stephen Ambrose documentary *Price for Peace* in its entirety. I was the only teacher in the country given permission by the D-Day Museum to show the film. So I was feeling pretty good as I drove home from the radio stations. This was going to be a special Saturday and a special event.

The promos went well, and I even succeeded in my getting my sister actress-singer Susan Anton's rendition of "Forever Young" from her new CD played on KATJ (Katt Country) by "Jimmer in the Morning" at about 7:20 a.m.

I remember pulling into the driveway of our home. It was a sunny spring day. The dew on the glass still glistened, the American flag was gently, and majestically, blowing in the breeze, and the front door was open, allowing the cool fresh air to bathe the inside of the house. Everything seemed so perfect as I strode up the walkway to the front door, anxious to get inside, say "hi" to my wife Sue and our son Jason, and get ready to go back to school to take over for my colleague, Wendi Rodriguez, who had agreed to cover my classes for the morning. (Naturally they were listening to my radio spots in class and becoming more excited about our upcoming event on Saturday).

When I approached the door, my wife, who had been sitting on

20

the couch, got up and moved toward the front door. As I opened the screen door, I noticed the fountain of tears in her eyes and the streaks of tears crisscrossing her reddened face. My heart sank. I knew immediately what was wrong. I said to Sue, "No, don't tell me this." She didn't have to tell me because I knew. I just knew. Her eyes told the story no son wants to hear: my father...my hero had died.

At that moment, you experience a lot of feelings, but I felt that this couldn't be happening to me, that it was happening to somebody else. Put it this way: a man that I had known my entire life was now "past tense." I couldn't fathom it. It was beyond surreal. I can't remember a lot of what transpired that day, but one thing that was vivid, and is to this day, was a recurring mantra that I kept thinking and saying in my mind: "Not yet, not yet. I wasn't done loving you."

I can remember sitting in the car on this beautiful "Chamber of Commerce" day, the kind of day that prompts so many people to want to move to California. As cars passed by on the way down the Cajon Pass, people everywhere seemed to be laughing and smiling, and chatting on cell phones as if they had no cares or worries. I recall being angry with these people and their jovial dispositions. I remember thinking, "What gives you the right to be happy?" My day had started off so wonderfully, and now I was beset by the darkness and gloominess that grief brings. "My dad is gone, and you people are laughing and smiling. What gives you the right?" I felt this resentment all the way to my parents' home in Calimesa, which is about one hour south of Victorville towards San Diego.

Sometime during the ride down, I gathered myself and muttered out loud to Sue, "That son of a bitch...do you know what today is?" She looked at me curiously, as if the significance was lost on her. "Sue, today is June 6! Today is D-Day!" The greatest man I have ever known in my life, my father, my hero, my mentor, obviously wasn't done teaching me yet. He died at 7:18 a.m. on June 6, 2002. He died on D-Day! I thought, "Wow! Of course, he would go out on this day. Of course he would do that."

Amazing.

A myriad of conversations past came flooding back in my mind as we made our way to Mom and Dad's, well, just Mom's now, to console each other and start the plans for Dad's farewell tour...his funeral. It felt strange to be thinking of Dad in this way. Sometimes in conversations, Dad would say he wanted to be cremated when that day came and wanted to have his ashes spread over the land he loved so much...Oak Glen, California. Dad had worked on this ranch since 1947, while doing other jobs like those long years of work for the county sheriff's office. This was the ranch he and my mom Lou Ellen fought so hard to save, after the death of my grandfather Blackie Wilshire had caused much of it to be sold. This ranch had been in our family since the late 1800s. This ranch meant so much to Dad. It was the only home he ever really knew.

Often as Dad would drive me up to the Oak Glen ranch from their new retirement home just 10 minutes down the hill in Calimesa, we would talk. I remember a conversation that we had just a few weeks before he died as he took a longer route home. When Dad took this route, I knew he had something to say, or something on his mind he needed to work out before he got home. So I just sat in the passenger seat in the white Ford truck he named "White Cloud." Dad had nicknames for everything at the ranch. Why? I'm not really sure.

I could tell he had something on his mind. He seemed fidgety on this late afternoon ride. He turned the radio on and off. He rolled up the window and then rolled it down again. What was wrong, I wondered? Then he broke the silence, and it was a topic for which I wasn't prepared.

"Todd, I want you to do something for me when 'that day' comes."

"Dad, can we talk about something else?" As the youngest of five kids, with siblings who were much older than me, I also grew up surrounded by my own friends' parents. They were much younger than mine, so I always had a fear of losing my parents, even at a very young age. I didn't like it when my dad talked about such matters. What kid does?

But Dad persisted.

"No. You have to listen to me, because I am asking you to do something for me. I want you to make sure of two things. I want you to make sure that when that day comes, you make sure that somehow a part of me is at Dodger Stadium because I love it there and I know you do too—all of us do. But we have something special there, don't we, Son?" You bet, Dad. Yes, we do.

"Now the second thing I want you to do and only you and I understand this, I want you to make sure some part of me makes it back to France so I can again be with the boys. Promise me."

Hesitantly, I said, "Okay, Dad. Okay."

This memory of our conversation was so real and so concrete that it helped me regain my composure and bring myself back to the present as the car Sue was driving bounced over a rough part on the long, endless road to a reality I had been wanting to avoid my entire life.

We finally got to Mom's house and there was that white Ford truck of Dad's parked in the front of the house like always. This just had to be a bad dream. Of course Dad was in there, his truck is here, right? But denial can't hide the obvious. I got out of the car wondering what attitude I needed to have. Should I be strong for Mom? Should I be the weeping baby everyone was expecting me to be? I went right in, bolting through the back door, rushing through the kitchen, and made my way towards the murmuring voices in the "sun room," which in reality was a large room with many windows, recliners, and their TV. I just threw my arms around Mom. She held me so tight and said, "Oh, honey, he loved you so much. You were his buddy. You had something special. Very special."

Finally, my brother Brent's voice cut through grayness, saying, "Todd, you are still doing your show."

My family was adamant, even at that moment of grief, that I go through with the D-Day event as scheduled. Originally, Brent wasn't planning to come, but now they would all be there. Somewhat stunned, I sat back when Brent asked me, "Can I have Dad's ticket?"

"God, I haven't even thought about it!" I muttered.... "Sure you can have Dad's ticket."

What did I mean I hadn't thought about it? Of course I had! For the last three months, I was consumed by my plans for hosting an event to raise funds for the National D-Day Museum in New Orleans.

I wanted to show them and myself that schools across America could be an integral part of their attempt to honor and celebrate the common American adage of World War II: "We are all in this together." We had been together in the 1940s and, I thought, we could be again.

But honestly, there was another reason. Who was I kidding? My father had been awarded the Bronze Star in World War II. Although he received the paperwork, acknowledging his "valor," he never received his actual medal. I had set aside a segment of this program where a US Army Honor Guard was going to award my dad with his long-overdue Bronze Star. I dreamt of this moment and I knew how Dad would react.

All I really wanted was to see him receive the salute of an Army Honor Guard and return that salute. I wanted to see his tears. It was going to be a magical moment. I wanted everyone to see the America that was quickly leaving us. I wanted my brothers and sisters to see that there was more to the man they called "Dad."

The event was shaping up to be an incredible one. The veterans I had arranged to speak were a remarkable bunch. I knew these people very well. All of them lived around the Phelan area or came into my life through my in-laws Herb and Bev Fuhrman: Ralph Browner, USMC and recipient of the Navy Cross for his actions at Tarawa, was going to speak about how he survived one of the bloodiest landings in the war. Ralph had attended many of my veterans dinners over the years. Alma Newsome Fornal, a real jewel, was a member of the Women's Air Force Service Pilots—better known as WASPs. She was going to show that World War II was a women's war, too. She accompanies my in-laws to many polka dances. Alma is the true definition of the word "lady" in my eyes.

Then there was Dutch Schultz of the famed 82nd Airborne Division. Dutch, let's just say he was one of my best friends. Anyone who has seen the movie *The Longest Day* will see Dutch featured in that film, and anyone who has read Stephen Ambrose's books will know about Dutch Schultz! Although it was a diverse panel, it was a uniquely American panel. It seemed like family.

As I planned this event, I kept Dad posted. I didn't tell him about his Bronze Star, of course, but we discussed the panel and who should be included. Dad didn't want to be up there. He didn't feel worthy. That was his way. I wasn't going to argue with him. I told him I was nervous and that I felt way in over my head.

"Pal, I understand exactly how you feel. That is what being drafted is all about. It, too, made you do things you've never done before and become things that you never thought were inside of you, and I'm glad to see you take on new challenges. It is the only way you'll ever be really happy." Then he began to cough and cough and cough. I hated listening to that smoker's cough.

Fifty-plus years of smoking at least two packs a day were really taking a toll on his lungs. Although he stopped smoking in 1995, the damage was done. Interestingly, the Army he fought for in World War II and again in Korea issued him not only shells, bullets, and rifles to kill the enemy, but cigarettes as well. Chesterfields and Lucky Strikes did more damage to him than the wounds he suffered on the hills of Spicheren, France on February 23, 1945 and the frostbite on the hills in Korea as he helped evacuate the Marines from the onrushing Chinese in 1953.

"Dad, you're coming Saturday, June 8th, aren't you?"

"Of course, Son. I'll be there."

I really gave him no option. It was for him I was doing this. My father. My hero. Some kids grow up with a dad who was a professional athlete or actor. My dad was a liberator: a citizen soldier who brought light to a darkened world. Millions like him destroyed Hitler, defeated Tojo's tyranny, and freed an enslaved world.

A Big Day

The D-Day event, at Serrano High School in Phelan, started on time. I had on my suit and started to walk out on stage with my guests. I was growing very close with Dutch, and he grabbed my arm and told me that I was showing as much courage as he'd ever seen to go through with this. "If you get weak, Todd, remember we are right here with you." I knew what he meant. They all gave me strength. That's why these veterans are the "Greatest Generation."

I walked out on stage and introduced everyone. To my amazement, I saw that the house was almost full...nearly 300 people. This meant we'd raised over $4,500. Not bad for an event run by ten middle school and high school kids and one crazy history teacher! Then it seemed all I could see was my brave Mom beaming at me, giving me the thumbs up. As our eyes met there was a dialogue of love that no words can describe. Beautiful.

When the soldiers of March Air Force Reserve Base entered carrying the colors, it set the mood for a very powerful moment. Everyone stood; the veterans saluted. It was at this moment that Dad's absence seemed so great. All I kept thinking was "Hold it together, Todd." To hear the Honor Guard call off the cadence was exciting, glorious, and sad all at once. Dad should be here, I kept muttering in my mind. The program went off flawlessly and the star attraction was Alma Newsome Fornal, the WASP pilot, who wowed the crowd with her story of the contributions of women in World War II. That night, many people learned for the first time about the work that so many women had done.

Ralph Browner of the Marines passionately told his story of fending off over 200 Japanese on the beaches of Tarawa by himself with his machine gun as the Navy Cross glistened from his suit jacket. His cocky, confident Marine challenge that night was for anyone in the crowd to say that dropping the A-Bomb was unnecessary...to his face! He wanted any of "those self appointed apologists or purveyors of political correctness" to look him in the face and say, in his words, "all this revisionist 'crap.'" His unit was slated to be among the first assault units to land in Japan for an invasion. The bomb saved his life.

Nobody spoke up.

"No guts," he said. "But I know you're out there."

Then there was Dutch. Rather than talk about himself, Dutch chose to honor two men he revered: General James Gavin, Commanding General of the 82nd Airborne and his buddy-in-arms Ray Gonzalez. In telling their stories, Dutch told his. It was a special night.

I was the co-host of the event, introducing each speaker. It was so hot on stage that I took off my suit jacket and draped it over my chair.

After the panel of speakers concluded, it was time for intermission. We brought the huge screen down for the movie *Price for Peace*, produced by Stephen Spielberg and Stephen Ambrose. Finally, I could sit down among my family and relax. Finally, it was coming to an end. Finally, I wasn't just the little brother anymore. It was so strange. My family looked at me differently. It was if I had grown up in their eyes.

As the movie ended, I left my seat in the crowd and I stood off to the side of the stage. There were about 10 minutes of the film to run. I looked at many of the faces in the crowd. Many were streaked with tears, mouths agape. I saw old men and women holding each other close with rediscovered affection and appreciation that they had survived those times. I was gathering myself for a final word of thanks and saying good night. I didn't want it to end. I wanted that feeling to go on. But it couldn't. I walked on to the stage and spoke a word of thanks to the crowd and they responded with a standing ovation that was led by my brave mother who shouted, "Bravo!" quickly followed by cheers from my family, and then everyone in the crowd stood.

The colors were retired and all in attendance either left to go home or joined us at our after-event dinner reception in the Diamondback cafeteria a few rooms away. The hall quickly emptied until I was alone on the stage in this vast room. As I went to pick up my suit jacket hanging over the back of a chair on stage, I noticed on the podium a small presentation case I had forgotten to pick up.

It was my father's Bronze Star.

4

Dodger Stadium

Okay Dad, One Last Game

Mickey Hatcher

Duke Snider was the hero of the Anton family, but that family didn't include me. I was born in 1964. Duke was long gone by the time I started playing ball in the early 1970s. Of course my team was the Dodgers and my childhood heroes were Steve Garvey and Ron Cey. But we really didn't have a family hero like we did with Duke—that is, until 1988 when we met Michael Vaughn Hatcher, better known as Mickey. Mickey played for the 1988 World Series Champion Los Angeles Dodgers. He was Dad's favorite player because he was, in Dad's opinion, "normal." If you know Mickey, there isn't anything normal about him, but Dad meant that Mickey had passion and desire for the game and that he was a regular guy, not a "prima donna" superstar. Mickey played the game as if every game was going to be his last. You could see how much he enjoyed playing the game, Dad said. Dad appreciated Mickey's passion.

Dad and Mick met on Hollywood Stars Night 1989. This is a game in which Hollywood movie stars, or other sports stars play in a pre-game exhibition match. My sister Susan Anton was invited to take part. We all went to see Susan play, and she was able to get Dad down on the field with her. I was so jealous. As she worked out, getting ready for the game, though, she was informed that women weren't allowed to play. She might get hurt. She would be the honorary bat person. She was incredulous. This was quite an decision from a team that brought the first black player into the majors, she thought. But she was a good sport and did her duty. Some of the Dodgers players were pretty angry, too, and one of them was Mickey. As a result of Susan not playing, Susan, Dad and Mickey were on the field for a longer time and he and Mickey talked for over an hour. Dad invited Mick up to the ranch the next day for a BBQ and to throw some horseshoes.

You would think that Mickey wouldn't come on up. Aren't baseball stars too busy?

He showed up.

We have all been friends ever since.

In 2002, as Dad and I watched Mickey's Angels play the Red Sox, he mentioned an idea he had—that I interview baseball's W.W. II veterans. Dad started to make his case. "You know, Todd, with all your interviewing of veterans you've got me thinking about those ballplayers I remember hearing about. Think about it, Todd. You are talking about Ted Williams, of course, Yogi Berra, Warren Spahn, Stan Musial. Todd, listen, the list goes on: Ralph Houk, Hank Bauer, Hank Greenberg, and Jackie Robinson. I just think a book or a TV special would make an interesting story because these ballplayers gave up everything and there are guys who didn't come home at all. Look, everyone is down on baseball. All these spoiled kids who don't know shit about how the veterans saved the game for them so they can make a ton of money. Remember when you spoke at the historical society? There was that guy who flew with Billy Southworth's kid. Those are the stories I am talking about. Indeed, it was a powerful one.

"Todd"—Dad looked right into my eyes, and said, "I am telling you. I think you should really do something with this baseball idea. Son, you've got to tell these stories."

Gold Star Manager

October 1942 saw America nearing the end of its first year at war. It was only a matter of time before baseball stars started to fill the ranks in the armed forces. Big league players and minor league players— some 4,500 in all—contributed to victory in World War II. Some even enlisted before the attack on Pearl Harbor. But the cost of victory was high. America lost over 400,000 of its best and brightest youth to war. One of the men who made the ultimate sacrifice was Billy Southworth, Jr.

The younger Southworth was probably the first professional ball player to join the World War II armed forces. He broke in to baseball with Martinsville, Virginia in the Bi-State League in 1936, progressing to Asheville in the Piedmont League, to Kinston, N.C. in the Coastal Plain League, and to Rome, N.Y. in the Canadian-American League. While with Rome, he won the 1939 Most Valuable Player award. In 1940, he was with the Toronto club when he won appointment as an Army air cadet, and began training as a B-17 pilot. He said farewell to baseball, at least for a while. Even before his playing days he'd been the batboy for his dad's teams, one of which was the St. Louis Cardinals.

Not large by today's standards, a Boeing B-17 bomber commanded respect back in 1942. It became known as the "Superfortress" and this powerful aircraft became the backbone of the Allied air assault on Fortress Europe. Billy loved flying it.

As Game Two of the 1942 World Series began, there was the roar of a four-engine B-17 bomber coming in low over Sportsman's Park in St. Louis. Violating all airspace rules, the young Billy Southworth Jr. brought his bomber in over the stadium to say goodbye not only to baseball, but also to his dad. As Cardinals players Stan Musial, Enos Slaughter, and manager Billy Southworth Sr. looked up, they saw a simple gesture, a wigwag of the wings, of Billy saying goodbye. An airman's salute. It was to be the last time Billy Jr. would ever see a ball game, a stadium, and his father's team in action. The Cards went on to upset the New York Yankees that year.

That flyover was a surprise in many ways. For what the Cardinals players saw that day was not that kid they remembered, who had traveled with them on the road wearing a Cardinals uniform, but a man and a Captain in the Army Air Corps in his twenties. As Billy flew mission after mission over Europe, he did so always wearing the St. Louis Cardinals cap his father sent him after winning the World Series. It brought him luck. He completed twenty-five bombing missions, and was awarded the Distinguished Flying Cross and air medal adorned with three oak leaf clusters signifying that he had been awarded it three times. Billy's proudest boast was that none of his crewmen in Europe were ever awarded the Purple Heart, for none had been wounded during the missions. Upon his return to the States in early 1945, Billy, now a Major, began training in the temperamental B-29 Superfortress. He died in an air crash in Flushing Bay, N.Y. in 1945.

Billy Southworth Jr. had given his life for his country, trying out the newly designed engines on the B-29s for the forming Atomic Air-Fleet. Cardinals manager Billy Southworth Sr. had given his son for the country, becoming a Gold Star father and manager. Freedom had come at a high price.

The name of Captain Billy Southworth Jr.'s. B-17 in World War II? "The Winning Run."

Something was becoming clearer to me. There was indeed a story here. This was powerful imagery. I can see that bomber coming in over Sportsman's Park wigwagging its wings. Saying goodbye...perhaps forever? What a story: fathers and sons, and the impact and cost of war. Somehow this was all wrapped around baseball and a Gold Star manager.

Not long thereafter, I called the Eisenhower Center and mentioned Dad's idea of writing a book on W.W. II baseball to my friends there. I told them they would be the ones to know if there would be any appeal for this story among the public and to check to see if Dr. Ambrose had interviewed any of the guys already. They told me that they did not have any oral histories from these guys. They suggested, "Why don't you get those? It would be great to have Ted Williams' story in here. It would be great to hear about Joe and Dom DiMaggio's service time too! Todd, what a terrific story!" Then my good friend at the Eisenhower Center, Mike Edwards, added, "Don't share this with anyone. This would be a great thing for you to do." I guess he was implying that I should write this book, not Dr. Ambrose or anyone else. I never saw myself as a writer/author, but I knew with Ambrose's talent this could be a big story. So I wanted to bring it to Stephen's attention and asked for him to call me about it. "Todd," Mike said, "Stephen is really busy and so is Doug." Ambrose was doing his Band of Brothers HBO tour and Douglas Brinkley was doing a book on

Henry Ford and starting a project on John Kerry's Vietnam experience. Simply put, they were busy.

Not only did Dad commission me to pursue this idea, but Stephen Ambrose also endorsed the commission. The more I looked into the experiences of ballplayers who went to off war, the more I realized that this story hadn't been told from an emotional perspective that we can relate to. There was no book or video about the ballplayers' specific personal experiences in war. Nowhere could I find anything that relayed the wartime experiences of these player/veterans in the first person, as an oral history, so that readers or viewers could understand their emotions and feelings over tragedies and triumphs and innings lost and nightmares gained. There was no vehicle for allowing these men to tell their stories in their own words.

Some baseball war books do exist, but they are told in the third person. That can bore people to tears. There is nothing out there that grabs a reader of history's attention more than a first-person account. That is why I have guest speakers, veterans, come into the classroom, to talk to kids. Anything like a textbook written in the third person is likely to lull students to sleep, and they won't care. So I thought to myself: "What a terrific idea, to talk to these ballplayers and get their stories." I wasn't sure how I was going to get there, but I would try nonetheless. Not long after this my dad was gone.

"Good night, everybody!"—Vin Scully at the close of every Dodgers broadcast

Dad asked me to take him to Dodger Stadium one more time. I remember that request and now that moment had arrived. I knew I was going to need some help. I knew I couldn't call up Dodger Stadium and ask them if I could place some of Dad's ashes on the field. They probably get that request all the time, and I was sure it wasn't allowed. But I wasn't going to be deterred.

So, I turned to my friend and Dad's favorite Dodger, Mickey Hatcher, to help me fulfill Dad's request.

By this time, 2002, Mickey was no longer wearing Dodger blue but rather donned the brilliant fire-engine red of the soon-to-be World

Champion Anaheim Angels, as their hitting coach. I knew I couldn't do this without him, and I also knew that he would understand what I was doing and why—in fact, Dad told me as much when we had one of those talks a few months earlier about what he wanted when he passed away. So I picked up the phone to give Mick a call, dreading the moment that I had to tell Mick that his number one fan was at home with Mickey's dad. What do you say? How do you start this conversation? Rather than over-think it, as I too often do, I just picked up the phone and called.

Mick answered in his usual jovial, upbeat manner.

"Hey you...hello! I knew I'd be hearing from ya! I bet you are looking to go to the game tomorrow...huh?"

I drew a blank. I didn't even know who they were playing. After all, I had been preoccupied. The Angels were playing the Los Angeles Dodgers at Dodger Stadium.

As usual, Mickey thought Dad and I would be coming...

"Aah heck, you don't even know what side to root for any more, do you? You bring that ol' geezer down here and we'll show him who to root for." Mickey chuckled.

"Well, Mickey, that is the reason that I am calling. I hate to have to tell you this, but Wally passed away on June 6."

There was a pause. I knew how much he loved Dad and how much Dad loved him.

"Wait, Todd, did you say June 6? Shit. That's D-Day?"

"I know, leave it to Dad to choose the 'Day of Days' to leave us.

"How's your Mom...how are all of you guys doing?"

"We are all numb. You can't explain it, Mick. You just feel numb." I knew he understood what I meant, losing his own father as he had years earlier. Then I seized the moment, the opportunity to ask Mick to help me fulfill one of Dad's wishes. I told him how Dad wanted his ashes spread on the field at Dodger Stadium. Since the Angels were playing the next night, I wondered if Mickey could help me make this wish a reality. When I asked him, his demeanor changed.

He seemed uneasy about the whole situation because he didn't know exactly what I was asking. This became apparent when he nervously asked, "Are we going to need a shovel and a bucket from the grounds crew?"

I laughed. "Nooo, Mick. This is just a small portion. I'm not cleaning out the fireplace!" I couldn't stop laughing at the image Mick had conjured up. "Mick, all I have is three 35-mm film canisters full." The reason I had three film canisters was that Dad wanted to be in center field, because that is where Duke Snider played. Dad then wanted to be at the mound and at home plate, because, as he said, that is where the game is decided. Don Drysdale pitched from that mound; so did Koufax. And home plate is where Mike Scioscia caught. We all loved Mike, too.

Mickey thought that getting ashes at home plate would be a problem or at least a distraction, because after all, batting practice would be going on. But it was a small amount.

"Anyway, Mick, I am not asking you to do it. We were just wondering if you knew who to ask to make this dream happen."

But now that he understood the small amount we were talking about, he insisted on being the one who helped. "No, no, I can do this . . . I want to do this. But I don't have to look, do I?"

"No," I answered, laughing. "It's no big deal, really."

Mickey said, "What I want you to do is to meet me at the front gate, you know the Elysian Park entrance, at noon tomorrow. I'll meet you there. Just bring what you need to bring and I'll take care of things. Need tickets?"

"Yes" I answered, "we will need a few. It's all six of us."

"No problem. Just make sure you get your family to the front office to get the tickets picked up! Also dress like you belong there."

I guessed that meant look like an athlete.

My sister Susan was seeing if she could sing the National Anthem that night as well, as a way of performing her own tribute. Things seemed to be coming together in a very powerful way.

The next day, I arrived at the front gate right on time. Mickey had been there a few minutes before me and talked to the guard, who waved me through. For the moment, I was struck by the thought that this is the way it used to be when Mickey would meet Dad and me early, so Dad could give him a rash of crap about what Mickey or the Dodgers were doing wrong and what they both needed to do to improve. I'm sure Tommy Lasorda and the O'Malleys appreciated the help. That's the way it had been since we met Mick in 1989.

As we drove over the huge parking lot of Dodger Stadium and finally parked, the memories were so deep, so happy that I felt a peace I hadn't felt in some time. Mickey and I parked directly behind the stadium near the center field entrance. I got out of my car and Mickey immediately noticed my attire, my Dodgers hat, and was compelled to comment. "Nice hat."

I bitterly responded... "It looked better on you."

"Don't worry, I'll convert you. Come on!" He added sarcastically, "Oh how cute, you even have a matching Dodgers bag."

Naturally all this sardonic ribbing was due to the fact that my matching hat and bag said Dodgers, and Mickey, cut by the Dodgers both as a player and coach was now an Angel. I followed him in and we walked through the outfield gates. And there it was! The emerald-hued majesty of Dodger Stadium's center field!

We walked straight in for about forty paces and stopped. Mickey, who seemed to be a little uneasy and fidgety, then asked, "So where do you want to do this thing?" He was looking around for who might interrupt us, but there was nobody around... absolutely nobody! It was great, we were all alone and it seemed as if the moment was somehow scripted, preordained to work out exactly as planned. Dad was somehow directing this.

Then Mickey interrupted my brief reverie by saying... "If you're going to do this, now is the time."

I knelt down, as Mickey kept a watchful eye out. While I feigned tying my shoe, I was gently opening these small cases and slowly turned them over in my fingers and I watched each grain gently, serenely fall to the grass as if the blades were calling him home to this place. I started to cry as I realized I was done. I knew I would never be at a game with Dad again.

As I kneeled there in center field, I began to gingerly spread Dad's ashes with my hand so that their gray hue didn't seem so conspicuous on the shimmering, verdant field. This entire process took about three minutes, if that much. But in my mind it took a long, long time.

I remembered all those special moments that Dad, Mickey, and I shared over the years. I clearly remember the last game just Dad and I saw together there. The Dodgers were playing the Houston Astros and Mickey was playing third base. Well, he hadn't played third in a long time. He made three errors...in one inning! Finally when a weakly hit foul ball rolled towards him he took off his glove and chucked it at the ball, as if to say, "I give up."

Dodger fans applauded as if to say, "We still love you Mick!" Then after the sound of the crowd subsided a voice bellowed... "You suck, Hatcher!" It was Dad.

Interrupting my daydreaming, Mickey piped up, "Eeew! That's more chunky than I thought." Mickey's compassionate commentary on my father's remains jarred me into the here and now. All I could do was laugh and realize, "That's the eulogy Dad would want."

I was done. I had one small canister left, so I put it in my pocket and headed back towards my car in the huge vacant parking lot. Mick began walking towards the dugout on the first-base side of Dodger Stadium. I was under the assumption that I was going to my car to wait for the game. I felt that I had bothered Mickey enough.

Mick yelled at me quizzically, "Hey numb nuts, where are you going?"

"I thought I was supposed to wait in my car," I called back.

"No, Mike [Scioscia, the Angels manager and former Dodgers great], and I want you to hang out with us today." So we walked across the infield—I just had to step on first base of course—and then Mickey pointed to the dugout and told me to sit there while he went in to get dressed.

"Todd, everybody knows you're allowed to be here. Mike's taking care of that...oh yeah, don't do anything stupid."

"Mickey Hatcher...is telling me not to do anything stupid? Boy if that is not the pot calling the kettle black!" He disappeared down the hallway tunnel into the clubhouse.

I was alone in the dugout at Dodger Stadium! How cool was this?

I had been through Dodger Stadium before, but it had been a while. I started to get happy; I started to get excited. I'm sitting there as Garrett Anderson, David Eckstein, and Troy Glaus passed by and said "hello," even though they didn't know me. I remember thinking at that moment, "I'm old!" All these guys were younger than I am. In fact, when Eckstein passed by, I felt like asking him if he had a hall pass from fourth period; he looked like one of my students.

All the players filed into the clubhouse eventually, and then Angels manager Mike Scioscia, came into the dugout. He said, "Hi, Todd. How are you and your family holding up?"

"We're doing fine. It is a shock. But we are fine...so far. We all are really looking forward to tonight." My entire family was going to be there later that evening; Mom, my sisters Susan and Peggy, and my brothers Greg and Brent. It was shaping up to be a magical night... it was Angels vs. Dodgers at Dodger Stadium and it was, of all things, ...Flag Day—June 14th—and the Dodgers were thrilled to have my sister, Susan Anton, sing the National Anthem.

Now that the awkwardness of talking about Dad's passing was out of the way, Mike took one look at my L.A. Dodgers hat and said... "What the hell's that hat doing on your head? Take it off!" Mike then playfully took it off and threw it to the ground. He told Ken, their clubhouse manager, "Throw that old hat away and get him something that belongs here!"

I think Mike was implying to me that his days as a Dodger were over and indirectly asking me, "Are yours?" At that moment I was torn; I was ambivalent. I felt like a kid with divorced parents having to choose whom to live with. Regardless of my present frame of mind, I did manage to blurt out, "My Dad gave me that hat!"

Then Mike said, "Put it in your bag, and while you're at it, get rid of the bag, too!"

Ken came back and asked me what my hat size was. He checked the inside of my old Dodgers hat and took off back into the clubhouse. He returned with an Angel hat. Ken put it on my head and added, "Todd, this is Tim Salmon's hat." Tim Salmon is an Angels superstar.

I sat down on the Anaheim Angels bench wearing Tim Salmon's

hat thinking this is pretty cool. I felt like a little kid all over again and I was in reality 38. Baseball does that to you. I gazed over towards center field, feeling its new special emotional value to me. I talked to the players as they waited for the grounds crew to set up the hitting cage and protective screens in the infield and outfield. The Angels were all so nice. So…genuine. Mike Scioscia looked at me and asked, "What the hell are you doing? You're not sitting on your ass in my dugout. You are going to work." So he throws me a glove—his Rawlings catcher's glove with "Mike Scioscia" stitched in Dodger blue twill. I was incredulous. In fact, I was speechless, and those who know me can tell you how rare an occurrence that is.

My indescribable afternoon was now bordering on the unbelievable. Mike Scioscia, in my mind the Dodgers' all-time greatest catcher, has just given me his glove…told me to get to work…doing what? I had no idea. After all the hell I had gone through since June 6, this was heaven. I must have looked rather bewildered, more like an ass, but Mike said, "Get out to center field, shag the balls, put them in the bucket, and bring them up to me so I can throw BP [batting practice]. What did you think? Do you think you are going to sit here for free? You have to earn your keep. Get out there."

I arrive at the screen and my job is to catch the balls tossed in by the outfielders, and then when the bucket is filled, run it up to Mike on the mound. Simple enough, I can do this. It was joy.

I kept saying in my mind, "This is one hell of a way to get me here, Dad, but thank you!"

I did feel like a total moron, though. Here I am, surrounded by all these uniformed professional ball players and I am wearing jean shorts, a D-Day T-shirt, and an Angels hat. Talk about feeling out of place! But I didn't care. I was at Dodger Stadium—no, I was on the field at Dodger Stadium! I'm sure that the Angels players were wondering who this chump was, running around looking like a school kid picking up marbles rolling all over the kitchen floor.

The Angels players liked to have a lot of fun and of course they like to razz the new guy. One of the things they like to do is give each other, or anyone new, a hard time by throwing the baseballs to him all at once. Now it was my turn. I was nearly pelted by four or five baseballs. One found its mark. I was nailed right in the chest by an Erstad fastball. God that hurt. Then all I heard was Mickey yelling at him.

"Damn it! What the hell are you doing?! He's out here putting his father's ashes out here, and you guys have to hit him with a ball? Don't you feel like crap?"

Erstad didn't believe him. "OK, where are they?" So Mickey took him over to the "chunks." "Hatcher, you are full of shit" and then he looked down and saw for once Mickey was telling the truth and loving every minute of his awkwardness.

Darin looked over at me and nodded as if to say "sorry," I waved back. In fact, I was laughing so damn hard and so was Mickey. Obviously, Darin didn't feel comfortable enough coming over to me to talk, but that was okay. If anyone wonders why Darin Erstad didn't dive for any balls in center that night, now you know. After batting practice, I went back to the dugout and was talking with Mickey, Ron Roenicke, the third base coach, and Mike. As we were talking, Dodgers pitcher Darren Dreifort came over to say hi. He saw us all together. Darren Dreifort was, at one time, a teammate of Mick and Mike. Darren had come up to our ranch many times with another good friend and Dodger, Todd Maulding, who used to coach in the Dodgers bullpen with Mark Creese. Darren knew Dad very well. In fact many Dodger players and coaches over the years would come up to the pond in Oak Glen, California's beautiful apple country, to relax and have fun throwing horsehoes, as a result of Dad's friendship with Mickey and Mickey constantly telling them about this beautiful place to get away from it all.

"Hey Todd, how's crazy Wally?" Darren asked.

"Well, Darren, that is why I am here tonight. Wally passed away and we put his ashes out there in center field. That's what he wanted done."

Darren looked towards center and wistfully replied, "I can't think of a better place for him to be."

"I can't either," I said, looking in the same direction. I then brought up Dad's idea while we were in the dugout. Darren, Mike, and Mick took me right out on the field and Mickey told me... "Hey Todd, shut up with that idea. There is media all through here; all these guys will steal you blind if they hear that story idea." Mike added, "Exactly. There is nobody we'd like to see do this more than you. You deserve it. You're doing it for all the right reasons. We will help you all we can."

Finally, the Dodgers usher came over and said, "Okay, Todd, it's time to go." I shook hands with the coaching staff and thanked them. What could I say? Thank you is not enough, but for that moment it was the best I could do. Ron Roenicke gave me a comforting pat on the back. I didn't want to leave, but I also knew I didn't belong anymore. My clock had struck midnight. So I went up to the seats where my family waited, minus Susan. She was waiting on the field to sing the National Anthem, not to the audience, but to Dad.

I finally got up to the seats and the field had changed. It was now full of soldiers, sailors, and Marines. Flags were everywhere. I hugged everyone and asked, pointing out to the field, "What's going on out there?" My strong, brave Mom forcefully said, "Well, honey, it's Flag Day. Don't you know that?" She gave me a small flag and on the stick were the words "Boeing Aircraft" and also "Made in China." Boeing Aircraft, a leading aircraft manufacturer in World War II, was sponsoring the pre-game program.

First, Dad dies on June 6. We have his full military service, and now we were at Dodger Stadium on Flag Day. The field was full of soldiers. Our entire family was holding small flags and looking up into the heavens when all of a sudden roaring overhead came a North American P-51 Mustang and a B-25 bomber and I thought, "Of course, Dad, of course, it would be this way." This was quite a send-off, a celebration for my Dad: Wallace Peter Anton. I finally watched the last plane fly off into the distance and my attention was drawn to the first striking chords of Dodgers organist Nancy Bea Hefley playing the National Anthem.

Standing at rapt attention as if I was a soldier, I watched my sister begin to sing Dad's favorite song. I was amazed at how everything had come together. It was so beautiful, so natural—and at this very moment Dodgers announcer Vin Scully provided my father's eulogy on Fox Sports West TV, although he didn't know it at the time.

Vin Scully's "Eulogy": Flag Night, June 14, 2002

For those of you not familiar with Dodger broadcasts, they always start out with Vin Scully's welcoming introduction: "It's tiiiiiiiiime for Dodger baseball."

When he does that, it's as if everything is OK and all is so familiar ...you know peace of mind. Then he started:

> "Hi everybody. Welcome to Dodger Stadium.
> Tonight. Flag night, and the Boeing Company has arranged
> for quite an air show.
> We had three Stearman Cadets, Four North American Texans;
> we had a B-25 Mitchell, a North American P-51 Mustang,
> and for good measure a Douglas DC-3.
> The military represented here on the field tonight:
> Army, Navy, Air Force, and Marines,
> and the B-25 comes overhead as we see
> the P-51 goes off in the distance...
> So we have started off in fine style
> here at Dodger Stadium.
> The fans receiving American flags
> and we have the Angels and the Dodgers.
> Two good ball clubs colliding for the first time this year...
> and now as the P-51 comes back, flying over Dodger Stadium
> the crowd again applauding.
> So this is a rather patriotic beginning
> here at Dodger Stadium as the crowd files in...
> It is a glorious time of day.
> Blue skies...a setting sun...
> beautiful Dodger Stadium."

Of course, Vinny didn't know how well his words fit. I often think of his fitting description and my heart is drawn to his comment on the "blue skies and a setting sun." It indeed was a setting sun. An ending, but somehow it didn't feel that way. It was as if I was beginning a tremendous journey.

Later that week on TV as Vinny was broadcasting, he made mention that the Red Sox were coming to town and he was reminded of a Father's Day story he read. The story was about a Brooklyn Dodgers pitcher who was drafted into the U.S. Army Air Corps in World War II. He was being shipped overseas and had stopped by Ebbets Field to say goodbye to his teammates. The other players presented him with a baseball and told him, "When you get over Germany, throw this out the bomb bay and hit 'em for the Dodgers."

Vinny continued... "Eventually he was assigned as a bombardier on a B-17. He got so busy on his first mission that he forgot to drop the ball. Once he remembered it tucked away in his flight jacket, his bomber was over the English Channel on its way back home.

"I'll do it on my next mission, he thought. Once again, he was so wrapped up in the mission that he forgot about the baseball. Eventually it became a good luck charm for him. After his 25th mission, he was rotated out and sent home. Not everyone in the crew was assigned to this B-17 at the same time. So he left for home before the others, keeping his lucky ball in hand. The next day his old ship, his B-17, was shot out of the sky.

"Nobody survived. The man came home and raised his family in Boston. After many years had passed, this aged veteran knew that the Boston Red Sox allow fathers and sons to come on to the field at Fenway Park on Father's Day to play catch. So this old man, this old Dodgers pitcher and old bombardier took his fully-grown son on to the field to play catch. The ball they used that day? The one he was supposed drop on Germany nearly sixty years earlier."

Not long after Vinny's story—on July 5, 2002—Ted Williams died. His passing convinced me all the more that the time to do this project was now. Ted Williams' death spurred me to action. I had missed another opportunity to interview a decorated veteran. Another bit of our history dies with each veteran whose story has not been told. Ted

Williams was one baseball/war veteran I would never be able to interview. I didn't want to let that happen with anyone else.

My sister Susan, who was in town on her way to a Palm Springs party for Suzanne Sommers, and I ate breakfast not long after Williams' passing. I mentioned my idea about honoring baseball's veterans and told her a few stories that I knew. She was dumbfounded that nobody had written about this baseball story in a style similar to Ambrose's. Later that night at the party she ran into an old friend of hers who was a literary agent, Al Lowman. Quickly he stepped in and told me to "get to work. This journey will take you places, kid."

This journey that I believed would send me all across America talking to legends of the game began in, of all places, Hesperia, California—just ten minutes from my front door.

5

Lt. Bert Shepard US Army Air Force

38th Squadron, 55th Fighter Group, Eighth Air Force;
Washington Senators 1945

Over the months since Dad passed away, I had both my good and bad moments. I kept reaching for the phone to call him. My heart told me he would answer, but of course he didn't. I wanted so bad to know what he thought of the Angels' success when they won the World Series on Dad's 78th birthday. I loved that coincidence. It was one of so many in the pursuit of my project that it borders on the spiritual.

As I watched the celebrations, my thoughts turned to Dad. I knew how thrilled he was to see Mickey Hatcher and Mike Scioscia doing so well. We all were, and I especially loved my World Series gift—a ball autographed by the entire Angels team. A gift from Mickey Hatcher. I was so happy and excited to hear the term "World Champion Anaheim Angels." It sounded so strange to me. It still seemed hard to believe that I was happy an American League team had won the Series. But why wouldn't I be? As a devout Dodgers fan, these Angels from Anaheim—led by former Dodger greats—had just beaten the San Francisco Giants in seven games. It was so sweet, so justified in so many ways. Perfect.

As I drove home from Mom's, I continued thinking about baseball, my veterans project, and all that lay before me. As I drove up the long monotonous Cajon Pass, a thought popped into my head. I remembered hearing about a baseball player who had lost a leg in W.W. II, yet somehow come back and pitched in the major leagues. I had seen this story on "This Week in Baseball" with Mel Allen a year or two earlier.

The memory kept nagging, really bothering me. I went to bed and woke up about 3:00 a.m., trying to remember details from that show. The landscape looked so familiar with the Joshua trees, sand, and

Bert Shepard ready for mission. Courtesy of Bill Swank.

stucco homes. I vaguely remember reading something about a man like this in my local newspaper. What was his name? Then it came to me, I "heard" his name as if somebody was audibly saying it...Bert Shepard.

I was already awake, so I went to the kitchen cupboard and got out the phonebook in the dark. I didn't want to wake anybody. I opened up the fridge and held the book up to its dim light. Awkwardly holding this massive book, it felt like holding water, but I paged to the "S" section and my eye started running down the list of names. I really didn't expect to find anything.

But I did.

There was a Bert Shepard who lived in Hesperia, 10 or 15 minutes from my house. I couldn't believe it. I called later that morning and a voice came over the phone. I could tell the person was older, and the adrenaline kicked in. I asked, "Excuse me for calling, but are you the

Bert Shepard who pitched for the Washington Senators and flew in World War II?"

"Hell, yes. You're talking to him."

Absolute shock set in. Are you kidding me? Trying to mask my shock and joy, I explained what I'd resolved to undertake and how his story would have a prominent place in the book. "God, that would be great," Bert said. "Where are you flying in from?"

I laughed and told him. "Victorville."

"No shit? You mean you're right up here?"

"You bet I am, I live about 15 minutes away."

"Get on over here, then." I did. I jumped in my Rodeo and sped off.

I arrived at his home but it looked like he was moving out. There was a crew of kids and young guys moving things around. They welcomed me in. Nobody was moving. A water pipe had burst and they were repairing the water damage and also making improvements. We went into the living room and Bert sat down in his green chair, leaned back, and crossed his legs.

I tried not to notice, but I could see this metal shaft sticking out of his shoe and climbing up his pant leg.

He noticed and started talking about his leg. He did this to make me feel at ease.

"Don't worry about it, Todd. This leg has been with me awhile now." He pulled his pant leg up revealing a plastic and metal leg full of cracks. I was shocked at its condition and said, "Bert, you deserve a better leg than this! Have you talked to the Veterans Administration about this?"

"Damn, Todd. That takes forever and unless it is falling off or stolen, they won't do anything about it."

"Have you asked them about it?" I was infuriated.

"Well, let me tell you, Todd, about the wonderful world of being a disabled veteran."

Bert told me a lot about HMOs and bureaucracy. I was totally shocked and angry. This noble warrior had given up so much. If I could have bought him a new leg right then, I would have. I just knew there had to be some MLB [Major League Baseball] retirement program or something. I committed myself to doing something about it. I thought of writing my congressman, Jerry Lewis. He takes care of veterans, I thought, and he knows my family too. "I'll call Jerry Lewis." I told Bert.

Oh, Hell, Todd, this leg is no big deal. My favorite leg was the one I had back in the late 1940s; it allowed me to become Ted Williams' favorite story. You know, after the war I had my moment in the majors and then I became a salesman in New York City. I had friends on the Yankees. My good friend was Phil Rizzuto and he asked me to come in and throw batting practice to him and Joe DiMaggio. "The Yankee Clipper," as Joe was called, was having trouble hitting left-handers.

So I often went in and threw. That was fun. Hell, it was Yankee Stadium! One day, I was at Yankee Stadium when the Boston Red Sox were in town. I faced them in my only game when I was with Washington. It was good to see Ted Williams. He told me to pitch to him, too. He could use the work. Nobody seemed to mind. The Sox were out of it anyway. So I started pitching to him. Each time I followed through and brought my wooden leg around there was this big cracking sound and a big crack, both coming from my leg.

I threw again and again...crack. It was again getting bigger-louder. Ted didn't notice, but each time I could see my fake foot beginning to turn inwards towards a 90-degree angle, totally abnormal to look at. I felt no pain at all. How could I?

Again I threw and followed through...crack! Now I knew the foot was totally disconnected. I was landing on the shaft, you know a peg leg. Ted was beginning to laugh.

Now I wound up for what I knew would be my final pitch. I lifted my leg and all my foot did was spin around and around.

Ted Williams fell down laughing so hard. I struck him out!

Bert was obviously enjoying this memory. He was laughing hard himself. It was nice to see.

What a character, I thought. I couldn't wait to hear the rest of his story.

We got down to work. It seemed like something from the movie *Field of Dreams*.

If You Build It, They Will Come

I figured *Field of Dreams* was right: If you build it, they will come. At least they did in Clinton, Indiana in 1937. Every day and every night—when the weather was good enough—the town's only ball field was full of men or boys throwing, hitting, catching, and having a good time. That's what Indiana men and Indiana boys did in 1937. Bert Shepard was no exception. It was the Great Depression; there wasn't much else to do according to Bert.

We had gone through the Depression and hadn't recovered very well. We got one pair of overalls and one shirt through all of school. That had to last us. Of course, my mother would patch it up. It was pretty ragged at the end of school, but that was all we got. We didn't know any different, so what the hell. There were six boys in my family and my dad had a pretty good load to carry. I was the one boy who was always there. Every day, after school got out, I ran to the field, home-made glove in hand. I usually had to wait for the other guys to catch up.

Summer vacation was even better, no school to get in the way. Sure, I had work to do at home, but the second I was finished, I sprinted out to the ball field. We had a sandlot team that would gather out at the park at ten o'clock in the morning. The boys would play all day until the men of the team would take over. I would do whatever I could, shag flies or anything, because they were grown men. I would get home about dark and there would be something warm in the oven for me. It wasn't long before the men recognized I was able to do more than carry their gloves and field batting practice. But it was out of the question to let me play with the big team.

One summer evening, another team—from nearby West Atherton—came to play the men of Clinton. But they were a man short. Rather than waste their time and forfeit, they took a look around the park.

I was throwing batting practice for my friends. Even though it was BP, they were having a hard time hitting me. I tried as hard as I could but I just couldn't take the snap off my fastball, or the curl off my slider. I'm too competitive. Figuring anything was better than a forfeit, I guess, the men of West Atherton called me over and asked me if I wanted to pitch. I couldn't even answer at first, I was that excited.

When I came to the mound to start the bottom of the first, I did everything I could to shut out the jeering and laughter of the men of Clinton. I tried, also, not to hear my pals on the sideline cheering me on against their own fathers.

I threw with everything that was in me. Whump! Strike! I looked at the batter's face. All I could see was shock. And fear. I knew it was no fluke. I knew I could do this.

I shut them out. We, West Atherton, won 3–0 and I became a popular man in Clinton, Indiana too! That suited me just fine!

It didn't end there. I started traveling with the men's team. They had a tournament in Terre Haute with this team that I had just beaten; of course, I wasn't scheduled to play because it seats 13,000 there. Some say I may have been the team's best pitcher, but no 17-year-old is going to be ready to play in front of a crowd like that, these men argued. I went along anyway, just in case.

[The Terre Haute team] had five players coming down from Danville, Illinois. They had some pro experience and they were very good players, but they had a car wreck. So our manager was going to call it off, and I said: "Hell, here is my friend that I am in high school with and here is another guy. Hell, we got nine players here. We will have a couple of pitchers in the outfield and my friend on shortstop," I said. "Hell. Let's play." By God, we did and I beat them 3–0—that sort of got things started. I had beaten the team that brought me! They thought I wasn't ready to play. Bullshit! Now there was no denying it. I was turning into…a legitimate ballplayer. I knew I could do it.

But before I could pursue any dreams I had to finish high school, and I had to make some money. When summer came in 1938 and '39, like many other young men, I went to a Civilian Conservation Camp, you know FDR's CCC program. These camps were a government make-work idea that kept plenty of men in pocket change by planting trees and cleaning waterways.

I also had another way to supplement the $30 a month I made at camp, $20 of which I sent to my parents. I charged 10 cents a haircut. I would go to a house and they would have six kids. That would be 60 cents; the old man would get a haircut, and that would be 70 cents. So I was a traveling barber. The barbers charged 25 cents and 50 cents, so I was undercutting them, but hell, if a guy has six kids at 60 cents, it helps him out. If he gets a haircut, then it's 70 cents. No tips or anything, just 70 cents.

Without much else to do, I moved to Bisbee, Arizona, where I drove a truck during the day and played a season of unpaid minor-league ball in the evenings. Maybe some scout would see me and sign me up to play for money. I used Bob Feller as a reference point, but so did a lot of us kids.

A Changing World

Bert leaned back in his chair and took a deep breath. "Todd, are you thirsty?" He got up, went to the kitchen and came back, sat down, stared out the window as if going back in time, and he started again.

In September 1939, Germany had stormed over Poland, and Britain and France immediately declared war. On the other side of the world, the Japanese had long since invaded China and had been threatening Western interests ever since. I knew what was going on. I just didn't expect to get in it, you know, I guess many other Americans like me felt—let the other countries have their wars. But then Pearl Harbor changed the whole picture, and we were way behind when the war started.

I signed up for the service right away. I wanted to fly, but so did countless others. The system was clogged. I passed the cadet exam, even though I only had a high school education. I was waiting to be called into cadets, but so many people were volunteering, they had to hold my application up. In the meantime, my draft number came up back in Indiana and I went in the Army at Fort Benjamin Harrison. From there, I was sent to the infamous Army training base in Biloxi, Mississippi. We had basic training and that was eight weeks, it was hot and it was that prickly heat, and you are out there marching in that heavy sand. "Turn real hard! Turn real hard!" they'd order, and you're doing that all day long. It was miserable and there was no air conditioning in the barracks and it was hot at night and this was in June and July. Oh God, it was miserable, so I would do anything to get out of there.

I completed basic in Biloxi, and I volunteered for anything to get out of there. The fact that I had passed my cadet exam now helped me immensely. So they sent me to Daniel Field, Georgia, which was a very mild U.S. Army Air Force Base

One of the benefits of Daniel Field was that we were allowed to play sports as we waited for our assignments. Baseball may be the national pastime, but these tough southern and mid-western boys wanted to play football. Hell, I jumped right in. I had never played a football game in my life, but I thought I would go out anyway. The coach said, "Where are you from?" I said, "Indiana." He thought I meant Indiana University; even now, I still laugh at this memory. So, he gave me a shot at first-string fullback, and I made the team.

I guess I was a good athlete, but playing the toughest position in the toughest game held a few surprises for me. Our first game was against some college in North Carolina. A guy stuck his knee right in my ribs and fractured them. I missed the next two games. The third game, we played Jacksonville Naval Training Station. They had George McAfee of the Bears, George Callen of the Cardinals. Six out of the starting eleven were out of the National Football League and none of our players had played pro ball, just college.

The talented swabbies did not take it easy on us recruits. I had never played before, but they thought I had. So, we went to play Jacksonville Naval Training Station and they beat us 50-something to nothing, but I was proud of my contribution in this massacre. I had made about eleven tackles and I was having a pretty good game. That was the first real game that I personally did not get injured in.

Just as I was getting used to it, my football season came to an abrupt finish. I got back to Daniel Field, and there were my orders to go to cadets.

Before I left, I had some owning up to do. I had to come clean about my football experience; one of coaches I had befriended was Joe Burnett, who had been something of a star himself at the University of Pennsylvania. I told him that the first time I'd ever played football was there at Daniel Field. After he stopped swearing, Burnett laughed and told me that I'd fooled a lot of people. He showed me that day's newspaper with a story all about how much I, the star fullback from Indiana, had added to the football team. Damn, that was funny!

From there, I took a train for preflight training at Santa Ana, California. You know, I may have fooled people into thinking I was a fullback, but I was no pilot yet. I had never been near an airplane. I had seen them fly, but I had never actually been near one.

As I was making friends among the other cadets, I realized that I was, again, the only one without prior experience. We're talking about flying and everybody else had flown with a Piper Cub or some little thing or they had their license and had flown quite a bit. That was four months of studying I knew nothing about.

Of course that was no barrier for me. I was ever-confident. Why? Don't know. I just was.

I didn't have to fake it, the time would come sooner than I expected when my inexperience would show. The instructor asked us how many hours we had flown. They all answered. That is, except me. One guy had 100 hours.

My silence made me stand out.

The instructor came face to face to me and asked me exactly how many hours I'd flown. There was no getting around it. I motioned toward the trainer on the runway outside and told the instructor that that was the closest I'd ever been to a plane in my life.

"Good!" The instructor smiled. "I'll take you first."

We walked all the way around the Ryan PT-22 Recruit primary trainer. The fuselage was highly polished, almost chrome, the wings were yellow and the nose—with five cylinder heads sticking out of it—was a gaudy red. I couldn't help notice that, despite the attention paid to the PT-22's appearance, it was a primitive machine—an open two-seat cockpit. This would be flying at its most basic.

It turns out that the instructor was a pretty good guy. So, he took me up, he took off, and I rode around with him for awhile and landed. "Nothing to it," I thought.

Although the instructors were pretty understanding about my lack of flying experience, my classmates weren't always so kind. After six flying hours, my regular instructor was sick, so I had to go with another instructor. He starts teaching takeoffs as soon as you get into the airplane and I had never tried takeoffs. One of the guys that went up before me said: "Boy, that torque sure takes off. You got to kick that foot in, it really will take off on you." So that was the only thing I had in mind. I had it all planned. In order to compensate for the torque from the propeller, I'd slam my foot down on the rudder. That way, I'd stay in a straight line. So I thought!

This guy started teaching takeoffs as soon as we got into the airplane and he thought I had been practicing takeoffs. Goddamn, I'd take off and the airplane and torque started taking it to the right. I would kick [on the rudder pedal] real hard and here it would come back across this way. I was laughing as I saw how the plane bounced sideways across the runway as I overcompensated for the pull of the propeller. I would let up on it, then it's this way now, and I would kick it this way. I was finally going sideways. I said; "Oh my God, I am going to wash out for sure."

Once we stopped the plane on the infield grass, I finally admitted that I only had six hours' experience and had never taken off before. The instructor told me not to worry about it. Then we— along with some other students—pushed the plane back to the starting point and we tried again. This time, I aced it.

I soloed an hour later. I was so relieved to just be alone in the air. You know, free.

When primary training was over, I moved to California to learn the finer points of flying. I had a rookie lieutenant, and I was in the first group that he had trained. He wasn't a real good instructor; the problem I had with him is that you would come in to land or do a maneuver and he always had his hands on the control, so you didn't get the feel of it. I was frustrated. When I went up with other instructors, they were more knowledgeable. I could learn a lot from them, but I couldn't learn anything from my regular instructor.

Although we had moved up in to a more advanced class, our planes didn't get much better. The Beech AT-10 Wichita certainly looked the part with its twin engines and enclosed canopy, but even we young pilots knew it was a third-rate aircraft. Underpowered and made largely of plywood, the AT-10 did not inspire confidence, and performed like a tractor. It would *fly at 120 mph straight, dive at 120; it just was not a good airplane to train in, and it was a wonder I didn't wash out. You are supposed to come in and keep the glide down low to the ground, because you don't know when it's going to finally level off. Well, I am up with another instructor flying nighttime and we went up and flew in this airplane. He broke the glide high and just came in nice and soft. He said, "Now break the glide at about 50 feet," which I didn't want to do, but I did. I got him going straight for the ground and his headset comes off and everything else. I said. "Goddamn it, I'm washed out now," but nothing broke. Not only hadn't I crashed, but I'd scared the instructor into passing me. The damned instructor didn't understand the airplanes, especially this piece of shit. I knew I was able to get through and graduate then.*

Every day, it was the same routine, not something I could stand for long. Although we were allowed to fly every afternoon and every evening, morning was reserved for a drudgery called ground school. This new captain, Captain Rand—he and I didn't get along too good—had his own strict ground school schedule and wanted us to fly in the morning. So, I went to the head of flying control and told them we flew yesterday afternoon and we flew last night and we are supposed to have ground school this morning and fly this afternoon. I told him, "I don't think it's good for safety reasons." I was never one to know my place. I knew I was right and I had to say something. I'm just a cadet, but, Goddamn it, when I see something wrong, I am going to speak up.

Cadet or not, the colonel agreed and shut down ground school.

Oh, that captain was furious! One of the cadets went back home and stopped to see Captain Rand, and Captain Rand wanted to know who all made it.

"How about Shepard?" Rand asked.

"Oh sure, he made it."

Captain Rand was shocked, and angry. Cursing, he said, "I did everything I could to keep him from graduating."

He admitted it! I knew it! Well, I wouldn't give in to him, you know.

The Forked-Tailed Devil

I asked about flying and the P-38. I wanted to get to his service in World War II. He became animated and stood up, telling me that he had to "stretch his leg." I noticed he made sure to keep it singular. It was approaching twilight time.

Finally, Todd, I got to fly the hotrod. In 1943, America's most potent fighter was easily the Lockheed P-38 Lightning. Man, I loved that plane. It was bigger and faster than anything else in the air at the time.The heavily armed P-38 had already established itself as one of the most dangerous opponents in the sky. The Germans, who often thought better than to tangle with the unique twin-boom fighter, called it the "Der Gabelschwanz Teufel" —the fork-tailed devil. It was still training for me, but it was in the Lightning and I wanted to fly it!

See, I was at Williams Field, Arizona, which is just south of Phoenix, and I head for Bisbee, where I played ball. The first time I soloed in a P-38, the town was down near a little gully. I buzzed the town, did a loop, and came out of the loop down between the buildings right in front of the baseball office at the Copper Queen Hotel.

The last thing I wanted was to lose my P-38, but I also was never one to play by other people's rules.

I knew I was lucky—thousands of young men were standing in line to get into a P-38. But I couldn't control myself. I was young, largely unsupervised, and had the hottest plane in the air. So the third or fourth time I got in a P-38, I headed for the Grand Canyon, After all, I was in Arizona. You could find it pretty easy and, of course, it was way out of our flying zone. I wanted to see what this P-38 was all about.

I saw that big ol' hole and I dove all the way down the bottom, about 5,000 feet. I said, "Climb, you son of a bitch, climb." I remember the terror of flying over 400 mph straight at a massive sheet of rock. So I climbed out of there, did a nice chandelle, got out of there and never told anybody. Well, until now that is.

That was the difference between me and other men—while some guys would be tempted to risk everything to take the Lightning into the Grand Canyon, I actually would. And did. I wasn't showing off. There was no one there to see me. I was just having fun.

My training soon finished and I found myself on a troop train to New York. We left on Christmas Eve. Goddamn, that was an awful cold ship. We set sail about two o'clock in the morning.

New York City: Point of Departure

We had about 10,000 American troops crossing the frigid, U-boat-infested waters of the North Atlantic in an old ocean liner, the R.M.S Aquitania. A four-stacker with a striking resemblance to the Titanic, the Aquitania was known as the "ship beautiful" during her luxury cruise career before the war, I was told. But that's not how I or my shipmates saw it. Stripped of virtually every amenity to increase capacity and speed, the Aquitania was like a huge iron prison.

Although I was one of the few who did not get seasick, I had terrible memories of one thing in particular: the food. One boy cut into a duck and it was raw inside because they hadn't learned you are supposed to let it thaw out before you cook it. So this one ole boy said; "Bring that chef here." The chef came over to us, and he said, "Hey this bird's not dead yet, I think you can save him." God damn, I thought there would be a riot!

Despite the ship's size and the Allies' desperate need for 10,000 Americans in Europe, the unarmed Aquitania crossed the unsecured Atlantic without any escort. We were counting on our speed and zigzagging. I guess they had rumors of some German submarines in the area, so they had to swing further up north. It took us nine days to cross. Normally, it was about five or six.

Once in England—we arrived near New Years Day—the twenty or so of us P-38 pilots from the Aquitania had to undergo another brief period of flight training because it had been three weeks since any of us had flown.

I, as usual, found trouble right away. But this time, the plane was to blame, not my attitude. The first airplane I took off in, the engine revved up and went wild on me, so I had to go back and land with hardly no engine power. The ground crew couldn't tell what was wrong, but they could see that I was coming in for an unscheduled landing. They cleared the runway. Everyone on the base watched as I gingerly put the plane down without incident. The red lights were going all over, but I was able to land.

I was kind of embarrassed, so I strode past the other pilots and ground crew and said to the crew chief, "Well, I only graduated six months ago, but I'm studying every night." I got stony silence for an answer.

I took off the next time, Goddamn, everything went wrong, and so I came back and landed. The proper maximum RPM is say 3,000, but mine was doing 3,600 RPM with no power. I had to nurse it back in. Those were the only two flights I got for training and then we went down to our combat outfit because they were short of pilots. If this bad luck had been a test, I guess I had somehow passed.

I was surprised at the welcome I received from the veteran pilots of the 38th Squadron of the 55th Fighter Group. It was the opposite of the cold shoulder that we replacements were told to expect. They were just wonderful to us. They were so glad to see us. They didn't have that kind of crap that they show in the movies. We weren't career officers. We were there to fight the war and get the hell out of there. We were well-accepted.

It wasn't simple courtesy. Combat losses and accidents had reduced the number of pilots in the 38th from 30 to 16. Since a squadron was required to put 16 planes in the air each day, every pilot was flying every day. That is what we were there to do. You know, share the load.

We were gonna give the veteran pilots some days off. They were glad to see us and they put us in flying right away.

News of the pilot losses didn't slow me down a bit. I just flew any damn thing they had ready. Some pilots had planes assigned to them and others took what they could get or sat it out. I flew more combat than anybody in the group, because, Hell, I wanted to fly.

Not all the pilots shared my enthusiasm; my unit had its share of sad sacks. They just didn't want to fly; maybe they felt a little woozy when they had to start out across the Channel. God, I remember some of the excuses guys would give. "Oh, the engine's running rough" and they would turn around and come back. We had a captain there that was very famous for that. They finally transferred him to headquarters. You know, promoted him!

Before I got there, they had some very poor leadership. I forget the colonel's name, but he was a stateside colonel and a little old. One of his great orders, that pissed us off, was when we were flying at about 20,000 feet coming home and we saw some enemy down below. He sent eight of us down to engage in a combat—and he stayed at 20,000 feet, and in a little while he said: "All those not engaged in combat set forth for home." He just left them there. I disobeyed and went in to help. That bastard just left us there.

He wasn't the most popular colonel—he led us for a little while and then he went to headquarters. You know—promote incompetence!

Even with that colonel gone, the leadership didn't improve much. Then we had a captain who talked a better fight than he flew. "Oh, we got a good mission today, boy, we'll go get 'em," he'd say, and he would always turn back. He would go to the Channel or the West Coast of France and turn back, saying his "engine's running rough."

I was the opposite. I flew every time I could. Hell, if some guy didn't want to fly I would say, "I'll take your place today." Goddamnit, I loved to fly. After all . . . It's my country.

The Mighty Eighth

Our job in the American Eighth Air Force was bombarding Germany and German-occupied cities in increasing numbers. Thousand-plane raids were becoming a regularity. Unlike the British Royal Air Force, which did its bombing under the cover of darkness, our giant B-17s and B-24s flew over the enemy in broad daylight. Although our big bombers were loaded with .50-caliber machine guns, their bloody experience showed that the only effective way to counter German fighters was with a fighter escort. That's where the Lightning came in. I loved being on this awesome team. Damn, that Eighth Air Force did a lot of work.

Never once were the bombers under attack when we were with them. The bombers would be flying, there would be some Germans over here, we would just turn into them, and they would take off. I'll tell you this, the pilots of the Luftwaffe had their own bloody experiences at the hands of our Eighth, and they knew better than to test the Lightnings.

A 38 wasn't a good airplane to make a head-on pass at. We had four .50 cal machine guns and a 20 mm right in the center of our nose in the 38. We would shoot the hell out of them, and he can't hit us, because he has guns that converge at 300 yards and two more that converge at 400 yards, so at 1,000 yards those Germans flyers can't touch us. There was a problem, though. The Lightning had only carried enough gas to get part of the way to some of the bomber's targets. We had to go back when the gas gauge says you better head home. That was about the last thing the bomber crews wanted to see.

One specific target city was within the Lightning's range.

Berlin.

When I found out that this day's mission was over Berlin, I felt no special anxiety. Aw, hell, we were just gonna go, you know, get it over with and come home. I got a P-38. I got guns and ammunition and if anybody gets in my way, I'll shoot his ass down.

I didn't fear the Luftwaffe; I did have other concerns. It was cold that day and probably 50 below in the cockpit. We didn't have a heater inside because our engines were outside. Goddamn, it was so cold in the cockpit.

Although the men of our 38th got credit for being the first Americans over Berlin, we didn't see any action. At 30,000 feet, we were too high for flak and not only didn't the Luftwaffe show up, neither did our bombers! We were supposed to escort B-17s, but they had to turn back and we didn't get the message. So, here we go all the way to Berlin and circle around Berlin and there are no bombers! There were a lot of screw-ups like this in World War II.

I also flew on missions the bomber pilots feared most—the heavily defended ball-bearings factories of Schweinfurt. One day on the way to Schweinfurt, there was a group of B-24s going down and we were pretty close to them, and then a B-24 just peels off north to Switzerland, where they landed and sat out the rest of the war. Another pilot and I followed them down; figured they need some escort in case the Germans come up to get them. So, they get leveled off, we fly up pretty close, and they are waving at us. They knew where they were going. They had already planned it. These men were deserting. Switzerland had managed to remain neutral in World War II and detained any combatants who ventured into its territory. The men would spend the rest of the war as civilians, guests of the Swiss government. Hell, some of them landed with their regular street clothes on and only wore their helmet and everything else. It was pre-planned, but who could prove it?

My own attitude couldn't have been further from theirs. Typically, when I saw a chance at action, I couldn't pass it up. Once we were on a mission and I am at about 25,000 and I saw a P-38 down below me with a German on his tail. I called it into my leader and he wasn't real eager to join in. So, hell, I just peel off and dove for the German Me-109. He sees me coming and he breaks off.

The airplane I flew in that day was because everybody else had turned it down. So I said: "Let me fly the damn thing." I took off with it and everything was going nice until I rolled over to put it in a dive. It just started shaking and bumping real bad, but I was able to scare the German off the P-38 down there.

Despite my willingness to fight, I was no ace. I never fired my gun at any enemy aircraft in the air. Never fired at them once. If you can't hit them, then there is no need firing. I'm not disappointed. I had them pass underneath me head-on, probably 100 feet below me, but I couldn't get my nose down fast enough, so there was no need to fire. So I never fired my guns once in 34 missions! Of course, I got it planned that if I live to be 95, I may get two or three victories by then, because there won't be anybody around who can deny it. There are a few people I know who picked up a few victories that way.

I remember the date I chased the Messerschmitt off my buddy's tail—May 21, 1944. It doesn't stick in my mind because I think this was an important event. It's because it happened to be opening day for the baseball team I'd organized.

I'll Be Back in Time for the Game!

This demonstrates what baseball meant to Bert. Here he was, going into warfare, and what is on his mind? Baseball. Indeed, this is America's sport.

It was an afternoon game, and we were taking off at eight o'clock in the morning. So I said, "I'll be back in time for the game." I never made it. I was shot down.

Ever the kidder, after I was exchanged from a German POW camp, when I got home, I decided to pull a pretty young reporter's leg that was there to cover our return. I said to this columnist from New York: "My players were very loyal and they waited two weeks there for me to return. Once somebody got a hold of the paper saying I was missing, they figured out that something had happened to me, so they called the game off after two weeks." She went ahead and put it in the column! What I didn't know was that the young journalist was Dorothy Kilgallen, whose nationally syndi-

cated column was read by virtually everyone. So all America read this BS of mine!

"But here is the true story, Todd," Bert said as he sat back down, grabbing a sip of water. He leaned back in his chair and brought up the footrest, again exposing his steel-shafted leg that had such a story behind it.

We sent up 3,000 aircraft to go in as far as we could and just go to the ground and strafe every damn thing we could, anything that moved. The Germans didn't send up any aircraft because they would have got clobbered, but they took care of us with ground fire. They knocked down 46 aircraft that day. That is a pretty good bunch of aircraft.

The 38th, my group, was hit especially hard. Six of the squadron went down and I happened to be one of them. We all survived. There was nothing wrong with the other guys. I was the only one that was injured.

I had been down shooting up some stuff, and I got word that there was some aircraft on the field up ahead. Some of our aircraft had strafed them, but there was more on the field. I just said to myself, "I'll just stay down straight and low and make a pass and keep on going." What I didn't see were the anti-aircraft guns. The Germans had made a clearing in a small forest and placed an 88-mm anti-aircraft gun among the trees. The only way to see the gun was from above—directly above. That's how I discovered it.

My attention fixed on the burning German aircraft on the airfield up ahead, I found out about that damn gun when my right foot was blown off.

A shell had come up through the floor of the cockpit and taken my foot off. I looked down to check the damage, but since I was only 25 feet off the ground, I couldn't look down for long. I called the colonel and told him I had a limb shot off and I would call him back later. In the meantime, I got hit in the chin. There is a scar there now. You can see it.

I guess I slumped over the controls and I don't remember anything until I woke up in the hospital. I possibly remember coming to, but I can't say for sure; you are in a daze. One thing I do remember, though, is that the Germans kept shooting at me long after I started going down.

The next thing I know, I had come to . . . in a German hospital. They had taken my leg off and put a metal plate up here in my chin and this face was all sewn-up like a baseball.

A German Luftwaffe surgeon, Dr. Ladislaus Loidl, was operating on some of the German civilians and soldiers injured in the attack. You know, my attack. Despite his best efforts, many of them were dying. In between operations, he received orders to go to the wreck of a P-38 and, if the pilot was alive, take him prisoner. He did as he was told.

Thank God.

But it wasn't easy for him to do so. The new emphasis on ground-attack had not endeared us American pilots to the German people. In an effort to cripple the German military, our Air Force had taken a terrible toll on civilians and their property. I guess we had earned a new name from the Germans... "Terrorflieger"—terror pilots.

When Dr. Loidl arrived at the wreck, it was surrounded by farmers, many of whom were wielding pitchforks and other makeshift weapons. They were going to run me through. Alone, Loidl chased them all away. He set aside his politics and saw a person.

He called the nearest hospital at Leutensweis [sic], which was about 10 miles away. He said, "I've got a flyer here that's down, an American."

They refused him. "We won't take him, he is a terrorflieger."

So he called Berlin, the office that had given him the orders in the first place, and told them to call a hospital for him. They, too, refused, saying: "You take him, you're responsible."

Loidl, who appears to have had a personality very much like me, took me to another nearby hospital. They might refuse him over the phone, but there's no way they'd say no to his face. I was unconscious the whole time!

Thank You for Saving My Life

I sat in rapture listening to Bert. He was so matter of fact about his experience I was amazed at how comfortable he was describing such a traumatic moment —the loss of his leg.

I finally woke up in a hospital about a week later—without my right leg. They had removed my leg up here, just below my knee. The leg had been amputated and it was in good shape. I don't know how long it took them to do it.

But I didn't panic. I finally woke up and tried to piece the events to-gether. Let's see, I remember flying and crashing, I am thinking, "Am I in heaven, you know...is this heaven?" I remember, smiling. Things are start-ing to sharpen up, and then there are the German doctors, the nurses. I looked up at them. They pulled back the sheet. There the leg is, off below the knee.

The hospital staff couldn't help but stare. There was silence, tension in the room. They expected hysterics. Here I was, a captured airman, wak-ing up in an enemy hospital, discovering that my right foot was gone. But I surprised them all. I looked up at them and smiled and I said, "Thank you for saving my life." That seemed to settle everything down, and they treated me wonderfully. I never, never once even thought I would be mis-treated.

Recovering, I found out that the Allies had succeeded in invading the European continent. We got the news about the Normandy landings about three weeks after D-Day. An orderly came in and said, "The war will be over soon."

As I recovered, I was sent to prison camps further and further into Ger-many as the Allies advanced. I was surprised at the general goodwill of the German people. One guard—this was at the Meiningen camp, the fourth or fifth prison camp I was in—rides by on a bicycle. He was a civilian guard. You could tell it by his uniform. He would ride by on his bicycle and he would say "hallo" in his German accent. We would say, "Oh you little fat so-and-so," and "Let's take him out and cut his nuts off." We'd yell a lot of dirty things. Hell, this Kraut doesn't understand us, we figured. We kept it up for about a week, until one day this guy stops at the fence and asks in perfect English: "How are the Dodgers doing?"

After the shock wore off, we started laughing. Turns out, he had lived in Brooklyn for 12 years and worked as a policeman there. He came back to Germany to take care of his mother and the war started. Damn, I still laugh at that one.

There Is a Big Difference between Germans and Nazis

As Bert was talking, I noted a distinct fondness for his former enemy: the Germans. Bert also was very critical of the ignorance in America towards the Germans as people. They weren't all evil; the Nazi government and its ideology was evil, but to Bert it was always about the people; the one-on-one interactions which he personally experienced.

I was also impressed with the medical care I received. They did a hell of a job on the surgery and I had no pain after I had gotten over the numbness (and that was four weeks later.) I was in pretty good shape, but I only weighed 125 pounds. I had lost a lot of weight. With the Allies constantly advancing, I was moved to a POW camp, on the Baltic Sea. They took me down to the train station on a two-wheel alley cart because they were short of transportation. They put me in the corner of the baggage car because that's the only place there was room. I wasn't alone in the car, either. They brought a crate of pigs in. The pigs never complained at all. [The guards] give me a couple of sandwiches and I ate with the pigs that day.

Despite my situation, my spirit never flagged. Here I'm laying there in a train station on the stretcher and, Goddamn, there was a good-looking German gal who was in the service and I waved at her and she waved back. She didn't know I was an American POW.

The effect of our bombing campaign was becoming apparent as the Germans were resorting to desperate measures to travel. They took me to the hospital in a wood-burning car. They had to utilize so many different ways that we don't even think of here.

There were just 10 prisoners at our new camp: one Englishman, the rest were American. I was hungry and they brought me a box of prunes that came in a Red Cross parcel. I was sitting there talking to the prisoners and I ate the whole damn box. I was pretty hungry. I was there about three or four weeks. While there, the prisoners made me a crude artificial leg for me to walk on, and then I was ready to go down to the interrogation center in Frankfurt.

There was a big difference this time, though. They sent a two-man guard with me. We were going through Hamburg, and Hamburg had just had the hell bombed out of it about 10 days earlier, so the trains are all fouled up. We had to stay there overnight. I am on crutches and I had that crude leg on. We go to get on a German trolley car to go where we need to go. We don't anymore than get on there, and a German lady jumps up and gives me her seat—and this is a town that had just been slaughtered 10 days earlier... by us! I took the seat and there was no problem whatsoever. I tell you, not all Germans were Nazis!

We couldn't find places to sleep so we slept in the men's room in the train station. We were going to sleep in a hotel, but there just wasn't anything available. After interrogation, I was sent back to camp. As we were getting off the wagon to go inside, here comes a guy coming out of the station calling my name out. "Hey Bert, how are you doing?" He was an American, I knew his voice, but he had been burned so badly. Finally, he told me his name and then I knew who he was. I had trained with him in flight school years ago. He had been burned so badly and I couldn't recognize him and that was not good. I felt pretty bad.

As the war came to a close, we were moved to Meiningen, which was more like a convalescent home. Because all of the prisoners were severely injured and since every available German soldier was needed at the front, security was very light. And there we were allowed to play ball. This English guy wanted to play catch with me, and I hit him right between the eyes and knocked him colder than Hell. The other guys thought I was trying to kill him. No hard feelings. This English guy challenged me. He was a nice fellow, but he would say, "C'mon, boy, put something on it, put something on it, put it right here." So I put something on it. They thought I had hit him on purpose. Of course I didn't, but he just wanted me to throw a little harder, and so I did.

By the time the war ended, I was back in America playing ball. I got out of there on a prisoner exchange. Not many people know that the U.S. government and the Nazi Government did such a thing. But we knew we were getting ready for the prisoner exchanges because the other type of prisoners were guys who all had legs and arms off, broken backs and stuff. They were all severely disabled so the governments agreed to the exchange. The Swiss came around and examined us. They go through the Germans over in America and choose those who are the disabled to where they wouldn't go to combat again and they needed medical care.

All of us prisoners wanted to be part of the exchange. Guys would be up at four o'clock in the morning lighting a match to see if his name was still on the order. Finally, they had the orders posted. I was on it! It took them three days to ship us all out. They had a lot of civilians, German civilians and Jewish civilians, too, coming out of Germany. When we got back to the States, it was all hush-hush. There wasn't any publicity about them. I guess that had been going on, the Germans sent back from the States to Germany, and Jewish-Americans being sent back over here and there wasn't any publicity on it. It was very, very, very quiet.

New York

We arrived in New York almost a month after I saw my name on the order back in Germany. We were coming up the Hudson River and here were two big boats with bands on them playing music. I had this crude artificial leg that was made in Germany, but I wasn't going to let it hold me back and I said: "Hell, lets go downtown."

After my experiences in Germany, I wanted to do New York right. We went into Brooks Brothers to get me a new suit, and my damn foot broke on me. I had about six salesmen running around trying to find a hammer and nails to nail it together. I tied up six salesmen for the whole afternoon and never bought a damn thing. I wanted to go to Brooks Brothers because one of the guys in prison camp was from New York and that was his favorite suit store.

None of my friends or family could afford to travel from Indiana to visit me at the veteran's hospital in New York, so I entertained myself by watching the other wounded guys get welcomed home by their loved ones. God, I remember one moment really well . . . Danny Daniels, who I was in prison camp with, is in the middle of the room and his wife comes in. She just puts her hands on her hips and said, "What the hell is this? There is nothing wrong with you. What is going on?" Since he had never written to her about his injury, and because his injuries were internal, she couldn't see what was wrong with him. She said, "I had made up my mind that if you got both legs off and both arms off, I was going to care for you the rest of your life." I couldn't help but laugh. It was a very, very touching scene. He was a handsome devil. He could write music as fast as he could write a letter. I was just sitting there at the side watching people greet each other and that's a scene I will never forget.

I was given three days' leave and took a train to Washington D.C., sim-

*ply because I had never been there and thought I should take the opportu-
nity to see it. Then I went to Walter Reed Veterans Hospital to see if any of
my pals ended up there.*

*As I arrived there, a limousine pulled up and this officer inside stopped
and started talking to me. They wanted two officers and two enlisted men
to go down and meet Secretary of War [Robert Porter] Patterson because
he wanted to do a press release on our treatment in prison camp and they
heard I was there. I was selected to be one of the officers involved. It changed
my life.*

Sir, I Want to Play Baseball!

Major League Baseball in 1945 had many of its best players serving
in the Armed Forces. The quality of play was diminished. Consequently, there were openings on many teams. Bert Shepard was to
benefit form the manpower shortage, albeit briefly. This was the most
amazing part of the story to me. A man with all the excuses still had
the desire to achieve his dream, and did it.

*We drove down in a big limousine over to the Pentagon to meet Assistant
Secretary of War Patterson. The Secretary asked all of us what we wanted
to do with our lives.*

The first guy said loudly he wanted to go duck hunting.

*Then he came to me and I said, "Well, if I can't fly combat in the South
Pacific, then I want to play baseball."*

Astonished, Patterson said, "Well, you can't play baseball, can you?"

*I noticed that Patterson was looking at the crude leg I had on, which
was made for me by a fellow prisoner in a POW camp. I told him, "Sure I
can. As soon as I get a new leg I am pretty sure I can."*

*Patterson was impressed. He called up Clark Griffith, the owner of the
Washington Senators, and said he had a prisoner of war there and, "He's
got a leg off and as soon as he gets a new leg he could play ball."*

*I knew that Griffith was not going to say no to the Assistant Secretary
of War. He told Patterson, "Send him over whenever his new leg [is] ready."
So I got a new leg and, about four days later, I was behind the barracks
practicing throwing and so forth, shifting and getting a balance. Then I go*

out to work out with the Senators. Of course, nobody, the players, fans, no-body knows I am coming out. I am a little late and I am in there dressing by myself and I go out to start to warm up.

With the war still raging, it's still 1945. There were just two sportswriters at Senators training camp that year. One of them noticed me working out and asked who I was.

One of the Senators' bat boys told him, "Well, that is a guy just back from prison camp and he's got a leg off, but he thinks he can play ball."

That reporter was none other than Ernie Harwell, reporter for the USMC's Leatherneck *magazine. Eventually Harwell became the Detroit Tigers broadcaster.*

He must have been a good reporter because, two hours later, the camp was teeming with journalists and cameramen.

Knowing that the extra attention was for me, I tried to put on a show. I put a uniform back on, going out and doing some running for them. I was showing them I could field bunts. Hell, I hadn't fielded bunts in four years, but I could do pretty damn good with the leg.

I was becoming a celebrity. I guess it went out in the service magazine and all the other newspapers and I guess it was all over the world. News of my achievement reached as far as Australia. That was my start in baseball.

I Made the Washington Senators: Dreams Do Come True

When Bert told me, "Dreams do come true," I listened intently. I wanted this dream of mine to come true, too. Listening to Bert, who did so much in life in spite of his injury, made me re-focus during this long interview. It was getting to be 6:00 p.m. and we were both getting hungry. But Bert had much more to say.

I made the Senators! I knew I was there as a token, but I didn't care. I wanted to use my status to make other injured men like me feel better. A lot of the amputees received me very well.

I was also able to recognize and thank those who had helped me make it. I sent Mr. Patterson, who had followed my career since the meeting in the Pentagon, four tickets to the practice game when I pitched against Brooklyn. I had to pay for those tickets! The Senators were a very cheap bunch.

But Patterson wasn't the only one. Later, I was in Detroit and the guy that made me the crude leg in prison camp got in touch with me and I said, "Come down to the ball game." I was happy he remembered me. I went in the Tigers office to get five tickets. I was going to pay for them, and they said, "No, these are for you and they're free." That was the difference between the club I was playing for and one I was visiting.

Although I was on the active roster, I never got out of the dugout. The Senators were in the middle of a pennant race with the Tigers and couldn't afford to risk having me on the mound. I knew I could do it.

Then, on August 4, 1945, we were getting hammered by the Red Sox. Boston broke out to a quick 5–0 lead. Our manager, Ossie Bluege, didn't want to waste any of his regular relievers, so he threw in rookie Joe Cleary. Seven runs and a strikeout later, we were down 12–0 and the fourth wasn't even over yet.

Bluege had nothing left to lose. So I went in. The crowd went wild. Although the Germans had surrendered back in May, the war in the Pacific was still very much active and costly. Seeing me trot out to the mound was a welcome diversion. I wasn't tearful, or scared. Hell, after what I'd been through, I was ready!

I pitched the rest of the game, and I didn't do bad at all. I faced 20 batters in all, allowing three singles, a walk, and an earned run. But I struck out two and recorded a very respectable 1.69 ERA. Much better than Cleary's 189.00—and he had both his legs!

I went to bat three times. I didn't get a hit, but I smacked the ball hard twice and, by all accounts, I was considered a tough out. I also covered first flawlessly. I was flying pretty high and even at that moment on the field, my thoughts drifted back to that kindly German doctor who saved my life.

Unfortunately, though, my good job on the mound wasn't enough to get me more playing time as we fought tough to the end and finished 87–67, a game and a half behind the Tigers. Those Tigers went on to beat the Cubs in the 1945 World Series.

It should have been us.

My lack of playing time didn't faze me. My major league debut more or less a success, I went to spring training with the Senators in 1946 assuming I'd make the team.

I pitched three innings three times, and I allowed one hit and no walks each time. I thought I would probably get a better chance this time, but the regular pitchers were coming back from the war and they had already made their mark, so I never got in any more games.

Although I understood my role, the lack of playing time began to get to me. I wanted to earn a spot, so I asked the Senators to send me down to their Triple-A affiliate in Chattanooga. I went down to Chattanooga, and I won two and lost two. I thought I had it made. But the call back to the big club never came.

I did, however, go barnstorming with the American League All-Stars. I played first base. Hell, I hit two home runs in Calgary. I am beginning to see I can hit. I always thought I could. But then, there wasn't much of anything I didn't think I could do. You're young. You can do anything! We played Feller's All-Stars in Seattle, and I got 1-for-2 off Feller, and 1-for-2 off Johnny Sain. I hit the ball hard every time.

Since many of the players didn't like flying, the All-Stars would sometimes have patchwork lineups. The next night we played Feller's All-Stars in Yakima; my outfield was Jackie Price, Denny Galehouse, a pitcher, and Jess Flores, another pitcher. That was my outfield. Naturally, we didn't beat Feller's All-Stars, but I pitched a full game after playing first base the night before.

I was feeling good. I was sure I could make it back to the majors, this time as a legitimate player. All I needed to get ready for next spring was a re-amputation and a new prosthesis.

I went back to Walter Reed, got a re-amputation by a real lame-ass doctor. It took him three times to cut my stump right. He screwed me up royally, and eventually I had to have four more amputations over a period of two years because of this prick. He did 26 botched operations on the ward that day and they all had to be done over.

Things got worse before they got better for me. The third doctor overlooked a bone spur. He didn't even operate on it. The fourth doctor got the bone spur out, but cut too close to a nerve. I would wear the leg a couple of days and I would start weeping. It really hurt.

As had happened in Germany, a compassionate doctor came to my rescue. Colonel Spintlers had heard about my problem. He was gonna go in there and "take care of things." Another operation? Jesus…again? He was probing around. He couldn't see anything really wrong, but he finally saw this cross section of this nerve and he got a hold of my nerve and pulled it out, cut it off and it flew back in. I haven't had any trouble since then. Except getting a leg that doesn't crack.

I'm not bitter. I was a victim of some very poor surgery, but what can you do about it? You can't sue anybody. You can't blame anybody. That was just the way it happened. By all rights, I should be dead. So what am I going to do…bitch about it? Hell no! Be a man and get on with life. My leg eventually recovered, but other problems set in. Being on crutches all that time just screwed the arm up.

Of course, I didn't give up. The only job [available] was managing. So I went to Waterbury Connecticut Class B, and I took that job just before the season started.

One of my first decisions as manager was to put myself in the starting rotation. I won five and lost five, but my arm just wasn't any good. I have to admit it. I played first base quite a bit because I was the manager! If a guy got hurt I would play first.

I was just 25. I still had dreams about the bigs. One night, I hit two home runs and drove in eight runs. I always felt like I could have helped the team as a pitcher, or be a substitute as a first baseman and outfielder, but that didn't materialize. But, I have no complaints.

I honestly think I could have made it, but with my arm growing tired, I packed it in. I played a few exhibitions after that, but nothing serious. I didn't want to play if I couldn't play as well as the others. Anybody that plays against me, I want him to do his very best. If he feels as if he can't then he hasn't got any guts! I would not go on the field unless I could do my share as well as anybody else.

That was it for me. I couldn't play any more, but I stayed close to the game. Years later, I was in Washington as a guest of the Senators. I ran

Bert Shepard shows off his Distinguished Flying Cross and Air Medal to his Washington Senators teammates after receiving them in a ceremony on the field from Under Secretary of War Patterson and General Omar Bradley. Left to right are Joe Judge, Roger Wolff, Mario Pieretti, and Bert Shepard. Courtesy of Justin Shepard.

into the secretary of my old ball club from way back in my playing days in Bisbee. We went out to dinner and I told him, "Gus, I was down to see you when I was in training, but I was doing about 450 mph in my P-38 and I couldn't stop."

Gus dropped his fork. "Was that you? I was sitting there at my desk in the Copper Queen Hotel, and I hear this damnedest roar come through ...and there was this plane right over the field."

You know, Todd, I may never have been a star in the major leagues, but you know, I can always say I was there. And I did it my way.

Hungry?

I looked up at Bert and I was speechless. This man symbolized exactly what and who it is I am trying to honor. There was an awkward silence. Bert asked me if I was all right. I was. I was just thinking

Cartoon presented to Bert Shepard. Courtesy of Justin Shepard.

about the uniqueness of this very improbable meeting. So heroic, and I felt so amazingly small. I told him how much I appreciated his story, his service, and what an example he is for all Americans. His response was typical Bert:

"Bullshit, Todd! You would have done the same thing. Your dad did. It's in your blood. You are an American, a child of a hero too."

God, I teared up at that moment. I was embarrassed. It was October and Dad had only been gone 24 weeks and Bert said, "You miss your old man, don't you?" "Tell you what, let's talk all about this over the dinner you're going to buy me. Let's go to Sizzler."

We did. I could tell he was a regular there. He flirted with the waitresses, just like my dad did. They all loved him. It was reassuring. We talked and it was great. I asked Bert about why his story hadn't made it to the big screen or TV.

He answered, "Well, there has been some interest, but the producers all want to depict the Germans as evil. Well, they sure as hell were not to me. So I just said, 'No,' not until someone will do it right. Todd, I wish it was you."

Me, too, Bert, I thought.

We ate and then I was upset with myself. In my haste to get to Bert's home, I left my ball for him to autograph back at home. I figured I had plenty of time. He was only a few minutes away. I went by his home a few times later on, but nobody was ever home. The gate around the house was locked. So I couldn't get to the front door. I finally got a message from his son telling me Bert had suffered a stroke and was back at home in the Midwest. He is still there and that baseball of mine remains blank.

6

Sergeant Ernie Harwell USMC

Hall of Fame Broadcaster, Always a Marine

A Date with Lou Ellen

I went to a Tigers/Angels game not long after Dad passed away. I took my mom—Lou Ellen. It was the first time I had ever been to a game with just my mom. This guy an aisle over consumed over 13 beers, providing entertainment, but we were there to see Todd Maulding, a dear friend of our family. He was the bullpen catcher for the Dodgers for many years working with Mark Cresse, out there from the 1980s through the 1990s. You had Mickey Hatcher, Todd Maulding in the bullpen, and Mike Scioscia catching for the Dodgers and it was just paradise. It was the best of times and everybody was so nice, generous, thoughtful, giving, and caring. Oh, those days in the "Blue Heaven" of Dodger Stadium. But all of them, my Dodger friends, were let go by the new owners at Fox after O'Malley sold the club. Now Todd was the bullpen coach for the Detroit Tigers.

I told Todd about the baseball and veterans idea, and he said, "You need to talk to Ernie. Ernie Harwell, our broadcaster. Ernie is a Marine." My ears perked up.

Todd mentioned it to Ernie. It is not every day you get a phone call from Ernie Harwell saying that he would love to help you.

I called Ernie right back and arranged an interview and flew to Detroit. As I walked up to his home, I noticed two seats from old Tiger Stadium on his porch. I walked into his house and he was so gracious. His wife, Lulu, was there. He was so kind and patient.

By his reverence and his carefully chosen words, you could sense the passion for baseball and the men of the game. Ernie told me about interviewing Christy Mathewson, about interviewing Babe Ruth, about what Ted Williams meant to him. I was like a kid in a candy store.

Ernie asked me, "Have you ever interviewed Jerry Coleman?" "Jerry Coleman? The Padres announcer?" He said, "Well, yeah, he wasn't just an announcer, he played for the Yankees. Not only does he live out your way, and not only did he fight in World War II, but he fought in Korea, too."

Ernie showed me around his house. It was simple. Decorated like my parents house. It seemed so familiar, so comfortable. I was relaxed. I had expected to see many baseball artifacts, but there was only one: a picture of Babe Ruth in front of Ebbets Field. More interesting was his other favorite picture: a panoramic scene of the skyline of Old Jerusalem in Israel.

We sat down and talked. It was magic, a real gift. Ernie started in his Georgian drawl, a melodic tone...

The Georgia Peach: Ernie Harwell

I grew up in Georgia. I was born in a little town called Washington, which is between Athens and Augusta, about 120 miles east of Atlanta. My family moved to Atlanta when I was four or five years old and I lived there until college. I broke into radio in Atlanta in 1940 and was working there when the war broke out. At that point, even before the war broke out, I was planning on getting married. I went to the Draft Board—a friend of mine was the head of the Draft Board—and I said "I am thinking about getting married and I don't want to get married if I'm gonna be drafted immediately."

My friend said "Well go ahead, I think you should get married and you probably won't have any problems."

After I got married, they put me in the 1A right away [chuckling]. That taught me a lesson about listening to marital advice. Because I was in 1A, I decided I'd like to, instead of being drafted, go into a branch of the service that I could select. I wanted to go into the Marines. I wanted to be an officer. I enlisted and went into the Marines in July of 1942.

December 7th, 1941: Everything Changes

Like everyone else, I really didn't know where Pearl Harbor even was. You know we found out in a hurry, but at that time I don't think we knew anything about Pearl Harbor. I went back to my work at WSB. I was a sports

Lulu and Ernie Harwell. Courtesy of Ernie Harwell.

announcer. I did whatever duties I had, which was generally a sports show every night, golf tournaments and things like that. I covered the Masters and I had done football there with WSB. I did my usual sports-casting duties. Then in July, I went to Parris Island for boot camp and that was the beginning of my career in the USMC.

Becoming a United States Marine: Parris Island

I got down to Beaufort, South Carolina, where they dumped you out of a train, you get in a cattle truck and go over to Parris Island, and you become a Marine. You lose your individuality and your identity as a person, at least for awhile, and you become a boot there in boot camp. This was July and August in South Carolina, but I made it through and I think it made a better man out of me.

Parris Island really felt like being in prison. You get down there and if you're a boot, even a Pfc. had to be saluted and it was a very grueling, intense kind of a training that you had. You are there about eight to ten weeks, I think, and we really didn't get out of the barracks to go anywhere all that time. You got very little sleep. You were drilling or carrying a rifle or you were ironing your pants or shirts and doing something all the time.

I didn't mind it at all. I was able to take it. I was a little older than most of the guys. I was around 23 or 24 years old at that time and most of the guys in my platoon were 18 and 19. I was the oldest guy in the whole platoon and I had a little bit more maturity than they did and I was able to handle it. The physical part wasn't too bad. I enjoyed the drilling. The part I didn't like was the spit and polish, because I'd been sort of a loose kind of a guy, clothes you know, I didn't dress up too much.

They sent me back to Atlanta on this sort of like PR duty and I stayed there for a year. I had it really too easy and it wasn't exactly right. I was sort of glad when I got sent back to line duty. I had applied to be a combat correspondent and was rejected. I was then sent to Camp Lejeune in North Carolina and I stayed there. I was a member of the 59th Battalion, re-placement battalion they called 'em, and we lived in what was framed as the "Tent City in the Camp Lejeune." The idea there was they tried to make you so miserable that you would want to go overseas and fight the Japanese, but I had a very, I think, interesting experience. When my wife, Lulu, came up to say goodbye, the 59th Battalion was shipping out and it was our final weekend there. We were shipping out on a Monday, and she showed up on Friday. That same afternoon, the order came into the 59th Battalion that they wanted two men pulled out for duty on the newspaper there at the base, the Camp LeJeune Globe. *I happened to be one of those two guys. The 59th went overseas and was decimated on one of those is-lands in the South Pacific. They weren't really well trained at that point, and most all the guys were killed. God just intervened and saved my life at that time.*

Marines Endure

When I went overseas, finally, I went over as a correspondent for Leather-neck. *I was Sports Editor and an overseas correspondent. I covered some of the surrenders of the Japanese to our troops. I covered the surrender of Wake Island, for instance, for* Leatherneck. *I covered the surrender of Mille.*

Mille is an island I was told was the most bombed island in World War II. What made this island so eerie, was that the Japanese soldiers on this besieged, surrounded rock were so well fed and happy. They passed the time watching captured American films and newsreels. I remember their com-

manding officer had a little Hitler type mustache. He was a real little guy. I didn't think anything about their good condition at the time. Come to find out these Japanese soldiers resorted to cannibalism. They ate captured Allied prisoners! Not long after Mille, I went into China. I didn't see a whole lot of combat with the guys, but I did see some of the surrenders. What I saw mostly was the dedication of our guys in the Marines. They put their country first. They gave up their families and their regular civilian life. They gave up their privacy, which I think is one of the big sacrifices. When you are in the service, you are always with somebody else. You really never have a moment to yourself. Whatever you do, you do with at least 64 other guys [chuckle] most of the time. And, of course, the physical hardships were certainly evident that came about when you were in the Marines, It was a great experience for me and I was really very fortunate in that I didn't get shot at. I didn't have any kind of a heroic career, certainly. I just served my four years and did what they told me to do. Some of the things I wanted to do I wasn't able to do, but in the long run I was probably lucky that I didn't get to do 'em because I might have been shot and killed.

Wake was such a symbol, a little island that had been surrendered by the US early in the war. A lot of guys suffered, captured as prisoners, tortured, and a lot of them died. It was also symbolic when the Marines went back there, because it was something they recaptured. They had a ceremony where they raised Old Glory back on Wake Island. Walter Bayler, the Colonel who was the last man off, was the first man back on that island. The Marines are pretty good with the propaganda and the public relations. So they set it up that way and when he landed on Wake Island, I was right behind him. We went around and inspected the hospitals and things like that.

During the war, many of us GIs stateside and many GIs overseas tried to follow the game. In fact, when I was overseas I did stories in Leatherneck, a lot of interviews with players. I did some work for The Sporting News. They had a great interest in baseball and I think it was a good diversion. Not only were they playing baseball on military teams, they were following the big leaguers that remained back and were able to keep the game going.

Ernie Harwell, Marine Correspondent, on Wake Island. Courtesy of Ernie Harwell.

As a reporter, I was curious about the baseball veterans that were in the service. The games are continuing back in the States; I'm wondering if there is a little jealousy on their part. It was a different response from each player that I talked to. Overall, they were patriots and good citizens who knew they were doing a much more important job than playing baseball.

China: The Stares of Vacant Souls

I did a short duty in China after Wake and Mille. Those few months there showed me the face of war and what that war did to the civilians. Although I was not in combat, I did see its aftermath and impact, especially on the kids and the women. Some of the women were scorned who collaborated (meaning slept with) with the Japanese and even the Americans. I remember seeing the lack of feeling in the kids' and women's eyes. Seeing an emptiness of a vacant soul is how I remember it. [He showed me his pictures from China too and started to tear up about it.] *Look here. Starving*

Ernie in China, 1945, with his "No. 1 boy" (note the Leatherneck *box). Courtesy of Ernie Harwell.*

kids, homeless kids, raped kids and women moved me to see that man left to his own devices will turn to evil. This experience in war, especially in China, made me appreciate our freedoms, more especially our Bill of Rights, and Free Speech. After being in China I better understood the cost of such freedoms and also what a nation looks like [which] has never had them. Also I know how imperative it is to speak out. It is the essential building block of a free society. I may not like what you have to say, but I'll defend your right to say it.

    This brings back memories of when I had Jose Feliciano play the National Anthem for the Tigers. Jose sang it such a contemporary way that many were offended and I was nearly fired over it. Heck, it was the American Vietnam era 1960s and all America was uptight. I am very proud of the fact that I was the one that invited Jose to sing that day. To me it was all about freedom and expression not taste. Not everyone liked it. I did. A new voice always gives me hope.

The USMC Is Always with Me

Ernie wasn't done, thank God. He had a lot more to say as I was trying to get to the essence of what it means to be a service veteran from Ernie.

What I remember the most is the patriotism of the guys and the sacrifices they made. Of course, a lot of my friends were killed. I was in a college class in 1940, where they were just ripe for the service. Most everybody in my graduating class went into the service one way or the other and a lot of the graduates that got their diplomas when I did were killed in different branches of the service—some of them in the Marines, some of them in the other branches, so I, personally, lost a lot of friends. I brought back from the Marines a sense of discipline, a sense of not only corporate discipline, but personal discipline, that you have to keep yourself in good shape, you have to keep yourself mentally alert, and you have to be ready for whatever might happen.

The war ended in August 1945. The atomic bombs? Did they help to bring about the end of the war and save lives? I think that was a good decision by President Truman. I think it saved a lot of lives, certainly a lot of American lives. I think probably a lot of Japanese lives, because they went in there and they used the Atom bomb. I think if America had to invade Japan, it would have been a long drawn-out process and a lot more fatalities.

After the War

When I got my discharge I came back to Atlanta and my job was waiting for me at the radio station. I decided I didn't want to go back there because they didn't have enough sports to do (although they were required to give me my job back). So, I decided I would freelance and I began to do play-by-play baseball with the Atlanta team, my hometown team, the Atlanta Crackers. The Atlanta Crackers was the first professional baseball team that I worked for. That was in 1946 when I came out of the Marines and that launched my baseball broadcasting career. From there I went to the Brooklyn Dodgers in 1948, and stayed two years. I went to the New York Giants for four years and the Baltimore Orioles when they came into the big league—their first big league team in 1954. I stayed there through 1959 and then I came to Detroit in 1960 and stayed there until I retired after the 2002 season.

The Dodgers—the Brooklyn Dodgers—was a great place to work. I loved working for them. Jackie Robinson was a fantastic player. Robinson was the ideal choice that Branch Rickey made to break the color line. I don't think many other people could have done it. Jackie had a terrible temper. He was very combative, but he was able to turn the cheek and make that noble experiment a success. I think it's the most significant thing that has ever happened, not only in baseball history, but also in sports history. The fact that he was able to break the color line and open the door for so many great athletes, not only from America, but also from countries all around the world.

Jackie was great to me. He was a very personable kind of a guy. I played cards with him. We played and talked a lot on the trains. I was in the clubhouse and in the airports when we did fly. I was pretty close to Jackie. I knew his family well. My wife Lulu and Rachel Robinson were good friends. I was very fond of Jackie and very proud that I was to be a part of that experiment.

I did both radio and TV when I first started. When I came to Detroit in 1965 the Tigers came up with an idea that they would split the radio and TV, because they had competing beer sponsors. They put me on the radio and they put my partner, George Kell, on the TV. Most of the time, since 1965, I have been a radioman.

The Detroit Tigers

Hank Greenberg was a good friend of mine. I didn't see him play much, but I knew him later on when he was an executive. He was a very intelligent guy, a very high-class person, and a fantastic hero in Detroit, especially to the Jewish population. He came along in the 1930s when the Jewish people in America were denigrated publicly and had a tough time. He was a hero to the young Jewish boys in Detroit. They looked up to him and he was practically a god to them because he gave them something to cheer for, and he was a good citizen who did his duty.

He went in the service twice. He was drafted into the service and dis-

charged before Pearl Harbor. After the Japanese attack, he went back in (when he didn't have to) for another tour. He got out in 1945, just in time to hit a home run, and win the pennant for the Tigers. Remarkable, a remarkable man, and a real example to America. We could use some people like him.

I think a lot of guys gave up their careers in baseball to fight. There are many examples of players who were either established big leaguers or great prospects who went to serve in the Marines, the Army, the Army Air Force, Navy, or whatever, and they left their baseball careers on the battlefield or wherever they fought. I think that is true with a lot of prospects that were great players. By the time they had finished their armed service, usually four years, their skills had eroded. When they came back, in 1946, 1947 or whenever they returned, they didn't have those skills anymore. So you might say that they sacrificed their whole careers to be in the service. There were other guys who came in and gave up two or three years maybe like Ted Williams or Bob Feller, Warren Spahn and some of those guys. They were able to come back and pick it back up. But even in those cases I think if they hadn't been in the service, they would have added to their stats, their records, and their place in baseball history. But these guys don't seem to mind . . . all for the good of the country you might say.

Ernie went on to talk about many of the great players he has met and explain his relationship with them, as well as how he interviewed them. He did this to help me, guide me, and train me to be a good listener. Here I was, sitting in Ernie Harwell's home, talking to this servant of God. It wasn't until I got home and started writing that I realized what a special gift I had been presented that October day in 2002 especially when Ernie Harwell was teaching this teacher.

I knew Bob Feller very well. I knew him when he played. I saw him pitch. I've been very friendly with him and been on a lot of cruises with Bob Feller. We've gotten along great together. I'd admired his naval career, as well as his career in pitching. He threw about as hard as anybody that I've ever seen. Bob Feller was unique in that when he graduated from high school in Van Meter, Iowa, I think they had a graduating class of 50. The

NBC radio network covered his graduation and then Bob went and pitched that night.

The biggest network in the country sent people out there to cover a high school graduation of the guy. You don't find that today with movie stars or anybody else, but they did it for Bob Feller. Then he went into the service not long thereafter.

He was very proud of his naval service. He wasn't a pencil pusher or a guy behind the scenes, he was right there with them on the ships and right in the battles. He was proud of that naval career. He should be.

Another great man was Stan Musial. I've been on cruises with Stan and he has been a good friend of mine for years. He is one of the great personalities of our game. I think he was underrated. He was one of the great hitters of all time. He wasn't a great all-around-player. He wasn't much of a fielder. He was a broken-down pitcher who became a great hitter, but he certainly could hit as well as anybody and was "Mr. St. Louis Cardinal" for most of his career. I think Stan is a Navy veteran like Feller.

Being a son of an Army officer, I wondered aloud with Ernie if any of the big names were in the Army. "Of course, I'm sure there had to have been." Ernie thought about it and gave me this answer: "Warren Spahn."

I knew Warren. He is the best left-handed pitcher I have ever seen. He won more games than any other [left-handed] pitcher and gave up some crucial years being in the service. He was in the Battle of the Bulge and was at the bridge at Remagen. He was a real a hero there.

Of course when speaking about heroes, you must mention Ted Williams. Like me, he was a Marine. Ted and I had sort of an affinity. When I was in Baltimore, we had a special day for Ted and he came to me and asked me if I would go over his speech with him and check it out and see if it was okay. I was proud of that. For years, I would be one of the introducers of the players that he would induct into the Ted Williams' Hitters Hall of Fame. I did an interview with Ted in 1942 at WSB in Atlanta. I've got a picture of Ted and me at the microphone in WSB studios. We were both so young. He just hit that .406 the year before, in 1941.

I heard Ted say that the two greatest days in his life was the day he went into the Hall of Fame and the day he became a Marine. He was proud of the Marines. A good friend of mine, General Larry Taylor, was at my Ernie Harwell Day when the Tigers honored me. General Taylor came and represented the Marines at this event and I was proud of that. I'm always a Marine.

My interview had lasted a long time. I think I was there for a good two hours. Ernie could see that I was a rookie, but he sensed a deep love and affection for what I was doing or trying to do. He brought out his scrapbooks from his service time and showed me pictures from his time in China. He even signed a few baseballs for me. Then we drove to his favorite restaurant, not too far from where his daughter Julie works. She joined us and we talked about teaching, and where I am from and what I am trying to accomplish.

All I remember about the restaurant was the affection and respect shown to Ernie by the owner and the restaurant patrons. Ernie is a big star in Detroit and even though he was asked for his autograph, as we talked and ate our steak sandwiches, it was done politely and Ernie responded kindly by always agreeing. Before getting into our cars, Ernie called out to me, and encouraged me to interview Jerry Coleman. He had given me some phone numbers earlier. I got back in to the car and made my way back to the airport. It was a remarkable 24 hours.

7

The Marine Colonel "Just Call Me Jerry"

Jerry Coleman, NY Yankees and Hall of Fame Broadcaster

Meeting a Yankees Legend

Lunch break is my favorite time of day at school. It gives me a few moments to catch my breath and gather my thoughts and get ready for my next class period. February 24, 2003 was no ordinary day, because the next day I was going to be interviewing Yankees great and Padres announcer Jerry Coleman. In addition to preparing for a substitute during my lunch break, I kept thinking about the Coleman interview and how totally overwhelmed I felt. Compounding my stress was the announcement over the intercom: "Attention Heritage Middle School students; due to the inclement weather, all students will now report back to your classrooms." "Great," I thought, "Not only have I not eaten lunch yet, I still haven't finished preparing for my sub." That takes a lot more work than people think. On top of all this, I was going to be losing a day's salary to do this interview, and I knew that wouldn't go over well at home. After all, I have a wife and two kids who depend on me. I felt guilty. Was I being selfish?

The students poured in as the rain poured down. They were visibly excited by the prospect of a snow day. Distracted, I never did eat my "Banquet Mexican Fiesta" TV dinner, something I realized when I opened my microwave three days later.

The next day, I set out for the 215-mile drive to San Diego. I had three hours before my appointment with Jerry Coleman and his agent Andy Strasberg, and wanted to stop to visit Dad's burial marker at the Riverside National Cemetery. Nestled deep in one of the pockets of my 82nd Airborne jacket was a gift for my father. Threading my way through the labyrinth of car paths that crisscross this hallowed place, I proceeded to search for my dad's marker. Is my dad really here? Disbelief. Denial. As I searched, I read the names of many others and thought, "People miss you too." Then I found it. The marker that reads:

Lt. Wallace Peter Anton+
Oct. 24, 1924–June 6, 2002
He served with honor

Here I am on my 39th birthday standing in a downpour in a muddy cemetery, holding a conversation with a slate-grey granite tablet, freckled with bits of variously colored gravel. This can't be real. Abruptly I exclaim to the marker, as if Dad really could hear my anguish, "Dad, I do not know what I am getting myself into. I'm going to interview a Yankees legend, this baseball star whom I know nothing about, and to be honest, I'm not versed in the Yankees religion."

Dad would have said, "Son, don't think of him as a ball player, think of him as a veteran. You've interviewed hundreds of THEM, and if you stay there (seeing Jerry as a veteran and not a baseball hero) it will be all right."

I felt my balance coming back, my confidence. Of course, I thought. I had interviewed many veterans for the D-Day Museum. That never made me nervous. I always get so worked up; it's my way of covering the bases, so to speak. Before leaving, I carefully removed my dad's present and placed it on his marker: a baseball on which I wrote: "Thanks for a great season. Love, Todd."

I reached Andy's office and while we made some small talk, I realized there was a third person in the room who I had failed to notice. Finally, he interrupted by blurting sarcastically, "Hey, I thought we were here to talk about me." Turning to this voice, a flash like a thunderbolt hit me. Sitting there, proudly attired in his A-2 USN flight jacket, was none other than Lt. Colonel Gerald Francis Coleman USMC!

Jerry, as he prefers to be called, leaned over with a wry grin on his face, reached out his hand, shook mine and said, "Hi, Todd. Thanks for coming today." I was amazed. "Mr. Coleman, you do not need to thank me! Thank you!"

"Please call me Jerry." He said.

Andy interjected, "You know, Jerry, I think what Todd is doing is along the lines of the book *The Glory of Their Times* [a first-hand account of baseball's early days in the players' own words by Lawrence S. Ritter]. Todd's book is going to be a military version of this. I don't think I've seen anything like it."

Jerry asked me, "Just who have you interviewed for this thing?" I replied, "I've interviewed Bert Shepard. You know who that is?"

Jerry said "Yeah, of course, that one legged pitcher with Washington." I then continued, "And I interviewed Ernie Harwell in Detroit." Jerry perked up and spoke glowingly about Ernie, a real "class act." I nodded in agreement and told Jerry, "Ernie was the one who suggested I talk to you."

As we sat down, I quickly established that indeed I was there to talk about Jerry Coleman, the veteran, not the Yankee, but it was hard to separate the two. As we starting getting into the meat of the interview, Jerry looked down a lot, never at me directly. It seemed he was far away. I thought I was boring him, that I wasn't doing well. Was I asking those old worn-out questions he had heard so many times before? I wasn't sure. I know that many veterans do not like to talk about themselves. They view it as disrespectful to those who made greater sacrifices than they did.

More than a Hero

To see Jerry Coleman behind the microphone broadcasting for the San Diego Padres today is a comforting sight. His wit, his cheer, and his selfless demeanor disguise his true character and the magnitude of his courage. Jerry Coleman is remembered for many things: World Series hero, an integral part of the Yankees dynasty of the 1950s, manager of the Padres, and a long-time broadcaster known for some of his expressions such as, "Oh Doctor" and "You can hang a star on that baby."

But Jerry Coleman is indeed a rarity. He is a decorated combat veteran of two wars, and he chose to remain active in the United States Marine reserves while still playing and pursuing professional baseball. Lieutenant Colonel Gerald Francis Coleman, United States Marines, is baseball's current highest ranking military veteran. What does Jerry say to such worthy accolades and acknowledgment? With typical humility he says, "So what? You know, I had some help!" Then he started talking. Softly, but talking nonetheless...

Wow, World War II. Baseball, and Korea. You know, that was almost 50–60 years ago?! All three of them are an important part of who and what I am. I'm not special. I tell you that. I just survived, that's all. I was a successful survivor of two wars and a career in baseball, but a hero? Never. Let me tell you something, Tom Brokaw wrote a book called The Greatest Generation, *or at least that is the argument he is making, but I see it differently. The greatest generation is now—it is every generation. It is every American kid meeting the challenges that face them. Name any challenge and they would, as sure as I am standing here, meet that challenge. These kids of today will come through. These kids today would have done the same thing my generation did. You bet they would.*

Making the Choice: Naval Aviator or USC?

Pearl Harbor changed my life. It changed everyone's. I was a senior in high school, and I was all set to go to USC on a basketball and baseball scholarship. I was all set to try out, but one day all senior boys were called in for a special assembly which was to be presented by the United States Navy. As we are all waiting, we were all saying what we were going to do in the war: Oh some would say, 'I am going into the commandos.'—you know, all that stuff movie star war heroes are made of. It was just nervous chatter. It's 1942, and we have only been at war a few months. Still it all seemed like the war was a game. Death, destruction, and tragedy were something that happened only in the films. It won't happen to us. Not me. I didn't even think about that stuff. But let me tell you, when those doors swung open and those naval aviators walked through wearing those wings, they looked like they were five feet wide, and God, those guys were huge! At that moment I knew what I wanted to be.

Obviously USC and all that stuff would have to wait. All I wanted then was to do one thing—become a U.S. Naval aviator. But hell, I was 17—

Jerry Coleman, strapped in. Courtesy Jerry Coleman.

you had to be 18. The only reason I played professional baseball in 1942 was because I had to kill a summer. Joe Devine was the Yankees scout that signed me, and I played ball in a place called Wellsville, New York, which is about as far away from San Francisco as I could get. My first season in the minors ended on September 8th and I took a train back to San Francisco and arrived home on my birthday. Immediately I went to the San Francisco Trade Building to get into this Naval Aviation V-5 program.

I am waiting in line and nervous, insecure. I just did school for the athletics. School was something I had to do to get onto that ball field. As I progressed through the induction process, I did well physically and mentally and finally got into an interview with the commander, who looked like Admiral Perry to me. He's got three stripes on his sleeve and he's talking on the phone and smiling and this and that and he finally gets to my high school transcripts, which are a disaster. Then he said "I can't sign this." My jaw fell right at my feet, and I said "Whoa...why not, sir?" He told me "You know how much it costs to train a Naval Aviator? Three hundred thousand dollars." In 1942, that was like three million dollars. "You are going to get part way through this program, and you are going to fail and it is going to cost the government X amount of dollars, and I'm not going to sign this." I spent about a half hour telling him I wasn't really a moron, I just didn't apply myself in school, but I could do this. I had like three sevens or three eights out of ten in my mental aptitude tests. My physical was fine. He said, "Well, it goes against my grain, but I guess I have to sign it. But let me tell you something kid. You are NOT going to make it."

Wings of Gold: World War II Training

I went to Alamosa, Colorado, where we took what we called WTS, War Training Service. Then we went to Adams State Teachers College, where we got ground school and we flew these little Piper cubs and first soloed. And I can still remember they cleared me to solo, and I'm going down the runway I took off and I said, "How am I going to get this thing down?" That's all I could think of. I must be nuts. How do I get down?

Surviving the physical training was one thing, but the mental challenge took greater effort. They took 25 of the top St. Mary's Preflight School students—I was one of them—and sent us to Kansas for primary flight training. That would be done in an old biplane that looked like it was built by the Wright Brothers. I called that plane "The Old Yellow Peril." Out of our group of 25, I think five or six got through. But there was also a process that changed a lot of the thoughts of the cadets at that time; if you washed out right now, before flight training, you'd go back to become a civilian, and you'd start over again. But now, if you washed out, while you're in training, you'd become a seaman first, or second class. Basically a grunt. So, some people quit. They didn't want to take the risk. I survived and was on my way to Texas, which was a three-month program that became a six-month program because of the horrible weather. A week of rain. Two weeks of rain. Finally we did get off the ground and as I flew, the plane felt good; like a pair of shoes that fit just right. And finally on April the first, which is April Fool's Day, 1944, they commissioned me. They gave me my wings.

Jacksonville, Florida was home for what they call operational training. It was there I was assigned to a plane called the SBD-Dauntless Divebomber. The next level was combat flight instruction at Cherry Point, North Carolina. They had a lot of pilots around there, and didn't know what to do with them. They used them for ferry duty. It looked to me as if I was never going to get my shot. These guys at Cherry Point, some of them were there for a year and all aching to get into combat. What I didn't know was they were fighter pilots and there was a big glut of people wanting to be fighter pilots.

It was decided that we all needed more basic training. So the Navy sent us out to what they call the boondocks running up and down getting mosquito-bitten and charging beaches and so forth. When I look back at it now, this wasn't basic training. It was survival training if you were ever shot down. They just didn't call it that. One day, Naval brass lined us up and said, "All right, the following officers step forward. Gerald F. Coleman, 036103. You're going to Miramar and El Toro, California and you'll pick up a squadron." Once I got to Miramar and El Toro, we flew around the clock for 20 days. There was an unbelievable rush of activity. Finally, I was in a replacement ship with the troops crossing the Pacific Ocean. I was still 19 at the time. I was going to war.

"MacArthur . . . He's a Pain in the Ass": World War II

We were on "cruise" to Pearl Harbor and from there we sailed all the way to Guadalcanal, which is just above Australia in a chain of islands called the Solomons. The lower you were in rank or officer grade, the worse job you got and I had the D-hole duty. Four days on, four days off. Everybody's upchucking all over the place and I can still remember it because the odor was incredible: vomit, diesel fuel, food odors, BO. I had to clean it up!

They assigned me to a squadron called VMSB 341, on Green Isle, a little north of Bouganville. We flew missions in the Solomon Islands area especially near Rabaul and other Japanese strongholds. While we were there they took our group and made us close ground support, a new tactic in W.W. II.

This type of air/ground communication was innovative and dangerous. Coleman's dive bomber (SBD) squadron was among the first in the Pacific Theater assigned to this task. Coleman explains it better.

We were the first group of close air support squadrons to be used specifically for helping our brothers on the ground. The Dauntless Dive-bomber (SBD) did the job. The reason I went to the Dauntless dive-bombers is be-

cause of Colonel Lloyd Mangrum. He was the first Marine pilot to land on Guadalcanal. Don't forget how special Guadalcanal is to the USMC. As a USMC hero, it made their base to have such a celebrity on site in Florida. Before our assignment overseas, the first thing he says was, "Why do you want to be a Marine?" I was really nervous. I told him I always had visions of sinking a Japanese carrier. I guess that is why I was assigned to the SBDs. People don't realize this, but this plane changed the war in the Pacific; they sunk the four carriers at Midway. It's a great plane for dive-bombing, had no speed but, I mean, they were very accurate. The Dauntless, you could really move it around with one finger and they had the great brakes and had a gunner behind. And, it always fascinated me. Even though I'm only 19, my gunner's 18, we knew what we were doing. That plane made us men. There's no way to see age in the sky. God, back home, we couldn't get the keys for the family car. Now I was given my own plane. You grow up fast . . . real fast.

I had visions of sinking a ship. I really wanted to do that. I was carrier-qualified . . . but I was a land-based pilot at Henderson Field, Guadalcanal in my squadron, the Torrid Turtles. How would you like to go to war as a turtle? And that's about how slow we flew.

In all wars you lose people—some good people. It didn't always happen in combat. Every now and then they sent us out on scouting missions to patrol or check a sector over the sea. Since there are no landmarks in the sea, you just went by compass and time readings. You fly an hour and half due north after takeoff, an hour and a half later, turn due west way and an hour and a half back. It was lonely even if I had a gunner at times. We really couldn't talk, as we needed to maintain radio silence. I felt like I was on the moon with nobody there, just water. The sheer vastness of the Pacific really scared the hell out of me. I'd rather dodge traffic than go out there alone. It's terrible. Homer Grasshorn, my best friend, disappeared and never come back on one of those damn patrols. I didn't know where the hell he was. He probably had engine trouble, or ran out of gas, or got lost. It was the first real time I could put a face with death. It was troubling, confusing and a very real message that I could get killed here.

Adjusting to war was a hard thing to do. With a name like Torrid Turtles we had to have a lot of good natured guys. Some of the higher-ranking

officers like us had tents; there were four of us and there were three first lieutenants. I did all the all dirty work, being the rookie. If we built a tent, I
had to get all the bamboo and crap and so forth and build it. God, it was
muggy. Those bugs? My God, they were as big as a house! Those guys just
loved yanking my chain. What can you do? Just say, "Yes, sir." But we were
all there for each other. We all lived this nightmare.

Combat experiences shaped us and bonded us together. These experiences are very personal and intimate and something you just learn to hide
away. Why explain them to anyone who hasn't experienced it? It's kind of
like a woman trying to explain having a baby to a man. He just doesn't
get it. But when she explains it to another woman, boy there is an unwrit-
ten degree of understanding. So it is with veterans. If you are not a veteran
(or a mother) you'll never understand. Never. But I'll share this...we were
trained specifically with interdiction stuff [air/ground directed combat].
While we were in the Solomons, we got orders to move and be ready to attack in the Philippines. Our air group came under the overall command of
General McArthur; he's a pain in the ass, you know. We could have wiped
out half the targets causing trouble in the Philippines in two days with the
bombing from our squadron with all the experience we had. But no,
MacArthur wanted his Army artillery to attack these targets. You know,
it's supposed to be some Army show.

The Army's 155s [howitzers] cannons compared to a USMC air squadron? Give me a break. We were misused. Good men died in the air and on
the ground. It takes front-line troops to clear the Japanese from positions
so the big guns could be brought up. The targets were not always buildings,
but this time...people. An artillery shell is much like a fastball in baseball.
Fast. Accurate. On target.

Our job in the Philippines was to drop white phosphorous shells from
our planes on Japanese troop concentrations. American ground troops were
very close by and they used colored panels as markers of their positions. We
had to be careful of the wind. I hated every mission when I used it. I'm
sure many of our own guys were burned because of it. Damn!

The Army's 155s were better equipped to do this very accurate mission.
Wind wouldn't really interfere with a projectile coming from a cannon. Our
bombs were just dropped and you hoped for the best. We complained about

our missions to superiors but nothing ever came back. There's leadership for you. It's just that I saw each guy down there as a brother and to be told to do something you knew would jeopardize their life was hard to deal with. It still is. God. Sometimes those radio messages directing us are still in my head. One time there was a forward air controller on the ground, in a jeep and he was the one who was directing the fire and when that happened he'd tell you what to do and where to drop it. When the wind shifted . . . can you imagine hearing those screams?! They called those forward spotters "mosquitoes." These guys circled around in their jeeps and they were always at the front line. They had a tough job, but using the air to perform this task was just flat out wrong. The artillery was in range, but who am I to question decisions of the Almighty, oh I mean Army command.

Finally in July of '45, they took all the qualified carrier pilots, of which I was one and sent us back to the States. That took forever. We had to go through every damn small island, and finally we arrived to Guam. From Guam, we got a plane to Kwajalein and on to Johnson Island, and on to Hawaii. And I had a buddy that was a sharp guy; he got us a trip home on a Clipper with sleepers for the four of us. So we finally got back to the States and they sent us home on leave for a week. Being a California boy, I was already home on leave when war ended in 1945. Toward the end of my leave I got a call. "Lieutenant, we're changing your orders to Cherry Point. . . .'

"But I live in San Francisco, come on."

"No. You are going to Cherry Point . . . that's an order." So, I ended up in Cherry Point until January '46; then I finally got back home.

As I look back at World War II, we were patriots. We really were. We were just kids, we were so young. When I got back, from one year overseas, I was 20. I remember we picked up some nurses and told some lie that I was 22. We walked into a bar, four of us with our dates and they threw me out. Too young for beer. It was embarrassing. I never lied again. Right here in San Diego, they wouldn't let me into bar. Not that I cared; I didn't drink anyway. It was the principle or the irony. Life is funny that way.

Another thing people don't talk about anymore was whether President Truman's decision to use the atomic bomb was justified. In 1945, I said yes. In 1955, somebody asked me that same question on TV. Remember the Jinx and Tex Show? Jinx Falconberg and Tex somebody was the idiot that

asked me that question. In 1955, I said no. I'm not sure why. Probably because while serving in Korea, I went to Japan and saw the faces of our former enemy. I am not sure why I changed my mind. But you know when
you think about it, yes, it had to be used. Think about it, were we going to
lose, a million of our own people? It's war. There's morality in war? The
whole situation in 1945 screamed "yes" for the deployment of this weapon.
The atomic bomb had to be used to save American lives and I'm an American. You have all these theorists today saying how wrong it was. Funny
thing is, maybe their father or granddad was scheduled to assault those
Japanese beaches and would have died, so they wouldn't be here. Also what
do you tell a parent of a son who died on Japan's shores whose death could
have been prevented by using the bomb? Answer that one, Poindexter! God,
if Truman ordered the invasion and then it got out about this bomb and
that we didn't use it, he would have been viewed as a criminal by the American people. War is tragic. If you spent four years in a war that may never
end, and you've got to hit the mainland of Japan, and you're talking about
maybe a million men being lost, you don't even think about it. Bomb!

"That Cheap-Ass Hit"

Adjustment to civilian life for many returning GIs was a gradual
process. In some ways it was and still is an ongoing process. Dream-
ing of returning and who was waiting for them kept men going.
Dreams of wives, children, and aspirations gave veterans something
to live for. Civilian Jerry Coleman was no different.

After surviving World War II my outlook on baseball didn't change. Not
at all. I'm 20 now instead of 18 coming back. I figured, you know, I'd start
right over again. It took a little longer than that. I still was property of the
Yankees and they sent me to Kansas City, which is Triple A, one step below
the big leagues. That was a very hot summer; it didn't get under 90 degrees
for weeks on end, and I ended up 146 pounds! I'm supposed to be 165!
I went to a doctor in the off-season and I said, "How can I keep my weight
at 165 pounds?" And he says, "Do you drink beer?" I said. "No. I don't
have to. I don't drink." He said, "Drink two beers every day." Damn thing
for a doctor to say. Well, I did, I never lost an ounce; what beer did for me,

it put the fluid back in my system, relaxed me so I could eat. What I'd been doing before in combat was so intense that I was never eating anything all that much and I was losing weight. Before my first season in the minors I was looking like a cadaver, so I started drinking beer. I never lost an ounce after that. And the last beer I had? 1957, before the last game I ever played. I hate beer.

Being a veteran allows you to see baseball in a different perspective. Baseball allowed me to raise my family and make a living. Baseball was a means to an end. And I happened to be very fortunate: I was a Yankee and we never came in second. We either won or we lost. Second was losing. We never had a good year when we came in second. A lot of clubs we played would consider .500 a good year. Let me put it this way: the Yankees were not our team, they were our religion. I was with the club at the end of '48; they didn't play good. We lost to the Red Sox in the final two games of the season and the Red Sox tied the Indians, who beat them in the playoff for the American League crown. We came in third. Unacceptable. It was the lowest finish of my career. It would have been the other way around had the Yankees won those two games. Nevertheless the Yankees won . . . most of the time. We dominated the American League, but we did have our miscues. The Yanks lost in '54 to Cleveland, which had a great year and to the Dodgers in 1955. I guess it was their turn. The Braves in 1957 took us to seven games. We lost. I remember my late inning bunt squeeze that helped us win Game One. But like Patton said, "Coming in second just means you are a first place loser." That is enough of that.

More importantly, we won a lot more than we lost ('49, '50, '51,'52,'53, and '56 Champs). World Championship rings, MVP of the 1950 Series, a few hits here and there, and all that really matters? Living. World War II and Korea taught me there are more important things than rings. Of course you want to be successful. Sure! I just mean that baseball became more of a way to support your family and provide them a future, but I got to do it by playing a game I loved on a team I loved. I was lucky. I don't want to get into each game. That's an old story. Pick up some Yankees history book. It's all there. I am not trying to minimize it. But listen to me. Baseball is a game. Living is life. Seeing friends die and families cry is enough to remind me of the proper place to put baseball. After my second time in the service during the Korean War and my age, the kids were taking over on the field. Billy Martin was the younger infielder. That is the way it is. Mr. Richardson put me in the front office, which I enjoyed. Baseball is how you made your living. But it wasn't saving your country. You know the Celtics won all those pennants. What does that do? Nothing. It didn't do anything for the population, maybe for the people in Boston. The Yankees today are still a dominant force which their fans appreciate and UCLA basketball was great. They built an image, but from the standpoint of what they did, what does that prove to anybody? What did it do for anybody? Not much, not compared to what you did in the war.

A favorite baseball memory? That's easy. It was the end of the 1949 season and the Red Sox were making a hard run at us. If I remember, they were actually one game up on us as they rolled in to Yankee Stadium. Joe DiMaggio was really sick. Williams hadn't been hitting all that well for the Sox. It was going to be a heck of a battle. It was! We won the first game, 5–4. God. Joe [DiMaggio] should have been in the hospital he was that sick, but he played, got a few hits if I remember correctly, and then Johnny Lindell hit his home run. I've seen pictures of Ted Williams in left after that homer. His heart was broken. I guess that's kind of hindsight. After all, we had just caught up to the Red Sox. So if Ted's heart was broken . . . I guess the next day it would be shattered. It came down to this one day at Yankee Stadium; it would decide the pennant. I remember it was one tight game. It was the bottom of eighth inning and the bases were loaded, and I came to bat. I just went up there hoping to make contact. I did. You know Williams will never forgive me for that hit. Because Ted Williams said, "That was the cheapest ass hit I ever saw."

I said, "Ted, let me tell you something, pal, you are out in left field." Yankee Stadium left field at that time of year is bright, you can't see. "What you saw was the cover of that ball fall, the core of that ball is still in orbit." He goes nuts. Nuts!

"Do Me a Favor . . . Take Me Right Now": Going to Korea

For millions of returning G.I.s, discharge from the service didn't necessarily mean you were free from future military obligations, particularly if you had a specialty that was needed. You could choose to be placed on one of two lists called *Inactive Reserve* or *Active Reserve*. *Active Reserve* meant you willingly joined a unit that trained once a month and trained six weeks in the summer and got paid for it. Inactive Status meant you were truly severed from the service, and received no military pay. In essence, you were done—but understood that there was a slim chance you might be called up again. With the Communist invasion of South Korea in 1950, one need was evident: the need for experienced pilots. Ted Williams of the Red Sox and Jerry Coleman of the New York Yankees were both experienced pilots and Uncle Sam came calling. Coleman remembers...

One of the greatest needs in Korea was pilots. After W.W. II, I went on inactive status. I was playing ball, you know. We [Yankees] were dominating everything. We really were. I wasn't in the service in any way...wanted no part of it. That's all. I never even thought about it, being recalled to duty. I thought, "I'm out of the service." The thing that frustrated me the most about my time in the service was I wanted to be a first lieutenant in the worst way, and I was two years as a second lieutenant; I didn't get my first lieutenant stripes until I was out of the service in March 1946. I got so tired of running around as a shavetail [second lieutenant.] Finally I got it—but then I went on inactive status. Go figure, I just felt I had bad luck.

In October of 1951, I got a call from the Alameda Naval Air Station in California. Major somebody. He said, "We want to talk to you. You wanna have lunch?"

I said, "Sure." I didn't know what the hell they wanted; I thought maybe they wanted to make a banquet or something.

So he said, "What do you think about going in the service?"

"Well, I hadn't given it much thought to be honest with you." But what happened was the Marines committed an entire air wing in the defense of Korea. That six-month war was now dragging on, and they didn't know when it was going to end and they needed experienced pilots. The Marines trained very few pilots from 1945 to 1950. In fact Truman tried to disband the Marine Corps, in 1947 or 1948. He was going to wipe it out all together. So I am dumbfounded at the moment. I hadn't thought about it. How long? A year and a half they said. "OK, do me a favor. Take me right

Reporting for duty—Jerry leaves Yankees in the middle of a doubleheader to go to Korea. Courtesy of Jerry Coleman.

now in October 1951 and let me out in March of 1953, and I'll miss a year."

No. They pulled me at the beginning of '52 and let me out at the end of '53, so I missed two years. In fact I left for the service in the middle of a doubleheader. I wanted just one more game. Just in case. But anyway, to me I thought, well if I live, it'll just be a little blip in my career; I'll come right back. I was never that good again. I never played as well.

Some people ask me if have regrets over that. No. Not a whisper. Couldn't care less. My country needed me and to say baseball was more important or let somebody else do it is wrong. I am an officer of the United States Marines, for Christsakes. They need me. I go. I was married. I had two children. In April 1952, about a week before I went back in the service, my son was born. We ended up in Laguna Beach with our infant. I went over to Korea in the December draft of '52 and came back in August of '53— after personally winning the war, of course.

Back then, reserve squadrons were called "the weekend warriors" but they had no combat experience. I never got in a plane between 1945 and 1952, but I had the experience. So these guys, the new recruits, are dying to get in. But they wouldn't even take them, it wasn't just my W.W. II combat experience. No, it's the other way. They didn't want to take the whole squadron; they wanted a replacement pilot, so I went to war. Again. I joined VMF 323: The Death Rattlers. God, doesn't that sound better than a Torrid Turtle?

My job in Korea was not much different than in W.W. II, but this time I flew Corsairs. We did dive bombing missions and close ground support. God, did they ever screw up the Corsair. Lindbergh, no relation, is the guy who screwed up the Corsair. He got over on one of those Wake Islands or Midway Islands and said, "Hey, this plane can carry a heavy bomb load." He was taking off with this Corsair fighter plane in World War II with two 1,000-pound bombs. And people said 'Gee whiz, let's do that.' So the Marines got a hold of that. We, at times, had 3,500 pounds of bombs strapped to our fighter planes in Korea. We were very, very, heavy. On a short runway, with, I guess, about 30-degree flaps we barely took off. Think about it. The B-17, that famous bomber in W.W. II, only carried 3,000 pounds of bombs for Christ's sake. But the Corsair. I will say this: if I was on the ground and I saw a Corsair coming down the course I'd move out of the way. They weren't nearly as accurate as the SBD which you could go within a hundred feet of and really nail it, if there wasn't a bad wind problem or whatever. Basically in Korea we were on call, which meant sit around the "Ready Room" and wait to be called in various shifts of four pilots. In Korea we were on call all the time.

One of the highlights of my service in Korea was going into the ready room. The attitude I had to have each time I entered was to act as if I was going into action right then. They called my particular group of pilots "Four plane jocks." We would wait to be called to duty when the phone rang from Joint Air Command wherever the hell they were and you would jump. "What's your plane availability?" "Jesus Christ—hurry!" I say it was a highlight because I knew I was helping my comrades. I was bringing help. That is why it was a thrill to stick it to those North Koreans who had been giving us such a hard time. I saw it like being on a team.

Jerry Coleman in Korea—always a Marine. Courtesy of Jerry Coleman.

You could be in that damn Ready Room from five in the morning till five at night and that damn phone would be going off all day long and by the time you got done you said, "Jesus Christ, I need a drink or something." But, basically when they had some hot action for us, we responded to any disturbance on the Korean peninsula. One time there was a place called [Haeju]. We were sent half way up to North Korea; it was a bad place to be, because if you're going to get shot down, you're in enemy territory and it was hell to be a captured airman. They had what they call these long runs, every now and then. Once a month, you'd go out on one of these missions and circle the east coast or the west coast of Korea with four of our planes.

If somebody got shot down, we would go in and help them get out. We would direct the rescuers to them and provide protective fire to keep the enemy away. In fact when Max Harper, my wing man, went down, I think it was an Army group that was on station nearby and they said, "Can we help? Can we help? We're here; we're ready to go."

And I said, "No, no, there's nothing to be done cause when he got hit; I circled and chased him down and…shit…he went straight in and blew up." There was no parachute. But had he gotten out, then you call these guys in and they can try to get him out. They bring in the choppers and corpsmen to aid the pilot. There is a movie kind of like what we did. Mickey Rooney is in it. It is called The Bridges of Toko Ri. *The choppers were the ones that really took the heat.*

I heard Ted Williams go down and his radio calls asking for assistance and his wing man talking to him. That shook me up, too. I knew Ted, of course. Too close to home. We were too far away to help. Ted made it safely back to earth. Thank God.

I'm not really sure how far north we got on our missions in Korea. We were really way up there when Nash, another buddy, got hit. But one area I clearly remember was the Siningue River. Well…there's a place that took a really heavy toll. You know people die in war. It's not pleasant. Sometimes they are your friends. It is a fact of life. Your emotions change, your spirit just…well, it kinds of dies a little. When things happen and they are bad, you kept it to yourself and there was a lot of drinking at night. Far away looks. These guys were hiding things. I didn't see any real compassion that I know of. I didn't drink, but I went just so I wouldn't be alone. Funny. In a way, it was really as if dead men were walking or drinking as the case may be.

"Merit Badges"

I had what I consider a marvelous baseball career even though it was dismantled by the Korean War, and I was with the Yankees for 20-some odd years in one capacity or another, but the defining moment of my life was my time in the service and, to me, the most important part of my life was my time in the United States Marine Corps. Getting your Navy wings of gold is, I don't know how to express it, except you're walking on air. You are ab-

solutely dumbfounded by the fact that you've become a Naval Aviator and that, to me, is the greatest thing that ever happened to me in my life, even the World Series and all the other stuff. Making the Yankees was wonderful, but that was an achievement thing that involved careers and dollars and so forth, whereas the Marines Corps was something that was sacred. It still is.

I flew 63 missions in Korea and then came home in 1953. Hell, I flew 57 missions in World War II, and everyone asks about the medals. Yes, I was awarded two Distinguished Flying Crosses and a few air medals. You know they don't mean that much to me. Merit badges. I was doing my duty. That's what you're supposed to do. I don't listen to the hero B.S.; it isn't about me. But I tell you the most scary moment of the war is when a guy comes home. It's then that those emotions start hitting you in the head, in your dreams, and even on the field.

"Tell me Jerry . . . is he dead?"

Jerry Coleman sat on a hill outside his quarters in Korea. Staring off into space trying to come to terms with the war, and the death of his wing man.

What can you do in a situation like that? I followed him down to see if he survived, but he just exploded. He just disappeared. So I returned to base and sat down on my bunk. I had experienced this before, as a combat pilot back in World War II. You know you just learn to stuff it. What the hell can you do? I can't change what happened, but I can change how I choose to deal with it.

"Captain Coleman! Phone!"

So I went and took the call. It was one of these cranking phones. It was the owner of the Yankees calling, saying, "'We need you, Jerry. We are in a hell of a pennant race and we need you. Now!" Jesus! I thought. Now? "Well, uh, I am kind of busy here, sir." After all, I was fighting in a damn war. "Well, then get in touch with your commanding officer." So I did, not knowing what he was going to say. Yankees ownership was persistent; it's the Yankees way. The Yanks knew my tour was just over a few weeks from ending, so ownership thought they would speed up the process.

I wrote a letter explaining all of this and I walked it through and handed it to a General Megee who was in charge of the air wing. He said, "We'll have you out of here in a few days." I'm sure they felt it was a good move for them, PR wise. You know, I can go back and help the Yankees win the pennant. Christ, I couldn't even walk across the infield then. Consequently the request came back disapproved. There was a General Hart who was the Assistant Commandant of the USMC who said, "No." Lem Shepherd (Commandant of the United States Marine Corps at that time, and a Yankees fan) came back and approved it—overruling his assistant. Yankees ownership called the Commandant of the United States Marine Corps and explained the situation and I was out of Korea and bound for the green grass of Yankee Stadium. They called me into the headquarters and said, "Give me your piece." I had a .38 revolver and I gave it to them. And he said, "You are on Flying Tigers Airlines out of here at two this afternoon." It was like 11 in the morning and they had me on a Flying Tiger—which was a flying boat that took 40 flying hours to get across the Pacific. You went from Korea to Guam Island to Johnson Islands to Hawaii and on and on. It took forever. I had been this way before in W.W. II. So they had me in the States in 48 hours and in New York 12 hours later.

About 72 hours after losing a friend and trusted buddy, Jerry Coleman stood on the field at Yankee Stadium wondering if he could even play again. He doubted his physical conditioning—and his state of mind.

I couldn't raise my arms. It's the day before my birthday, September 14, and I'm in the clubhouse dying, like I'm going to save the Yankees. The first day after I worked out, I couldn't get out of bed; I had to crawl out of bed. I was killed; it was ridiculous.

The Yanks were going to welcome me back in grand style with a "Jerry Coleman Day." Christ, I thought. It's just enough to be home, and I had to make a speech and play on top of that. So I went to my hotel room and sweated it out for the next day nervous and just wanting to get it over with. Jerry Coleman Day arrived. The phone rang…with a request from a woman to come down to the lobby. So I did. Her name seemed familiar, but with all the changes and emotions in my mind I didn't put it together. Life at that time was a fog.

Once in the lobby, Jerry recognized a woman he had seen so many times in pictures, pictures in which she was surrounded by her five children. Jerry had just come face to face with the wife of his wing man, Max Harper, who asked...

"Tell me, Jerry. Is he dead?"

"Yes" was all I could say. That was about all I could say and then she asked if I could sign some military death benefits papers, which would start the process of care for these kids. She was much stronger than I. She hugged me and thanked me. Thanked me! Can you believe that? That was the worst experience of my life. Now I had to go to Yankee Stadium and play in a game...a game!

I'm in the clubhouse. I'm dying, and I've got to make a speech. I'd just been with Max Harper's wife, and I'm feeling really shitty. Gene Woodling was really giving me a tough time about my speech: "Stop watching the clock, Jerry. You'd think you were going to be shot instead of honored this afternoon." It wasn't a comment I needed after the experience I had just had at the hotel. I didn't owe him or anyone an explanation.

"It's the toughest spot of all," I whispered back to him.

At that moment, Ed Fisher, who was the P.R. director, said, "There's a Marine out there who wants to talk to you."

"Christ, Ed what's his name?" I didn't want to talk to anybody at that moment. I know nobody out there...but I stroll out there to make sure. It's Lem Shepherd, the Commandant of the Marine Corps, for Christ's sakes! He needed tickets. "Yes, sir!" I went back in and I said to Fisher, "Hey, you dumb-son-of-a-bitch, that was the Commandant of the Marine Corps; he's the guy who got me out."

Jerry Coleman Day went off without a hitch. The pre-game show opened with Mel Allen in command of the event. The USMC precision drill corps and band played, a squadron of eight planes—some flown by his buddies from Korea—flew over the house that Ruth built. Gifts were showered upon Mr. and Mrs. Coleman. Allie Reynolds, representing the players, and Ben Epstein, representing the New York writers, presented Jerry with a silver plate, a new china set, a trip to Bermuda, watches, new wardrobes, rugs, radios, TV sets, and even a new car, a cream-colored Lincoln Capri. The greatest ovation of the day wasn't for Coleman; it was for his old W.W. II boss: Admiral William "Bull" Halsey, who stepped up to the microphone to pay tribute to a true "American hero." Smiling and thanking those great New York fans, Jerry Coleman performed his task. That is what officers do. When number 42, Jerry Coleman, was announced as starting at second, the place went wild. The Yankees went on to win that day on a home run by Johnny Mize in the 10th inning.

Reporters, and those around, might have noted somberness in Jerry's demeanor. They failed to ascertain why. They attributed it to his shyness, but even if the reporters pressed him, Jerry wouldn't have told them all the facts anyway. Marines don't whine. To do so was perceived as a sign of weakness. "God, all I really wanted to do at that time was just play ball." For it was baseball that gave him healing and purpose and it still does. Jerry has continued his involvement in the game as a broadcaster for the San Diego Padres. When asked about his veteran status today, Jerry wryly comments, "You really have the time for me to tell you how I won the war? OK, grab a seat."

Jerry Coleman did more than play ball during those early days of that pennant race for the Yanks. He took the time to help a family overcome tragedy on the road to a new life.

The interview ended. Jerry looked me straight in the eye and said, "Well now, let's get some lunch. I'm starving." Jerry shouted back to Andy's office, "Andy, wake up! Let's go eat," and we were on our way, the three of us.

Andy and Jerry, in deep conversation, went and sat at our table in the back corner of the room near the window. I lagged behind and went over to the waitress and told her, "I am paying this bill. If they ask, tell them it is taken care of." I thought it was the least I could do ... are you kidding? I sat down and the conversation was about the Hall of Fame and the announcement that Bob Uecker was to be inducted as a broadcaster and whether Roger Maris would ever make it to Cooperstown.

We got ready to leave and it began to rain hard. The storm I thought I had outran had arrived, but this time it was a blessing. We had to stay inside and wait it out. So we talked about what I did. Jerry was really interested in education. He loves kids. His daughter Chelsea, born to him and his second wife Margaret, was graduating from high school that spring. As the storm let up, Andy was telling this great story about Jerry. Seems that when Chelsea was born, not many of his old Yankees friends knew about it or that Jerry had a new wife. They knew that he had a daughter from his previous marriage who was by now a grown adult. His buddies asked how his daughter was doing. But the excited new father Jerry thought they were talking about his newborn. His new love. Well, that wasn't the case. His friends Yogi Berra, Whitey Ford, and others looked on in amazement as Jerry exclaimed, "Oh, she is doing great! She is sleeping through the night, sitting up and eating solid foods. You know, the diapers are a drag! But it's great, really!"

Did she have some sort of terrible accident? his Yankee friends wondered. Did they miss something? Jerry's friends were totally baffled. Laughing, all of us, I realized what an incredible journey life is as we walked out the door into the streets of San Diego.

They thanked me for lunch and it was time to go. The sun was out. Jerry asked me where I was parked and if he could "give me a lift."

No, I said, I need to walk a bit. Actually, I didn't want them to see my old faded black Rodeo. I thought this might just blow my attempt at being a legitimate interviewer. Funny how your mind works.

"Well…good-bye then, Todd, and I hope this all works out for you and you make a million bucks. Teachers like you deserve it. You do the real work in this country, I tell ya."

We shook hands and it was over. Jerry took out his keys opened his car door, and got in. I stood back and waved and realized that it was a Lt. Colonel, Jerry Coleman, who had offered me a ride and I blew some more time with him.

Like I said, it is funny how life works out.

Although Jerry Coleman served in almost 60 combat/close support sorties in W.W. II, survived an additional 60 combat sorties and a crash in Korea, was awarded two Distinguished Flying Crosses, 13 Air Medals and over a dozen Navy citations, he never thinks of himself or his accomplishments. "Heck, in World War II, I was just one of 11 million men who did their duty," he says, but then quickly adds, "...as a Marine pilot, however. I am very proud of that."

Cooperstown Calls

If you ever wondered if Mayberry really exists, it does. All you need to do is go to Cooperstown, New York. Cooperstown is more than just home to baseball's Hall of Fame. It is home to traditional America, Main Street, old fashioned values, neighborly people, tree-lined streets and reflection back to a time so often forgotten, or that never existed. I heard Dad and other World War II veterans talk about such a time and a place, and old fashioned values, and here they were right in front of me: Main Street, baseball, hot dogs, apple pie and baseball's men of character. I wasn't in Cooperstown for a vacation.

I was a guest.

Cooperstown finally called Jerry Coleman telling him he was chosen by his peers to be inducted in Baseball's broadcasters wing of the Hall of Fame.

I got a call also, from Andy Strasberg, asking if I'd like to attend as Jerry's guest.

Overwhelmed by the invitation to be included in such a prestigious event, all I could muster in my answer was a simple "sure."

On July 31, 2005, Jerry Coleman received the Ford Frick Award for broadcasting. Jerry's broadcasting career started in 1960 when he handled pre-game interviews for CBS television's Game of the Week for Dizzy Dean and Pee Wee Reese. In 1963 he worked "with" Phil Rizzuto, Joe Garagiola and "between" Mel Allen and Red Barber. Jerry used the words " with" and "between" intentionally. Sounds like more than broadcasting went on there, and according to Jerry it did. Jerry was even the voice of the Angels, but all that is background. Jerry is known today as the voice of the Padres, although he left the booth for a one year stint as manager in 1980 and then went back to the booth. "That tells you how well I did, doesn't it?" he says laughing.

Now the San Diego community was turning all out to tell Jerry just how much he meant to them. Although they call him "The Colonel"

Wally Anton, 18, served in the 70th Infantry Division's
882 Field Artillery Batallion 'Trailblazers'
in World War II fighting in eastern France.

Wally Anton was a member of the 715th Transportation Truck Company and was responsible for the quick deployment and evacuation of American and South Korean troops from combat areas along the 38th parallel.

Lieutenant Anton with troops, Korea

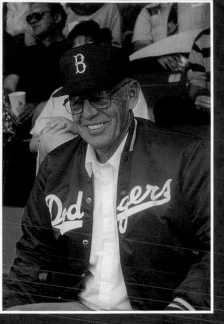

My True Blue Dad
(courtesy of Lou Ellen Anton)

Oh, to be young again!
Local students welcome veterans
to 12th annual Veterans Dinner.

A long overdue honor –
Jerry Coleman is inducted in to the
broadcaster wing of the Hall of Fame
in Cooperstown.
(courtesy of Jerry Coleman)

The show must go on:
'In the Company of Heroes' D-Day event
raising money for the museum 48 hours after
Dad died. Pictured from left to right are
Dutch Schultz, Ralph Browner
and Alma Newsome Fornal

82nd Airborne veteran Dutch Schultz (between Todd Anton and Mickey Hatcher) throws out
the first pitch on the 60th Anniversary of D-Day at Angels Stadium, June 6, 2004

My moment with Mr. Red Sox, Johnny Pesky

"I served because when your country calls, you answer!" – Don Newcombe

Among the greatest thrills ever – talking baseball with Vin Scully

Wally and Todd: Our last photo together –
the Dedication of the Korean War Memorial in San Bernardino, CA.

Joe Foss, Jerry Coleman's hero, meets up with Todd at the dedication of the
D-Day Museum June 2000. Any time spent with the late Joe Foss was an experience.
His stories of Guadalcanal still should inspire every American.

A long way from the classroom in Phelan to New Orleans —
Todd at podium, National WWII Museum

Teach me baseball —
Todd with Jonas Kirsch in Spicheren, France

W. P. Anton and flag in the sands of Normandy — Mission Accomplished —
Omaha Beach, June 2006

Jerry means a lot more to so many. I knew what Jerry had gone through for our nation, I knew the horrors he had seen, and yet he retains his decency, his humor, and, most of all, his faith in the future and his love of family. Although San Diego was honoring Jerry Coleman's service in the Marines, I don't think they ever experienced a moment like I did with Jerry in that rainstorm interview back on my birthday in February 2003. In that moment I got to feel the emotion of a man who saw so much and feels it so deeply that, for him, to talk about it somehow dishonors the men who sacrificed even more than he did. Jerry's humility is real. It's born out of a sense of seeing men die and give all, that makes anything he has ever done or achieved pale in comparison. It is a very special moment when someone tells you about what his or her life means to them. Now here was Jerry's moment to ascend the podium in front of America and yet I still felt as if everyone just didn't get who it was talking—a real American treasure.

I know I am not alone in this feeling. Jerry's broadcasting partner, Ted Leitner often asks him if the players and others "know just who it is they are talking to?" I know what Ted means. He is really saying, "Hey Jerry, does anyone know when they are talking to you, they are talking to a REAL American hero?"

"Why should they?" Jerry asks.

And all of us just stare back at Jerry in amazement.

Are you serious, Jerry?

He just shrugs his shoulders.

I wanted to give Jerry something, too. I had been working on this book for what seemed an eternity. I wanted to get Jerry something that perhaps might open his eyes to see his uniqueness to us all. When I talked to Jerry back in 2003 he mentioned that his two Distinguished Flying Crosses and 13 Air Medals and three navy Citations are really just "merit badges." Awards do not mean anything to most combat veterans. How can a piece of metal sum it all up? What does a ribbon actually mean after watching friends die? This doesn't mean it is not appreciated. Jerry told me, "The awards are really for the person giving it rather than the one receiving it. The honoree has gotten to live a long life, in most cases raise a family. That is reward enough for me."

It is statements like that which motivated me to write to President Bush, my congressman Jerry Lewis and others in government to consider awarding Jerry Coleman the Presidential Medal of Freedom. With President Bush being a former owner of the Texas Rangers and his dad such a baseball fan, I thought if the President *really* saw my letter it would happen. So I sat at my computer and "penned" the following letter...

President George W. Bush
1600 Pennsylvania Avenue
Washington, D.C.
Dear Mr. President:

Some 48 hours after his last Korean combat sortie for his "Death Rattlers" squadron and watching the death of his trusted wing man, Max Harper, Corsair pilot and New York Yankee second baseman Jerry Coleman was again standing on the verdant green fields of Yankee Stadium in 1953. The Yankees were welcoming Jerry back in fine style honoring him with a "Jerry Coleman Day." Legendary Admiral "Bull" Halsey was going to be there to host the occasion. That morning Coleman's mind was awash with a myriad of emotions as he prepared for his big day, and his thoughts were interrupted by a phone call as he dressed in his N.Y. hotel room. A woman wanted desperately to talk to him, so Jerry went to see who it was. Awaiting Jerry in the lobby was a woman holding the hand of the youngest of her many kids. Jerry recognized the face. It was the wife of Max Harper. "Tell me Jerry... is he dead?" she asked. Jerry Coleman, holding back the tears, said "yes" and stayed and consoled this brave woman and her kids as long as he could. Then he had to go on with his first day back in baseball, stand in front of 50,000 fans and receive their praise. "This was the toughest job of all," Jerry said. "All I wanted to do at that moment was just play ball."

Jerry Coleman is a baseball hero and broadcasting legend for the N.Y. Yankees and San Diego Padres. The 1949 Rookie of the Year, 1950 All-Star and 1950 World Series MVP appeared in six World Series in nine seasons. Jerry's on-air sayings: "Oh Doctor!" or "You can hang a star on that one!"

have endeared him to millions of listeners over the years. On July 31, 2005 Jerry will be inducted into the broadcasters' wing of the Hall of Fame. Jerry Coleman is excited about this honor, but his real pride rests in his status as a U.S. Marine combat pilot of two wars: World War II and Korea. The fact that Jerry volunteered to return to military service again in Korea causes him no regrets about his diminished baseball career. He doesn't complain. He isn't bitter. In spite of his baseball fame, he again told the Marines, "Okay, I'll go. I love my country more." Although he returned to baseball in 1953, he stayed active in the USMC reserves, retiring as a Lieutenant Colonel, making him baseball's highest ranking veteran and one of only a very few men alive in baseball to see combat in two wars. Officially Jerry flew 120 missions, received two distinguished flying crosses, thirteen Air Medals and three Navy citations. Jerry is not boastful; he calls these awards "merit badges."

That is the purpose of my writing to you. Lt. Col. Jerry Coleman's story touches me deeply and his humility and sacrifice compels me to ask you to consider him for The Presidential Medal of Freedom. I am Todd Anton, a U.S. History teacher, and World War II historian living in Southern California. Like you, I too am a proud son of a war veteran. My father served in W.W. II and Korea. Like you and your father, Jerry was also a pilot and lover of our "National Pastime." Currently in the editing phase of my book, No Greater Love, the title taken from my favorite scripture of John 15:13, I allow the baseball veterans to tell their stories in a personal firsthand perspective before we lose them. Some of these brave men are no longer with us now, but their stories are. Jerry is 80 years old and time is not our friend. That is what has inspired me to take on this challenge and write my book and contact you.

America and Major League Baseball today could use the gentle reminder of just how great of a sport it is and consider the American values it embodies. Just look at the character of the men who saved it. Thank you for your consideration. I stand ready to serve Jerry and you in this hoped for honor. He is a great, humble and worthy man. I hope you "hang a star" on him.

Sincerely,
Todd W. Anton

I never heard back. Of course, seeing those who got the award on the news after I sent this letter made me even angrier. I just knew if the President actually saw this letter he'd honor Jerry. I just knew it. I am not giving up either. I still see Jerry at the White House and the President awarding him this highest of all civilian awards, but somehow, in some way, I bet Jerry would think he was "undeserving." These were just some of my emotions as I watched Jerry sitting on the stage with ESPN's Peter Gammons who received the J. G. Taylor Spink Award honoring baseball writers. Soon Jerry and Peter were joined on stage by the 2005 player inductees, Wade Boggs and Ryne Sandberg. Acting as the backdrop were the 52 Hall of Fame members. It was baseball heaven. I was sitting right behind Jerry's family who were in the front row... beaming. Then it was his turn to speak.

Jerry had much to say, but, simply put, his was a message of thanks that day to all who have been a part of his life and his journey to Cooperstown. He honored his wife, his kids, his former Yankee teammates Yogi Berra, Whitey Ford, the Padres organization which made his life so complete, and the Marines (who inducted Jerry in to their own USMC Hall of Fame). At one point Jerry paused—with emotion—stepped back, and just for an instant I really felt he understood the love and respect everyone has for him. In his humble manner he finished. I knew he was grateful to be done with it all. Jerry doesn't like the attention, but always for the right reasons. When Jerry concluded, the crowd rose to its feet. He waved and sat down. Relieved. Then it was time for the "7th Inning Stretch" and the 30 thousand of us stood and sang "Take Me Out to the Ball Game" while Stan Musial played it on his harmonica. Truly a special moment—a gift from God, I believed.

After the induction ceremony concluded, there was a reception for Jerry in town. I quickly changed into my suit and made my way over to the party. Just as I was arriving, the heavens opened up and a summer cloudburst poured down upon us all. It was a simple but elegant reception. As I entered Andy made his way over to say "hello" and show me around and introduced me to Jerry's family and friends. As it is with any reception the honoree is busy, bombarded with guests and well-wishers. I just had to tell Jerry "hi" and that I was there. As I made my way over, there was Jerry posing proudly, beaming, with two enlisted men of the United States Marine Corps, in attendance representing the USMC. It was a great picture. For me it summed up Jerry's life and this moment. As I went over to Jerry, he extended his hand to me and said how much he liked the chapter I had written about him for this book and how much it touched him to see how much I loved my dad. "You're a good kid, Todd, and thanks." Just then on the other side of Jerry was Hall of Famer Dave Winfield, who, like me, is 6'7", and he stood on one side and I on the other and we made perfect book ends. We all laughed at the "midget" between us.

The heavens boomed again spilling even more water and I smiled.

It's good to get caught in the rain with Jerry Coleman.

8

Navy Chief Bob Feller, Cleveland Indians

Now I Know Why Hitters Feared Him

For those who do not know baseball or its lore, there is a pitcher whose dedication, talent and devotion to America and the US Navy has no rival. That man is Bob Feller. Make no mistake about it, Ted Williams served, after the 1942 season and after much controversy about his draft status. Joe DiMaggio served, albeit in Honolulu, Hawaii and he mostly played exhibition games for the US Army Air Force. Their cases were not unlike those of many major leaguers.

Bob Feller had every reason to sit out the war. His father—his mentor—was dying from inoperable brain cancer. Bob was the only provider for his family. Bob was the only one who could save the family farm. He was even offered a change in his draft status, with no questions about it. Everyone understood. But one clear hallmark of Bob Feller's character is to never, never offer excuses, nor make any, nor accept any. "Our nation was attacked and if you had any guts at all you get into it," Bob told me. He said he had "wanted to throw a few strikes for Uncle Sam. Not as some rear echelon soldier, but up front making a difference."

It was Dad who first told me about Bob Feller, and he used those very words: "Todd, Bob Feller had every reason to sit it out and he didn't. He was a team player. He was a member of Uncle Sam's team, Son, as we all were. You know the war, as bad as it was, did do some good things and one was to make us GIs all equal in the eyes of the government and also in the eyes of the enemy."

I was definitely looking forward to this interview. I wrote Mr. Feller a letter explaining what I was doing and asked for his time, referring to my relationship with the Eisenhower Center and the D-Day Museum. By the time I called the Eisenhower Center to let them know that they might even hear from him, I was too late. Bob Feller had

Chief Petty Officer Bob Feller and KC Monarch Satchel Paige, 1945. Courtesy of Bill Swank.

called a few hours before, checking up on me and my references. The people who took his calls didn't know of my project. I worried that Mr. Feller would think I was pretending to be something I was not. I was disappointed because it was now something I had to clear up. So I called him and learned the meaning of the word "intimidation."

Bullet Bob!

He answered and made sure he was in control. "Look, I assume you are writing a book? Let me tell you there is no money in books. Don't know why you would want to even do that. Books are a lot of work for little return. People do not even read anymore. I've done a lot of these types of things and I don't see that you are doing anything different. You understand me? So I guess I'll just pass after all!"

I was in shock! Working on this project, I had never been talked to this way. Startled.... I was becoming fearful that a man I thought essential seemed to be slipping away. I don't like controversy, or arguing, but I am not going to let anyone tell me what I am all about or question my motives. He didn't even know me! I figured I had nothing to lose, so I got angry and responded to his aggressive demeanor. I felt the blood rushing to my head and my pulse quicken. I broke out in a sweat. I looked around my bedroom in exasperation, running my fingers though my hair. I saw my dad's picture near my nightstand; he has this smart-ass grin on his face, and somehow I knew my dad was laughing at all of this. I could hear him say, "Son, this is what a Drill Instructor was like. Intimidating, isn't it?"

I took a deep breath and I stood firm. Wow, I thought, if talking to Feller was anything like hitting against him, no wonder he was so successful!

"Mr. Feller," I said, keeping my composure. "I know you may get bothered all the time about your career, but I believe what I am doing is different. I want you to tell me and my students about the sacrifice you and so many other sailors made for the freedom my generation and younger ones take for granted. If you feel that that your sacrifice is not worth your time, I will not bother you. But, sir, you were there and I wasn't. You saw men die for freedom. I didn't. You were there for a purpose and it just may be to teach all of us about the price for freedom. If that is too much to ask, I am sorry. My motives are about getting all of you veteran/players a long overdue 'thank you' from America and perhaps from current MLB players too.

"I am not a professional writer, sir, nor sports interviewer, but I am a historian, a teacher, and the son of a W.W. II/Korean veteran. I know that you have much to offer the youth I teach. Don't you think so?"

It was quiet.

I thought he had hung up.

"Thirty minutes!" He said, "I'll give you thirty minutes. Call back next Saturday at 2 in the afternoon, my time…and I'll be here."

Click.

I said goodbye to dead air.

Cy Strikes Gold

It all starts with a guy named Cy. Cy Slapnicka struck gold. He broke the bank, he won the lottery. He got a huge something for next to nothing.

Don't feel bad about not remembering Cy. As a pitcher, he was no

Cy Young. He spent 18 seasons toiling away in the minors, and his major-league pitching career was, at best, undistinguished. Called up twice by desperate teams way out of contention—the 1911 Cubs and 1918 Pirates—he managed to win a game, but lost six more.

But Cy did a great thing for baseball, and himself. In 1935 he went down to Iowa corn country, outside a little town called Van Meter, to look at some hard-throwing young righty the locals had been raving about.

At a farm with a homemade backstop, a tall, skinny kid stood on a lovingly maintained mound. There was a small square painted on the backstop about sixty feet away. After some brief necessities, Cy told the kid to throw.

He wasn't even looking when the first one hit. But he knew from the bang it made what radar guns tell scouts today. The kid had heat. Cy looked up. The kid was winding up again. This time, the bang was even louder. The ball hit well within the square. And it didn't take a straight line to get there.

He knew what he had right away, but he made the kid keep throwing. The kid never failed. Cy signed him up, paid him a small sum of money, and gave Bob a ball, a genuine major-league baseball signed by none other than Cy Slapnicka.

The kid wasn't just a thrower, he was a pitcher. People would hear more from the kid from Van Meter; people would remember the name Bob Feller.

Without the benefit of so much as one minor-league inning, the Indians put him up against the Cardinals' much feared Gashouse Gang. Sure it was just an exhibition, but for a 17-year-old farmboy to face the likes of recognized major-league stars like Beau Bell, Moose Solters, and Harlond Clift seemed unfair.

And it was. In three innings of work, Feller struck out eight confused Cardinals. When asked about how he was able to freeze big-league batters like that, Bob innocently replied: "I just reared back and let them go." He was ready.

In his first official start later that month, he gunned down 15 St. Louis Browns on his way to a 4–1 win.

When Commissioner Judge Kenesaw Mountain Landis found out that the Indians' promising young right-hander had yet to finish high school—it was clearly against baseball rules to sign underclassmen—he declared Feller a free agent and fined the Indians $7,500.

Slapnicka had a heart attack when he heard the news.

As big-money teams like the Yankees, Tigers and Giants moved in, newspapers speculated that the bidding war could push Feller's signing bonus to an almost incomprehensible $100,000.

But the newspapers never asked Bob what he thought. He knew that money wasn't his. He'd signed a deal with the Indians and he meant to honor it. It didn't matter that Cy had broken the rules. Bob Feller was, at 17, a man of his word and he only wanted to do what he knew was the right thing. He was a Cleveland Indian.

And the Indians benefited from his loyalty. At 18, Bob—whose fastball had already earned him the nicknames "Rapid Robert" and "Bullet Bob"—joined the Indians' starting rotation halfway through the season. He was still a bit wild, and the Indians didn't hit much or field well, but he won nine games. But it was his torrid fastball that brought him fame and respect. He froze 150 mystified major-leaguers in their tracks and continued his dominance up through 1941.

In just more than five seasons with the talent-starved Indians, he'd been able to win 107 games and find the time to save 10 more. He'd also struck out 1,233 major-leaguers, sending them back to the dugout shaking their heads and cursing his fastball or wishing they hadn't chased his changeup. Perhaps the best illustration of how fearsome his fastball was came when Washington Senators manager Bucky Harris told his batters when they faced Feller: "Go up and hit what you see, and if you don't see it, just come on back."

Things changed after that season. Pearl Harbor changed everything.

My Interview with "Rapid Robert"

I don't like doing phone interviews. They are too impersonal. I'd like to think that all the years of teaching have allowed me the opportunity to be good with people and get them to open up. I do it in class, but talking to a legend and war hero is different. I recalled my anxiety over Jerry Coleman and how I kept thinking of him as a war veteran, not a Yankee star. I tried this mental approach and I was feeling better.

Then my phone rang.

It was my literary agent Al Lowman. He was coaching me on what I should do and expect. Al has had a most remarkable career in getting the famous to open up. He was offering his experience, which is substantial, and also his love. To have such important people like my students and such a literary figure at my side as Al Lowman was reassuring. I was feeling more and more confident. That is, until I picked up the phone to call Bob Feller.

"Phones can be very heavy. Time can pass so slowly. How can you break out in a sweat so fast?" were all thoughts running through my mind. So I picked up the phone, gripped the receiver in my hand and dialed the numbers.

The line was busy.

I called back in about 20 minutes and there he was. Hearing that voice, my insecurities came flooding back. It felt like being back in school when the math teacher asks you to come work out a problem on the board and you are not ready for it.

Bob asks, "Well, how long do you need on this thing? You know, I'll just give you what I think is reasonable and that will be enough. Got it?"

I started in and even though Bob told me he'd give me 30 minutes, it ended up being almost 50. It was stressful and I did ask some of my students' questions and the response from Bob Feller was exceptional. He started with what he called the day everything changed ... December 7, 1941.

The Day Everything Changed

On December 7, 1941, the Japanese attacked the U.S. Naval base at Pearl Harbor, Hawaii. Like many American men, Bob Feller wanted to strike back. And he knew how.

Todd, I was in Chicago that day to meet the general manager of the Cleveland Indians. He was meeting me that night for dinner to sign my contract for 1942. I found out about the attack just before my meeting. When I met

For love of country—Feller takes his oath as a Chief Petty Officer in 1942.

him that night I said, "I already called and I am going to join the Navy."

All my former boss could say was "Congratulations."

I had called my friend Gene Tunney, who was not only world heavy-weight boxing champion, but also head of the U.S. Navy's physical fitness program. Tunney put me in contact with Frank Knox, Secretary of the Navy. Yes, they would be more than delighted to have me on their team. So, I volunteered. My mother wasn't all that excited, but my dad was very proud of me. Even though he had brain cancer, he said, "Go."

Some people wonder why I didn't sit the war out, since I had legitimate excuses, but I still can't understand why anyone would not want to serve their country. After the Pearl Harbor attack, I thought: "If you have any guts, if you have any respect for the sovereignty of the United States of America then you are going to do what you can do, no matter what and how little it may be."

Although the transition from baseball, where I was admired and paid

Bob Feller, a member of the Great Lakes Naval Baseball team, shouts encouragement to his teammates. Feller had requested combat duty and was about to get it aboard the USS Alabama.

very well, compared to the life of a raw recruit was sharp, I took it in stride. I didn't miss baseball at all, I never complained, I went straight to boot camp in Norfolk, Virginia.

The drive and intelligence I showed at boot made it clear to the Navy that I should be an officer. So I was sent to the US Navy's War College at Newport, Rhode Island. When I came out of the war college I was a Chief Gunner's Mate, even though I was always technically a Chief Specialist, a specialist in athletics.

By summer, I was on the deck of the USS Alabama, a brand-new state-class battleship and one of the most powerful war machines the world had ever seen. At just 680 feet long and 35,000 tons displacement, she was armed to the teeth. Her main armament consisted of nine 16-inch guns capable of firing a shell weighing as much as a small car 20 miles away. Complementing this awesome salvo was a set of 20 five-inch guns, 48 40-mm cannon, and 52 20-mm cannon. Her firepower was roughly equivalent to an entire Army division.

From America to Britain to Russia: Convoy Duty

The Alabama's first assignment was to provide escort on the all-important Murmansk convoys. A vital link from Britain to Russia, the convoys kept the Red Army supplied with American weapons to keep the Germans from overrunning the East. But the only way to get to Russia was to sail up the coast of Nazi-occupied Norway—braving the wolfpacks of U-boats and the deadly reach of the Luftwaffe—past the Arctic Circle and on to the northern coast of the Soviet Union. It was always cold. Icebergs and storms were as much a threat as the Germans. Polar bears were not an uncommon sight.

But Russia had to be able to defend herself if the war was to be won.

I was an antiaircraft gunner, spent all of my active duty outside. We had to stay with the slowest Liberty Ship, and, of course, we zigzagged all the way. We had aircraft cover. We had a couple of big carriers with us. We also had land-based aircraft dropping depth charges around the area to protect the cargo-carrying Liberty Ships from German submarines and aircraft. You know, I only ever saw one Liberty Ship go down in a whole year. I only saw one. We lost one. We rescued the crew.

You ask what my first combat was like? It depends what you want to call combat. I recall one time on convoy.... If combat is shooting at an airplane, shooting at a submarine, or being in a zone on a general quarters on alert, or condition one, if you want to call that combat, then I guess I was in it. Usually nothing is going on, but you are waiting for something to happen. It was stressful, however. Naturally, you are scared, you're worried, and you're concerned. We practiced a lot with loading the guns blindfolded so we could do it at night. Naturally, you are very concerned. You know that if you meet a bullet with your name on it—that's the way it is. Some never meet a bullet with their name on it; some of them will.

War is not glory, Todd, but you do see men at their best and a nation at its finest.

Besides leading my gunners, I helped with fitness and morale. My duties aboard ship including giving exercises twice a day if conditions permitted to the crew—about 2,900 in all. I had helpers all over the ship do the exercises if conditions permitted with their men.

We needed to always remain sharp. With the U.S. and Royal navies effectively countering the U-boat menace, the last real threat to the USS Alabama on its Murmansk convoys was the Tirpitz, a German battleship even more fearsome than the Alabama. The British had been trying to sink it for years and finally succeeded when a squadron of Lancaster heavy bombers raining 12,000-pound "tallboy" bombs finally sank her. We got it hiding in a fjord in Norway and put it to the bottom and they never got off a shot; the crew fled. The German Navy, as far as the British were concerned, were finished. They didn't need us [the Alabama] any longer; we went to the Pacific.

Task Force 58

As soon as the Alabama joined Task Force 58, it was back to combat. It was pounding Japanese garrisons with her 16-inch cannon while Marines stormed the beaches on islands throughout the Carolines and Marianas. The Americans were steadily and unstoppably island hoping towards Japan. We did it all. I am referring to how many battles the Alabama saw in the Pacific. We earned eight battle citations aboard the big ship.

But it wasn't all fighting. We played ball games on the islands over there in the Pacific when we were in port. These weren't just local sandlots. As often as not, the makeshift ball fields were just cleared of Japanese soldiers. We'd come in for three or fours days to rearm, reload, and lick the wounds if there were any, then go back and take another island.

Because of my baseball career I was in charge of the whole Third Fleet—their sports program on the beaches when we came into port. I was the one running the show. It wasn't all that much; it was mostly all baseball, of course.

I made sure the men had a good time. Baseball in the Navy always was much more fun than it had been in the Major Leagues. I wasn't all that serious about winning. You were just an amateur there. Not that I took it easy on them. Our crew's baseball team became feared by the other American ships in the Pacific. Sometimes we played the battleship Missouri or maybe a carrier, or the South Dakota, or some of the other big ships, the Wisconsin or the Massachusetts come to mind. We had large crowds of sailors on the beaches, but most of them were there just re-supplying, just like us and getting ready for the next invasion.

Bob Feller was chief gunner of a 40 mm gun crew aboard the USS Alabama.
Photo courtesy of Heritage School's Veterans Project.

I got a chance to leave combat and go back to Pearl Harbor to partici-
pate in an Army-Navy exhibition series. The captain asked me if I wanted
to go back. We were way out there between the Philippines and the Marianas at the time and he asked me if I wanted to go back? I wasn't surprised;
I knew something like this would come up. But I knew where my duty was.
"I don't want to go back," I said. "I am going to stay with you."

Captain George B. Wilson sighed and said, "When I asked you that
question, after I received the radiogram from Honolulu, I knew you weren't
going back. I knew you were going to stay with me before I even asked you
the question."

So I went back to the guns. Although Japanese air attacks weren't uncommon —my men and I had to fight off two attacks in one night more
than once—the night of February 21-22 was a very long night.

For 13 hours, the Imperial Japanese Navy threw every plane it could at
our taskforce. And the 2,900 of us on the Alabama fought them off. I was
the gun captain on a 40-mm quad, with about 25 sailors throwing in the
ammunition. We fired eight rounds a second and opened up at 4,000

yards. For all 13 hours, we stayed at our guns. We had our sea rations to eat and we just stayed there and waited for whatever was going to happen. You grow up fast, I guarantee you that. When somebody starts shooting at you, you can grow up fast.

The worst damage the great ship suffered was when one of its own five-inch guns accidentally misfired. Five men died and 11 more were wounded. That's all I have to say about that. Let's leave that story alone.

Battered but still potent, the flagship of Task Force 58, our ship, protected the carriers—especially the Yorktown—from the Japanese by putting our firepower between the Japanese and the flat-tops. The carriers were launching all-important air strikes against Japanese positions on Palau, Yap, Ulithi, and Woleai. Every strike made the enemy weaker and the invasions safer. That was our job.

On the sky just above the sea horizon I spotted dots; four of them. They could be anything—perhaps American SBDs dive bombers, Hellcat fighters, maybe. Probably it's just another protective air patrol. I blinked hard, rubbed my eyes. Nope. These were twin engine, high tail. These were Betties—Mitsubishi G4Ms, the enemy's most lethal attack aircraft. The alarm was raised, the gunners prepared. When the Betties got close enough, we opened fire.

The sky turned alternately black from smoke and bright white from tracer fire. The smell of cordite overpowered the sea air. The Japanese sent bombers, and we sent up a wall of white-hot metal to meet them.

I kept my four guns blazing. I never hesitated, never thought. I didn't feel fear or have a moment's indecision. That didn't surprise me at all. That's because [of] perhaps my experience in baseball. Two of the Betties disintegrated and the others turned around and fled. We were relieved for the moment. Then news came.

A blot as big as a hurricane showed up on radar, and it was approaching the task force. The ships that the Alabama were protecting were about to come under a massive and intense attack. Actually, we were prepared for it when that happened. We got the radar reports and we saw them with our naked eye. The horizon began to blacken with the approaching aircraft. It looked like a swarm of killer bees.

The Divine Wind: The Kamikazes

A combined squadron of torpedo bombers and dive-bombers swung in to attack our group. But they had to get by the fighter cover provided by the Yorktown's Hellcats.

Those enemy planes that got through had to brave the horrifying blast of our guns. Even our own American planes broke off the aerial combat to avoid being chewed up by their own ships' guns.

Two enemy dive-bombers made it through. A 250-pound bomb landed on the Alabama's sister ship, the South Dakota, and caused minimal damage.

An hour later, another wave came through. Again the Alabama put up a devastating barrage of fire. The two bombs dropped by the one Japanese plane that survived to press its attack fell harmlessly in the water beside the Alabama, causing nothing more damaging than waves.

The Alabama had just taken part in what later became known as the "Great Marianas Turkey Shoot"—a prolonged and lopsided battle that for all intents and purposes ended the aerial threat of the Imperial Japanese Navy. It was something! Of the 430 Japanese aircraft that attacked the Task Force 58 on July 19, 1944, just 35 came back in one piece. The gunners of the screening ships, including the Alabama, claimed 27 enemy planes. The Japanese Naval Air Force didn't exist anymore when the sun went down. We sunk four carriers and shot down almost all their airplanes. After that, the back of the Japanese offensive threat was broken.

Providing cover for the US carrier-based attacks at Cebu, Leyte, Bohol and Negros, the Alabama kept what remained of Japan's air power—including kamikazes—off the carriers. The guns of the Alabama took down three enemy aircraft and damaged another.

After that we had a short break for refitting in the recently liberated Philippines, and joined the battle for Okinawa—the last island before the invasion of Japan where we claimed another two Japanese planes and shared in the destruction of two more.

Nature's Fury

There would be no period of calm for us on the Alabama despite a short break in combat. Although the South Pacific couldn't match the North

Atlantic's icebergs, our ship saw its share of weather trouble there, too. One typhoon was a big one that sunk three destroyers because they ran out of fuel. They would have come alongside the battleship to refuel, but they were dead in the water and the swells rolled them over. The typhoon broke off the bow of the USS Pittsburgh, about 50 feet of it, took all the airplanes off the baby carriers and smashed in some of the flight decks on some of the big aircraft carriers. It did a lot of damage to the Third Fleet.

Although our massive ship wasn't in danger of swamping, our crew was hampered in their desperate attempt to save crewmen from the stricken vessels. We couldn't see anything because the salt spray was up to about four or five decks high. We saved 17 men off of the three destroyers that rolled over.

So we took over the Pittsburgh's mission. The Alabama was the first Allied ship to attack one of the Japanese home islands when we bombarded Minami Daito Shima on June 10, 1945. A that point, it was becoming increasingly obvious that the invasion of Japan was imminent. It was also clear that our ship, the Alabama—which was spending the summer of 1945 [with] cover air strikes on the Japanese home islands—was going to be right at the pointed end of that inevitably bloody battle. We prepared ourselves for what they were sure was going to be a long, fanatical battle.

But President Truman made a choice. He dropped two atomic bombs on the Japanese homeland, demonstrating the unprecedented power they were up against.

I knew that Truman had made the right choice. It saved five million lives. It was the right thing to do! Truman was a great President. He had guts. When you go into a war, you have to go in to win. That is what we were doing. He made a great decision.

A week after the second bomb, we received word that the Japanese had surrendered. The celebration was muted; we still had work to do. As the nearest battleship to the Japanese mainland, the Alabama had the curious honor of delivering the first Marines and Bluejackets for the initial occupation of the Yokosuka-Tokyo area. After that, we escorted carriers full of reconnaissance aircraft as the Americans desperately tried to find remote prisoner-of-war camps.

Then it was home. The second I was on land, the Indians called me. Would I be interested in coming back ASAP? Of course!

Taking the Mound: At Home, at Ease, at Last

Nine days after the Japanese had surrendered and a week before the documents were actually signed, I was on the mound in Cleveland.

It was Friday, August 24, 1945, and we [Indians] were going nowhere. But Cleveland Stadium was packed to the rafters as a crowd of 46,477 showed up to see me. I struck out 12 and give up just four hits in a 4–2 win over Detroit's Hal Newhouser.

Over the rest of 1945, I threw a one-hitter and two four-hitters. But our offense could only generate enough scoring to win five of my nine starts. We finished 11 games out.

Despite the nearly four seasons out of the majors, I did well. I won 26 games in 1946 and broke Rube Waddell's strikeout record with 348. More satisfying, though, was the fact that I threw my second no-hitter, this time against the Yankees. I would rather beat the Yankees regularly than pitch a no-hit game. I mean it. Finally management began to surround us with talent. With pitchers like Bob Lemon, Mike Garcia, Early Wynn and even Satchel Paige around, the Indians would get consistent pitching even when I wasn't on the mound.

And, in 1948, the Indians won 97 games and edged the Red Sox for the American League pennant by one game. We had finally made the World Series!

I started Game One. The pressure of performing on this grand stage didn't affect me in the slightest. I was facing the Boston Braves lineup, not a squadron of suicidal torpedo-bomber pilots hell-bent on my destruction.

In the eighth, I allowed my first hit of the day—a weak single to Phil Masi. A couple of pitches later, Eddie Robinson dropped my pickoff attempt and Masi was ruled safe at second. A single by Tommy Holmes scored the Braves' only run of the game. I felt I had done my job. But Boston's Johnny Sain allowed just four singles. The Braves took the game, 1–0. We came back to take the Series, but some of the magic was gone for me. After a '49 season that did not match my standards, I went just 15–14, I asked management to cut my pay from $65,000 to $45,000. I just wasn't worth it.

My major league career wound down in '56, but I continued to barn-storm through the country for charity. Often I'd reunite old war buddies or give otherwise unemployed veterans a chance to play. That was very satisfying.

In '57, the Indians retired my number. I was a first-ballot choice for the Hall of Fame in 1962. So I guess you could say I have seen it all.

There's no doubt to me that Bob Feller was an all-time great, the hardest-throwing right-hander of his era, a tough competitor who always came through in the clutch and backed down from no challenge.

But when you look at his stat sheet, besides the 266 wins, the 3.26 ERA and the 2,581 strikeouts, you see a big hole. The numbers for the '42, '43, '44 and virtually all of the '45 seasons are conspicuous by their absence. These were nothing if not Bob's prime baseball years. He left when he was 22 and came back when he was 26. He won 27 games in '40, 25 in '41, and then 26 in '46. There's no telling what he could have done had he not gone to war. Though a first-ballot Hall of Famer, he could have been the best ever. Pitchers now could be receiving the Bob Feller award for excellence instead of the Cy Young. But I know what Bob would say: "My country always comes first."

Any Regrets?

Does Bob have any regrets when he looks back on his clearly spectacular, but obviously gutted, baseball career?

Of course not.

I didn't miss baseball at all. I wanted to do what little I could to help this country. I did what most any good red-blooded American should have done. This is not to say that I didn't do a lot of praying during my tour of duty. There are times when it sure comes in handy. Like when you see the kamikazes coming at you. Like they say, no one's an atheist in war. There's the old gag about the atheist, when he died, he had put on his tombstone, "I'm going to see for myself." For myself, I believe in a Supreme Being. I'm not against anyone who wants to believe in any supreme being or if they don't. If they want to be an atheist, that's OK, too. In my experience that's much less likely in a theater of war.

As far as today's athletes are concerned, I don't think September 11 is a situation that is anything close to what the danger was for America during my time. We had a greater emergency then. We had Pearl Harbor and were losing big in Europe. We were getting pushed around, all over the world, and had a "now or never" mentality.

Today is nothing like the days of Pearl Harbor or Hitler. There is no national crisis. But I am sure that if we were threatened with a loss of sovereignty, an awful lot of good, young Americans would probably do what I did, or at least serve their country and go to war.

My advice to athletes would be to save your money and learn your job. And appreciate what the Good Lord gave you. Get the most out of your ability. Use a lot of self-discipline. Be able to say no to these fair-weather friends and hangers-on, the people trying to bask in your reflection and glory by following you around. Use your sharp elbows, get your guard up and don't get involved in a lot of controversy . . . things you don't know anything about.

This really helped me understand a lot. Bob Feller wasn't testing me at all. I was testing myself. He made me better and a more confident person. Thanks, Bob.

As for myself, I believe I gained much more than I lost from my military service. There are probably some records I could have had, like no-hitters, wins or strikeouts. There's a fellow who lives in Washington state named Ralph Winney who, about 20 years ago, wrote a "what if?" pamphlet. What if there were no wars, what records those who served might have broken. He dealt with more than 100 ballplayers. He projected his numbers on a 162-game schedule as well as 154 games. On this basis, I would have had potentially 100 or more wins. It was all speculation, of course, but interesting, nonetheless.

Ted Williams would have been way ahead of almost everyone in batting average, home runs, runs scored and runs batted in if he hadn't spent two years in Korea in addition to his tour of duty in World War II. But he served his time, just like I served my time. No regrets. We served our flag and our country without question and with honor.

It is, after all, about winning. Whether it's on the ball field or the battlefield. We're Americans. We always play to win.

Wow. I was so reassured by this confidence. I was at peace. It was OK. Would I like to call Bob again? No. I would like to shake his hand, look him in the eye and say, "Thank you for your service to America, Mr. Feller." You bet I would.

When I went back to class the next Monday, the kids all wanted to know how my interview went. I said "fine" and concluded my story with this:

"You know what, kids? Cy Slapnicka didn't just find a ballplayer when he went to that cornfield all those years ago. He found what made America great."

9

Sergeant Max West, United States Army Air Force, Boston Braves

The Throwback

Ted Williams Day in San Diego: Have We Met Before?

After my moment in the sun and rain with Andy Strasberg and Jerry Coleman I felt I was on my way. This project WAS going to happen. It was on that day in the restaurant in San Diego that I learned that these two men had a deep respect for Ted Williams. One of the conversations at the table centered on an upcoming event Andy was helping to host.

San Diego was Ted Williams' hometown. He grew up there. He went to Hoover High School, was a star player and went on and played ball for the Pacific Coast League's San Diego Padres. Andy was talking about ESPN coming out to cover the event and Jerry was going to be a speaker. I just tuned out the conversation, as I thought they were doing business and scheduling. So as I drove home my cell phone rings and I notice it is a San Diego number. Andy's number. My first thought was "What did I do wrong?"

It wasn't that at all.

Andy was calling to ask me to be a speaker at this upcoming tribute honoring Ted Williams. "Todd," Andy said to me, "I think you are the right one to speak about Ted's military career on Ted Williams Day. You won't speak long, about 15–20 minutes."

"Andy, who will be there?" I asked.

"Well, we have many guys who played with Ted talking about their time with him. Men like Jack Harshman, Ray Boone, and Max West. I think an ESPN film crew is covering that portion of the event. I'm not sure. But you can contribute greatly to this day."

What could I say that could be different or fresh? I just went and wrote about something that struck me about Ted. He was a very competitive man. He liked to know where he measured up as a player, as a fisherman, and also as a Marine.

In World War II, Ted Williams trained pilots in Florida. He was a good teacher. As a result, his deployment for combat duty was delayed until 1945. After arriving in Hawaii, the war was winding down. New combat pilots were not needed.

Ted didn't get to see how he measured up in combat. He trained for it. He trained others for it. But he didn't get to use his skills himself in the ultimate test of combat. That was it. Can you imagine Ted Williams, the greatest hitter in baseball, training others to hit but never getting to hit for himself? I'm sure not seeing any action after training for it was a letdown. Thankfully the war was over. It appeared Ted would never know how he would have measured up.

When the Korean War started, many Marine Corps pilots on reserve status were reactivated. Reluctantly Ted returned to duty. But his country called and he answered, and now Ted would have the opportunity to see how he measured up. He left the game...again. So did Jerry Coleman.

Earlier in the event that day, Jerry Coleman spoke about Ted. Jerry's honoring of Ted's heroism just floored me—I thought Jerry was the superstar in courage.

I asked Andy if people knew about Jerry's service and what he really did in *both* wars. "Not like you do," was Andy's response. So that they would understand Ted Williams' character and the men of that era, I thought that I'd remind the audience of just who was in their presence a few minutes earlier. So I told them about Jerry Coleman Day and his compassionate act for the family of Max Harper in a New York hotel. People were spellbound. It was a story none of them had ever heard. Veterans do not talk about themselves. So I talked about these two great baseball veteran/heroes: Ted Williams and Jerry Coleman.

Jerry had left by this time. He did not hear the accolades due him. Nor did he hear my presentation on Ted. However, Ted's friends did.

One such friend was Max West who came right up to me and gave me a thumbs up. He said I got it just right. I was relieved. Bill Swank, probably one of the best baseball historians around, and a devout Padres fan, took me over to Max. "Todd, Max is perfect for your book." he said. "Max is a real throwback."

"To be honest, Bill, I have no clue of what Max is all about." I said. "I am a military historian, not a baseball historian." "Todd, just hang out with him and you'll see." Bill Swank was right.

Max lived in Highland, California—about 30 minutes from my home in Victorville. Max had lived there a long time and he asked me a question I was very familiar with. "Your last name rings a bell...." OK, I thought, he was going to ask me about my singer/actress sister Susan Anton. Again I was wrong. "Is your dad a sheriff's officer in Yucaipa?"

I just stopped. It was all so confusing. "Yes, yes, Max. He was."

"Then you must be Blackie Wilshire's grandson, too, and Susan Anton's brother."

"What the hell is going on here?" I wondered. How does this old guy know all about me? Especially my mother's side of the family.

Max continued, "Yeah, Todd, your grandfather was an apple rancher."

"He sure was, Max. My 'Papa' was born in 1900, and was a pioneer in Oak Glen, California. That is where I grew up, Max. I lived there for 25 years, until the day I was married. Max, how do you know this? Who did you talk to?" He could tell he was really bothering me. He was laughing by this time.

"Well, I got one more thing for you then, Todd, your dad's captain at the Sheriff's Office in Yucaipa should have been a man named Willard Farquhar." Then Max fessed up. He said his girlfriend, Maggie, was a Farquhar, and then I started to connect the dots. Max even told me about buying apples at my grandfather's apple shed back in the 1970s. The Farquhars grew oranges in the neighboring city of Redlands and they were friends with the Wilshires for years. Max and I got together not long thereafter. This entire journey was really taking some strange turns and I thought how small this world really is.

Max West: 1940 All Star Hero

I'll start from the beginning. Some call me an MVP even though that award didn't exist then. Before I left for the 1940 All-Star Game, we—the Boston Braves—were playing an afternoon game. There was my manager Casey Stengel, myself, and Eddie Miller picked from the Braves. We were playing at Philadelphia and it was about the seventh inning. We had to take the train from Philadelphia to St. Louis. The game was dragging on and we would miss our train, so Casey said, "Well, we gotta go." He put in a left-handed pitcher named Johnson, we got him from Holy Cross. He was wilder than the March Hare. Casey did this because he didn't like the home plate umpire, who also had to go to the All-Star Game, and wanted him to miss the train. Most of us didn't like him; I think his name was Bill Klem. So Casey puts this wild left-hander in to pitch and then we leave. I think that inning lasted almost 50 minutes! That's the last I heard of Bill for the moment. But anyway we got on the train, the three of us and we got into St. Louis. Bill told us the next day he wouldn't forget that damn joke and was going to take that up with the league. It took Klem an extra day to get to St. Louis. God, I loved Casey's sense of humor.

You know, the All-Star Game's not a big deal. It's another day, another game. We get to St. Louis and we take the cab over to the [stadium], we're the home team. And we had a little bag with our white uniform in it. So the three of us go to Sportsman's Park and go in the clubhouse and put our uniforms on. And go out and take batting practice and play the game. The reason I got into the game was because the right-fielder who was supposed to start the game, Mel Ott, was sick or something, so Casey put me in. The rest is history. I hit a home run my first time at bat against Red Ruffing who played for the Yankees. I took that first pitch and the next one was just what I was looking for. Whaaaap! It really felt good. I'd seen Ruffing before in an exhibition game and he made me look pretty foolish. I am glad I got him this time. I drove in a few runs, hurt my hip a little and came out and watched. People say I was the difference.

Going to War: From Pearl Harbor to Tinian

I'll never forget Pearl Harbor Day. It was really hot and I had this orange grove which covered a couple of acres. My dad, myself, and a friend of his

Max West, 1939 Boston Braves. Courtesy of Bill Swank.

had just built this nice little ranch house. For me. It had a porch along in the front, two roads back from the street. It was out in the countryside of California. My wife and I had really worked hard on the landscaping, too. We left one little tree, a small orange tree in by the drive in the parking area of the driveway. My wife had bricked it in for a planter so she went down and got a bunch of pansies and had me planting them in this planter surrounding this tree and I had the radio going. And I heard, while planting these pansies, that Pearl Harbor was attacked. I said, "That's it, I'm going to be in the service pretty soon. I have to go." There was a lot at stake for America: our way of life. We lose this war, we're gone. Forever.

I tell you this, you have never seen anything like the fear that gripped the West Coast.

Everybody thought that Japan was gonna land on the West Coast. The

Japs keep us guessing. Where they were going to strike next. Los Angeles? San Diego? It was really scary.

Some people would think I have regrets about changing my baseball uniform for one from Uncle Sam, but I do not. I do not have any regrets about doing that whatsoever! We were all doing it. I'm nothing special. Of course, it wasn't easy. But it was the right thing to do. I got home in November of '42 after I went to Lake Tahoe to see a friend of mine. The draft letter was in the mailbox when I came home. So I went down and they inducted me and I got leave until January and then I was in active duty in January in '43. I did my basic training down in Long Beach US Army Air Base with guys I knew from baseball: Red Ruffing, Danning and others. I didn't know Ruffing that well except I could get a home run off of him . . . with ease. We got to be good friends later on, but he never said a word about my homers. Harry Danning was a New York Giants catcher. Nanny Fernandez was there and Chuck Stevens was there and Al Olsen was there. There were a lot of guys in the same boat. You know we lost three years of our lives. The most productive years of our lives, we lost it. So what? It really was a matter of survival.

I was in the United States Army Air Corps. Down in Long Beach was what is called ferry command where they ferried all the airplanes. All the planes came in and they were accepted and we ground crewmen drained the planes of all fluids and helped pack the plane up for overseas shipment. We would service new planes and then they were flown to new destinations. Really all I did was serve on the ground crew in good ol' Southern Cal, but that good fortune didn't last.

As the advance went forward, so did we. I am not taking away what we did in L.A.; it wasn't easy. Once we went overseas, it was a long tough job. It takes a lot more than a pilot to keep a plane in the sky. I tell you that. You see all these aces on the TV, but not once do you hear those Chuck Yeager types go on about their ground crew. Hell, I am biased, I know, but we really did a lot.

We flew a lot too. I flew quite a bit on B-24 Liberators and the famous B-29s. I was a scanner sometimes. Not too many people know what a scanner does. In the B-29 there's a pilot and a copilot and they can't see the engines or bomb bays. They do not know if all the bombs have been dropped or not, so behind the bomb bays a guy on each side made sure there was no stuck ordnance in the racks, and we also watch the engines to visually inspect their performance. I monitored the electrical part of it. I made sure that the doors shut. Just because the instrument panel said everything was OK didn't mean it was. The reason I say this is because I saw some horrific crashes that could have been prevented. And we on the ground crew would have to go in and, in all honesty, mop up the human carnage.

The crashes are hard to deal with. You try to forget those types of things, but you don't. I remember every one of those crashes. Tinian Island was a mesa, a huge mesa about twenty-five or thirty feet above the ocean. If I remember correctly, it was the busiest airport in the world.

Sometimes these crashes would happen on takeoff. The planes didn't have enough power...when they take off loaded with bombs and fuel, they'd go down real fast over the horizon of the runway. And then you'd wait and hold your breath until you see them come up again. Well, when they went down, there was nothing you could do for them. They'd always blow up. You'd think the crash crews and all of us would be going to help recover, but...NO, you didn't, there was nothing...nothing left. Why endanger all of us? Those were our orders. So we watched men and plane alike burn. It gets to you, but I only saw it from a distance, you know, it was almost like fireworks. Remember it was an island. Are we going to swim out and endanger more of us? No.

Once in a while, we would disobey orders and get somebody out, but very seldom would they survive. One time I went in to help, we pulled out this pilot. I do not remember his name, but he had just flown all of us to Saipan for a ball game a few days before. We pulled him out and got him on a stretcher. He was burned pretty badly, and all I saw were his eyes. They were so white and he looked right at me, his lips kind of smiled and he just died. His face just went blank. I never offered to help on rescue missions after that. I still see him even today and it keeps me awake on those very long nights when it all comes back.

We would just go back to work and load planes for the next mission. The napalm we loaded were these aluminum hexagon things and then they're tied in a bundle, and they'd just go up into bomb bay. You had to be really careful in the bomb bay of those B-29s, you know those things need

An Army team that played in Long Beach, 1943. Max West in center. Red Ruffing, to his right. Nanny Fernandez, to Ruffing's right. Courtesy of Bill Swank.

room. They'd just release those down in pieces, like matchsticks. Those 29s really wiped those Jap cities out; they destroyed Kobe and Tokyo with the napalms. It was called firebombing. Those GIs that went in first after the surrender to play ball in Tokyo said they couldn't find the city. It was gone.

Sometimes I'd even fly with a captain who was from Atlanta. I'd fly with him a little bit. What would I do on those flights? I would just scout bombs. It was something to do. Between missions it got pretty boring. We would fly or sometimes they'd go and drop bombs on abandoned roads, test-bombing and stuff like that. Sometimes we'd take a practice trip with them. And it was kind of boring, all they'd do is put it in autopilot and go to sleep and let the bombardier do his thing. Like I said I did a lot more than just become a gas jockey for the B-29s.

Most of the time we were flying from island to island and playing baseball for the Army. There were three baseball teams initially for each base in Hawaii; they thought it would be a great morale boost to have us play across the Pacific for the boys. The problem is that we had a job to do as *flight/grounds crewmen and the other problem was they'd tell us about nine o'clock at night and say, "You're leaving at six o'clock in the morning for wherever." We didn't know if we were playing ball or getting reassigned to a new squadron. It was, all in all, a pain in the ass. So then they'd send us to Guam and we would play ball, then they sent us to Iwo Jima and all over the place... just to play baseball.*

You might think that was easy for me to just play ball, but it wasn't. Sometimes I felt uncomfortable doing this. I look at these GIs and thought they were thinking, "Yeah, look at him just playing ball while we are all getting the hell shot out of us." I wanted to tell them what I had been through, but I couldn't. I wanted to tell them that playing was sometimes a burden, not an escape. But that's the way it is. God, we traveled all the time. We'd go and come into an island, we didn't know where the hell we were, so we'd get in line and say we had flight fatigue and get a shot of whiskey. That's my kind of medicine. We were all trying to forget this war. When we got back to Tinian, there was a new plane in the squadron. The Enola Gay. That's right. The Enola Gay was in our squadron.

I witnessed the bomb being placed in that pit where they loaded the bomb into the plane.

I was there! We were within 200 yards of it. You know much is made out of us dropping the bomb. It's all a bunch a crap. We had to do it. It saved American lives. It's a damn war. We save our own. If it was the other way around, would the Japs even think about it? Hell, no! Think about the war in the early years. The Japs were killing our guys on that Death March, they were starving our GIs in prison camps. They were ruthless— and now in 1945 we are supposed to not fight back with all we got? I tell you this, what if we had not used the bomb? There would be less Americans alive today because either their daddy or granddad was killed invading Japan. They wouldn't even be born. For people to criticize the bomb... it is just [Monday morning] quarterbacking.

The war ended. I was feeling like, "OK, now what? Get me home."

You had to have a certain amount of points to get out. For every Bronze Star, you get five points and we had quite a few because of everything we did. You know, we fought in the Asian Pacific Theater and did a lot of tough duty at Saipan and Tinian and got a Bronze Star for that. We were a part of the squadron that dropped the A-bomb which got us one more Bronze Star and then dropping mines in the Sea of Japan got us our last Bronze Star. So we got all these awards. So what? We had five or six of them before we were through, and it helped me accumulate way over the points necessary, but the orders hadn't come through yet. So we stayed in the Army until it was all worked out. No early outs! Not even for us ball players. So we were late getting to spring training.

Fear

It's hard after all these years to remember specific details about fear. Hell, I was afraid most of the time I was either in the air or at sea. On land I was OK. But one time stands out when I had a moment of fear, I mean where I felt helpless. Aboard ship, we were told that there was supposedly a submarine following us and there we were, down there in the bottom of this ship and this submarine's around and you know you can't get out unless you go through a hole in the bottom of the thing. That's the only time when I felt helpless. There is a difference between fear and [being] scared. Fear is a healthy respect for the danger around you. Being scared implies a sense of cowardice in the face of the danger around. One keeps you on your toes and the other can kill you and destroy morale and your buddies' trust in you. All in all I would say my time in the service was positive, yeah. I think they made a man out of me, I'll tell you that.

Some Call It Baseball's Greatest Game

It was hard to follow baseball overseas. We didn't have satellites beaming in everything on radio. It was getting close to World Series time and I really wanted a piece of home. We had come from Guam to Saipan. And the Cardinals were playing the St. Louis Browns. It was early in the morning, I remember. And we were in an eight-man tent and my buddy Lodigiani was next to me, Dario Lodigiani. We carried in a load of bananas. I woke up and this typhoon hit. And we had a wooden floor with wooden sides and then they had these two by fours with screens to keep the flies out. Those blew right out of the tent and instead of sides of the tent going down to the ground, you had them rolled up for cooling. And this frame of two by fours started bending, folding, and came right across me. I saw it and I grabbed ahold of it and it pulled me right out of bed. And then it came back and I started letting go of it and it fell on my cot and I said, "Lodi! Let's get out of here!"

He and I ran to the mess hall, and the tar paper on the mess hall roof was flying all over the place. We went in there and they were preparing for breakfast and, my golly, on the radio they had the World Series between the Cardinals and Browns! We listened to the World Series as the roof was blowing off during the typhoon. This radio was hooked up to some sort of generator powered by someone pedaling it and somehow it generated power. So we grab some food, ate real quick, and Dario got on that generator bike thing and pedaled his heart out. I held on to the radio. I held on real tight and turned the volume up real high. We heard the entire game as the building just blew down around us and when it was over, nothing was left. Nothing—except our clothes, and the radio and generator. Everything was gone, but we heard the World Series and that's all that mattered.

Unbelievable. Two stupid kids, I'll tell you that, but baseball, the World Series, kept us going. Thank God for AFN [Armed Forces Radio]. Not long after that we went to Tinian to work the flight lines—and play ball when asked. One game I played in was real special. You don't hear much about it. Actually it shows just how damn important baseball was. If an idiot like me will wrestle with a radio in a hurricane to hear the World Series, it is remarkable what guys will do for a game of baseball and what it means to them.

One day, the Army staff just came to us players on Tinian. Apparently, they must have had like an all-star team they were putting together to play around the Pacific. Catcher Birdie Tebbetts was ordered to put this team together and I think the order came from Hap Arnold who told General so-and-so and General so-and-so told Tebbetts to get these guys together. Players were scattered all over on different islands. So finally we were all together; of course we didn't know at the time we were going to play ball. Army brass came to us and said, "Pack your gear, you're leaving in the morning." We left at four, five o'clock in the morning. And of course you never knew where you were going to go. They put us in B-29s.

I sat in my usual scanner spot. Now, we flew a good ways and what I remember is the ground, when I looked down, it looked like a pork chop. This island was called Iwo Jima.

We came around and landed and the runway ran into Mt. Suribachi. Everybody said, "What are we doing here? This is a bunch of black sand and destroyed crap everywhere." And Tebbetts said, "Max, I mean Sergeant West, we're supposed to play a game. And there's another group coming in on another plane." I said, "Birdie, I mean Captain, there's no way we are going to be playing in a game. Where is the field?" At the end of the runway, they had some Quonset huts and when they built the runway, they dug these deep pits, put in these huts, just covered the Quonsets over with dirt. That's where we had to stay. God, it was so hot in there. No ventilation. Stuffy. So we walked out front to get some air. The front of the Quonset was open— facing Suribachi. I saw that flag up there. My God, what a sight. All that grime and crap everywhere and you see that red white and blue flag...boy, that looked good! Real bright, real bright. A lot of stuff was going on as we arrived.

We were all standing around smoking and this Marine—Jesus he looked like he was 13 years old—told us to get back in our quarters, because Jap snipers were all over the place!

It was hard to sleep. All I heard were these tractors all night. But the next morning by golly they got the Seabees in there and they made a diamond out of this black sand. Amazing. When we got up that morning, there was a ball field, but no backstop and nothing else. But they leveled it all out and had it striped and everything else. The chalk lines were so bright. They even had USMC snipers posted in the outfield looking for Jap snipers in case one of us went down in this game. We had our helmets with us on the bench. Some guys wanted to wear them in the outfield. They tried real hard to make a game out of it for the boys. They even had an announcer who announced us as we lined up on the first base line and when they announced Captain Tebbetts, they booed him. I guess because he was an officer. All of us regular guys were cheered real loud. It felt good to line up again on a field. It all seemed strange. Weird. You look around and see all these kids who are hurt or bandaged up. Some guys have scars in their minds, too, and I am worried about playing baseball in a combat zone. I wasn't worried about my safety after that, but Birdie and I were worried about some of the guys sitting right behind home plate.

They didn't have a backstop. Remember these guys were bloody and everything else. Combat had just ended. In fact, the area was really not secure for some time and, like I said, [they] had riflemen around [in case] Japs came out of the ground to pick us off—those bastards were all under the ground like gophers. And there were still some of them down there. So anyway, we went over to these Marines behind the plate, and Birdie Tebbetts says to these guys, "You better move back or something or you're going to get hurt." And this Marine, I'll always remember him, was wearing a cast and was really beat up says, "After what we have gone through, we're gonna get hurt by a baseball?" We felt so stupid, so they stayed there for the whole game. I do not remember who won, but it was really special. It was called the greatest game ever played or something like that. And the Marine officers came around to us and said, "This is the greatest thing that ever happened, you guys coming here like this, because you know these guys are all shot up and everything else. They took a hell of a beating here."

Yes. Yes, it made us feel pretty good.

Back to Ball

Well I finally got out of the Pacific, but was a couple weeks late getting into the spring training. And Southworth was the new manager for the Braves. I got starting in and then . . . my dad died. I had to go to Miami and try to fly back home. In those days, flying across the country was a chore. It took me about a week to go from Miami to California. Wartime travel restrictions were still going on. So, anyway I got home and nothing was done. So I had to arrange everything. By the time the season opened, I had to play myself into shape. I guess they figured I was hurt. I was even called lazy and they traded me to Cincinnati.

I still wasn't in shape. But I played. They put me in left field and there's a famous incline in left that went up like four feet high and then leveled off to the fence and I'd never played there. I had to play short for those short fly balls and when the ball was hit over your head, you had to look to see how you were going up this hill. Well, I didn't do very well . . . you're going up this damn hill and one leg is uneven. I came down and hurt my back. I didn't play much after that. And they wanted to operate on me and because of some of the other ball players—Vander Meer and a few of them—told *me stay away from the knife. So I did. This pissed off owner Warren Giles. He and I didn't see eye-to-eye. So he sold me to San Diego. And the funny thing about it, he thought he was really giving me the shaft.*

I got a telegram from him and it said, "You didn't like it here and I know you're not going to like it where you're going." The only way I found out where I was going, one of the top sportswriters down there at San Diego, called me and told me I was sold to San Diego. I said, "Ooh, boy. The two places I [would have liked] to finish with were San Diego or Los Angeles and I went to both of them. San Diego is unbelievable. I did really well. I got back on my feet and then it was back to the majors. Pittsburgh. I was just there one year and then...I was kind of like a free-agent then. And they tried to waive me. So Leo Durocher, damn fine man, kept me on the roster of the New York Giants. So when they called me back to NY, they kept me. It seems that many of the military veteran ball players who were coming up on their 10 years were getting cut so they didn't qualify for benefits.

Several baseball organizations were dropping players just before they reached the 10-year mark, so they wouldn't have to pay their benefits. Bob Feller and a number of other returning players talked about organizing a walkout of some sort, to see that all service players got credit for their wartime service. Feller called it a slap in the face to America's fighting men. Of course, players needed a minimum amount of years in MLB prior to their military service to qualify. The threat of bad publicity likely helped; ballplayers received full credit for their time in the service.

Let Me Tell You about Bob Feller...

Now I want to tell you something rarely mentioned. There was a bunch of military ball players that got done in by asshole owners. I was lucky. The league really did nothing to help us either. But Bob Feller put a stop to that. Nobody knows anything about that, about how he and others got the war years to count as part of your total years of service in baseball.

The pension plan, however, started before the War. Yeah, we all put in a hundred dollars each season, now some of the players didn't like this idea.

Amidst flightline duty and tragedy, men needed to blow off steam—they did! Max West, far right in skivvies, drinking beer after a baseball game on Tinian in 1945. Also in the photo, Rugger Ardizoia; seated third from left, and Al Olsen, PCL San Diego Padres, seated far left. Courtesy of Bill Swank.

So they didn't benefit. But we had no options then. There was no union protecting us. So anyway, I thought, "That ought to be a pretty good deal." So I did it. Thank God I did. Then the war comes along, well, you're still in the pension plan. I paid into it even in the service.

A hundred dollars was no big deal. Yeah afterwards we had to pay, depending on our years of service in baseball, I think I was a 10-year man, I had to pay something like eight hundred dollars. So I paid, I guess in one or two years. And then it really looked like this pension plan was going to fold and the owners tried like hell to break it. Owners thought there were too many guys in it who really were not going to be real big players, or in fact were really done with their careers. So why should they pay for them? Government rules said for business owners to give jobs back to returning veterans. The owners did that—and then cut them. That's what they were trying to do to me. Feller didn't like it one bit.

What Baseball Means to Me

What does baseball mean to me? Not much, really. I wasn't all that nuts about baseball. I went out and did a job and that was it. I wasn't . . . sentimental. I was a good player. I wanted to get paid. I had a life to lead, and a family to raise. Baseball was a means to an end. That doesn't mean I do not appreciate it. I do, but I keep it in its proper perspective. I guess the war did that to me. Changed me that way, I guess. Before the war, we didn't have two nickels to rub together. I didn't have a car, I didn't have anything. My folks didn't have anything and this opportunity to play ball came up, and when scouts said we'll give you five hundred dollars, I said, "How much is that?" I'd never seen more than a dollar in my life, you know? My parents were disappointed. I had a scholarship to USC—an education and a future. My parents understood that. But playing pro baseball? I know they thought it was too risky. They never said a word about it. My dad played a little bit of amateur baseball, with the Pasadena Merchants or something like that. I never saw him play. No, my parents seemed to be ambivalent, they never said anything bad or good about it. They did come around to see me play. As I became successful before the war, I bought my mother a dining room set and whatever she wanted. That's what sons should do.

What I Miss . . .

Do I miss the game . . . baseball? The thing is, in those days life was different than it is now. We didn't have all the things given to us like you get today. Of course, we didn't know any different. You don't know the Depression's on or whatever. And everybody was in the same boat. I didn't know how bad it all was until I was told about the Depression by my dad. But what do I miss? That's easy: I miss Lane Field in San Diego. I miss the San Diego Padres, I miss the Pacific Coast League [PCL], I miss the jokes, being with the guys, but most of all I miss being young. Damn . . . there is an old saying: "Youth is wasted on the young." Boy, is that ever true!

Max looked at me, eyes full of mischief, and sarcastically said . . . "Looking at you, Todd, I know that saying is true. Todd, that's about it. You got time for dinner? Sizzler is right down the hill from here."

I glanced at my watch and noted that I was running pretty late. I tried coming up with an excuse I could call home and use, but I answered him, "I promised my wife, Max, I'd be home so we could all get to church tonight...*as a family.*" He understood.

I wanted to go eat with Max so bad. He was buying too, but I wanted to keep my promise to Sue. Her support of my journey is probably the strongest of them all. So I thought, "I'll catch up with Max later and keep Sue on my side." It was the right thing to do. I kept in contact with Max over the next few weeks and his schedule was very busy. He was being inducted into the PCL Hall of Fame and he was going up north for a trip. I figured I had plenty of time. I didn't. Max didn't make it home from his trip. He became ill and passed away and I was left to wonder about that dinner that never happened with the hero of the 1940 All-Star Game.

10

Ensign Johnny Pesky, US Navy

Mr. Red Sox

Boston

After my terrific opportunity to speak on Ted Williams Day in San Diego, Ted Williams historian Bill Nowlin suggested that I talk to Johnny Pesky in Boston. I knew all about Johnny Pesky; I had seen him many times over the years on Red Sox games and also on ESPN. I especially enjoyed the TV special *The Teammates* based on author David Halberstam's wonderful book by the same name.

I've learned that the love we all share for this game inspires us to serve it. I thought that the writing industry would be full of competitive people looking for an angle. I didn't run in to that with any writer or baseball organization. But I've learned a lot, and people like Bill Swank, Andy Strasberg, Bill Nowlin, and Jeff Idelson have inspired me to go on and fight the good fight and finish this tribute to baseball and America.

With all the research I did on Ted Williams, Johnny's name kept coming up and there was an obvious bond between these men, and between Johnny and Boston. Bill also suggested I talk with Dominic DiMaggio.

I felt a rush go through my body; this means I get to go to Fenway Park, the home of the Red Sox, a team whose history I began to love. You can't help but have a heart for them. Granted, I want the Angels or the Dodgers to hand them their hat, but I have a heart for them. I root for them when I can.

I invited my buddy Morgan to come along. He and I have both been teaching history in the same district for 14 years. We grew up together in Yucaipa and have known each other since third grade. Morgan loves baseball and its history.

Working around our school schedules, we chose to go to Boston during Memorial Day weekend. I was going to have a witness to this grand occasion, and to share it with my best friend who is closer to me than a brother was indeed a treat.

Fenway

I have always wanted to go to Fenway Park, because my dad always said, "Real baseball is played at Wrigley Field, Fenway Park, and Yankee Stadium." He said, "But if you want to see a real baseball field, you need to go to Fenway Park." I guess it was because of the tradition or because of the men who were there, and I would always ask why. He would say, "Because Ted Williams played there." Then he would tell me about Ted Williams. That Ted Williams was a war hero and that he was in Korea, like he was.

"Son, I have always wanted to go to Fenway Park too. How could you not want to go to Fenway Park? Lou Gehrig played there. Babe Ruth played there. Ted Williams played there. A lot of history happened there. It has seen the passage of time and yet it still stands. Just like America. Todd…you want to see America? Go to Fenway. Want to see real baseball? Go to Fenway. You've got to love it, Son. It hasn't been knocked down for some retro ballfield or anything like that."

It was an amazing experience. There is something surreal about being at a place you've always dreamt of seeing. The old adage "pinch me" seemed to fit. It was all a dream. We arrived at the hotel and I wanted to go straight over to Fenway Park. That night we were not going to go to the game, because we had tickets to the following two games and I was going to interview Johnny Pesky. Shouldn't that be enough? NO. Out of my window I could see Fenway Park. It was maybe five or six blocks away from where we were staying. It was calling me. I looked over at my friend, Morgan, and I said, "I gotta go… now!"

I think it was the second inning. Somebody on the street had extra tickets and needed to get rid of them. We walked up to the gate, presented our tickets, and went on in, got our hot dogs. We started to walk to the tunnel entrance to the seats, but I paused for a moment and said, "Here I go." My first view of one of baseball's most hallowed grounds. This was a big moment in my life. I felt more than just the presence of my best friend, I felt the presence of my brothers and my father, who were in some small way saying, "Go in and check it out."

I did, and what I found was the most beautiful baseball field I had ever seen.

Fenway Park became a reality. I had tears. Great men played here. As an historian, I know to appreciate where I am. I've stood at Gettysburg, I've stood before the Korean and Vietnam War memorials and sobbed in my heart, I've stood over the rusty remains of the USS *Arizona* in Pearl Harbor and felt humble in what it means to be a citizen.

Now I was becoming a citizen of baseball.

We sat in right field under the overhang. It was a remarkable time. The Sox were playing the Cleveland Indians. When we got there, the score was close. When we sat down, the Red Sox scored all these runs and it was amazing. People were going crazy. The Red Sox were winning and blowing the Indians out and all that everybody would yell at that top of their lungs was: "Yankees suck!" "Yankees suck!" They're not even playing the Yankees, I thought. What is going on here? What I'd failed to notice was that the Yankees score update had been posted on the manual scoreboard in left field showing that the Yankees were behind.

Of course, I know the Red Sox hate the Yankees and I know the Yankees hate the Red Sox. Of course, I understand that rivalry. As a Dodger fan we all hate the Giants and as an Angels fan we are developing a rivalry with the Yankees.

Then singer Neil Diamond's "Sweet Caroline" filled the air between innings. Why was this played at a baseball game? I was in a different world. Welcome to Fenway Park.

The Fan

Naturally, I had my Dodgers hat on, and as Morgan got up to go and get something else to eat, I was officially baptized by one of the most passionate fans I have ever seen.

A "lady"—a woman in her late '60s, or early '70s—sat behind me.

She looked like a wool-clothed librarian, and she slapped my shoulder. I was pretty startled, but with that Boston accent she said, "Whatcha got that Daaaadger hat on for?" I was explaining why I was there. That we were visiting and that I always wanted to come here. She asked me, "Well, do you like the Yankees or do you like the Red Sox?"

I said, "I like the Dodgers and the Angels."

She said, "That is not what I asked you. I asked you if you like the Yankees or the Red Sox."

I said, "Well, I am writing a book on veterans and there are a lot of veterans on the Yankees and a lot of veterans on the Red Sox so I've got to be careful."

She said, "You California boys can't answer a damn question. I asked you if you liked the Yankees or the Red Sox."

I said, "Well, I am a Dodger fan and the Yankees have screwed the Dodgers so many times in their history that I would have to honestly say that I would have to root for the Red Sox because I don't like what the Yankees have done to my Dodgers."

She said, "Well, I tell ya, let me tell you something. You are wearing that Daaadger hat. Have you even been to Daaadger Stadium?"

I said, "Yeah, many times."

She said, "Well, I've been coming here before Daaadger Stadium was ever built."

Then she went on to lecture me. I think she said she was 70. She said, "My family have had these same damn seats here for 65 years. I haven't missed many games here. My father brought me here. My mother brought me here. I haven't missed a game in many, many years, let me tell you something, and I saw Ted Williams play out there. You can't tell me that you got a legacy like that, sitting out there in California with your palm trees and your fans that leave in the sixth inning and all that kind of stuff. It's about time you saw what a real ballpark was like." She said, "Let me tell you, my father sat here, my grandfather even had these seats, but I have been in these seats for years."

I thought, this is really cool. The way she was dressed, she looked like she could have been a librarian, but my God the language that was coming out of her mouth. She was yelling at everybody and was telling them that they sucked if they didn't measure up. I have not ever seen or heard anything like this. This was amazing.

I was done being nice. I did remind her that out in L.A. we have our own names, like Snider, Koufax, Drysdale, Podres, Hodges, Howard, Wills, Alston, Gibson, and Hershisher. MANY of whom, I stressed, WON a World Series more than once!

She was quiet after that. 1918 was a long time ago.

She laughed and bought me a beer welcoming me to the house, in her words, "that misery built."

"Alone" in Fenway

The next day I arrived early at Fenway Park. Bill Nowlin was going to meet me at the front entrance and we would go in together. He has interviewed Johnny many times, especially for his book called *Mr. Red Sox: The Johnny Pesky Story.* Yawkey Way was shut down. Bratwurst, ribs, hot dogs, onions and smoke were filling the air. I was dying to eat. I watched young kids get bats made with their names on them. It was really remarkable; neither Angel nor Dodger Stadium has a climate like this. The city surrounded the park. I loved it. I went in to a Red Sox sports shop and came face to face with a jersey I had to have: a brilliant red number 9 on pristine white with "Red Sox" on the front. I felt justified in wearing a Ted Williams jersey. It was him and his fellow veterans I was honoring after all, I kept looking for Bill out in front of the main gate. He wasn't there yet.

A Red Sox official at the front gate asked me if I needed something. I must have looked out of place, lost and loitering. I told him what I was doing and whom I was waiting for. "Oh, you're on the list or at least Bill is! Bill will be here." I told him we were going to be interviewing Johnny Pesky about his experience in the service.

"Well, I can tell by your voice that you are not from here, where are you from?"

I said, "I am a Dodger/Angel fan from California."

Then this person said, "Well, are you leaving in the fourth inning tonight?"

I said, "No, I always stay for every inning of every game."

Johnny Pesky

Bill and I waited outside the locker room entrance. Players were all going in to get dressed after batting practice. Nomar Garciaparra walked by; I was in awe of where I was. Then here comes this small older man out of the clubhouse door into this anteroom we're standing in, away from the public, wearing nothing but his Red Sox jersey and his underwear. "Hey guys, I'll be right with you. I'll meet you right here." He went back inside.

Bill reminded Johnny, in jest, to "put your pants on." That was my first glimpse of Johnny Pesky. I knew there was a real character here. I thought: this is going to be fun. A few minutes later, out he came wearing his uniform, tennis shoes, Red Sox jacket and a warm and friendly smile.

"Hi, Todd. I'm Johnny." We shook hands.

We started with a little friendly conversation, getting to know each other, and we got to work. Johnny actually got us started, reminding me that I didn't come all the way to Boston to make small talk. "I've got a game in a few hours and you spent money on seeing me. Let's make it count." I told him about 30 minutes should do it. Fine, he said and then asked me "Todd, what can I do for you?"

So I pulled out my list of questions and we talked our way through them. We sat along the first base line. I had on my D-Day powder blue denim shirt and jeans. I also pulled out my digital recorder, plugged it in, and got to work. I kept checking to see if it was recording...if everything was OK. I could see myself coming all this way and forgetting to turn it on or something going wrong. After the interview, I even ran the recorder back to my hotel room shortly before the game to see that I had indeed got it. I had. Now I could enjoy the game.

I started with the reason I was there: his service in World War II.

World War II

Well, Todd, I just got back from our Louisville minor league season, and we all registered for the draft. It was the law in 1941. Luckily I had a high number or I would have got drafted. So it's early December and I was com-

ing home from church in Oregon, and I was just walking up and down the street, and when I finally got in the house, they had the radio on and the family was listening to it pretty loud.

The Japs had attacked Pearl Harbor.

What can you do? You wait your turn, and I was waiting my turn like everybody else to get my notice. I did go to spring training in 1942. I made the club, and then in about July of that '42 season there was a guy by the name of Lieutenant Fuller, who had this V5 program going on, and it was a great program. This program was a fast track to learning to fly and becoming an officer. I was interested.

It was pretty tough at times in 1942. If you weren't in a uniform, people would say, "What the hell are you doing out of the service?" Unless you were classified 4-F. Well, hell, there was nothing wrong with me. Dominic [DiMaggio] wore glasses, but a lot of guys wore glasses. He had to fight to get in. Which he eventually did. Ted Williams talked me into joining this V5 program. We signed up at 150 Causeway Street in downtown Boston. Together.

Other players joined up too. Johnny Sain, Joe Coleman, and Buddy Gremp enlisted. Sain and Gremp were with the Braves, and Coleman was with the A's, and of course Ted and I were here from Boston. We thought we were going to get called at the end of the month. The Navy was trying to build up its aviation wing. They swore us in at the end of July, but we weren't called for about a month-and-a-half in August, September. I was waiting for a call, and didn't hear anything so I went home. I was there about 10 days, then I got a call to come back. Ted and me and others, went up to WTS, which was War Training Service up at Amherst College, I think we were there for three months, and then from there we went to Chapel Hill to fly. Hell, yes, I was nervous.

Ted went on to get his wings, but I was a little…in arrears about my navigation, so I had to stay two extra weeks. My navigation officer was a pretty good guy, but then the captain of the base called me and some other guys in for an interview, and there was a kid from MIT, Harvard, Colby College, and myself, I was the only high school graduate of the four. I'll never forget his name, his name was Roy Callahan, and he said to me, he said, "Johnny, we're opening this operations school down in Georgia." He said, "I'd like you to go and you'll get your commission there." When he said commission, I was all for it.

"You'll learn how to operate in the field. We go all over the world." We were getting so many kids and so many flyers, they needed guys to work on air stations, casualty units, carrier aircraft service units. They put these Operations officers into areas where they needed someone with a little rank. I said, "Yeah." I just wanted to get my commission. I went to this school and I really bore down. I never left the base. I wasn't in the top of my class, but I got my commission. That was one of the proudest things I've ever experienced—I made it to the big leagues as a player, and then I got my commission in spite of just having a high school diploma.

Flight School

Flight school was a difficult experience for me. Things just didn't come easy for me. I marveled at Ted Williams' capacity to learn. He had a photographic memory. Ted was intense at everything he wanted to do well. In class, he'd absorb it all—a damn human recorder. Ted even tried to help me out. I used to see Ted reading all the time. I'd go get something to eat. I just couldn't discipline myself the way he could. I needed somebody to show me. That's how I learn. My approach must have frustrated Ted. After two or three weeks, Ted said to me "Shit, why can't you get this?" I said, "Well, Ted, I'm not you! Your mind is much quicker than mine." "Well" he said, "when you eventually get it, you'll retain it." Which was a left-handed compliment. He worried about me.

Todd, Ted Williams wrote in My Turn at Bat *that I "flew an airplane like I had stone arms" and Ted told about one day when I had to make eight approaches to land my Cub observation plane. Go look it up.*

I did. Ted Williams writes: *"It looked like they were going to have to shoot him down. They finally got Pesky out of there. In an airplane he was a menace to himself and everybody else, but he was certainly officer material so they moved him into Officers Candidate School [O.C.S.] and he actually got his rank before I did. But he couldn't fly an airplane for shit!"*

Johnny continued: *Todd, let me be honest. Six weeks into training, I was soloing and working on navigation flying on a predetermined course*

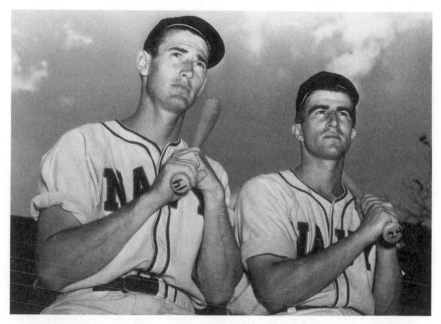

Ted Williams (left) and Johnny Pesky, U.S. Navy Baseball Team in World War II: always teammates. Courtesy Bill Nowlin.

and schedule. I got lost. I looked at my watch and realized I had to get back to the airport but, damn it, I couldn't find it. I had no idea where it was. I was running low on fuel, so I picked out a farmer's field to land in—a good landing, too! I climbed out of the plane and had tucked my parachute under the wheel when the farmer wandered over.

"What's the matter, sonny? You lost?"

"Yeah," I said.

It turns out the airport was straight ahead and just a couple of miles away. I climbed back into the cockpit, put my goggles back on, gave it full throttle and pulled up from the farm, returning an hour late. My instructor Bill Barwick said he'd seen my acrobatics and that I'd done his maneuvers pretty well, but then had to ask why I'd come back an hour behind schedule.

"I got lost."

"You goddamn ballplayers get every break around here," cracked Barwick.

"Maybe Ted was right," I kept thinking.

But I was single and what the hell, I was giving it my best shot. We all were. My brother Vinnie, he went up to Seattle for training, he was a fast go. He moved around. He was in Pearl Harbor. I saw him in Pearl Harbor when I was out there. He was stationed on Bora Bora.

Mine was a Navy family. I couldn't see myself in the Army. My father, when he came over to this country, was in the Austro-Hungarian Navy. Many guys were joining the Navy. Ted was here… Dominic went in the Navy; I went in; Ted was one of the first three guys in our lineup who went into the Navy. When you're 21 years old, you think nothing's ever going to happen to you, and luckily I was very fortunate how my Navy career turned out.

The hardest lesson that the service taught me? Discipline. When you get a group of people, you have to have certain rules and regulations, and you have to abide by them. They had places where they put kids who got in problems. They put a blue shirt on them with a "P" on their back and march them around the area, and the guys see that and say, "I don't want that to happen to me." The rules were made and I abided by them. We had duties to do when we first went in. The thing I remember the most about my duties was I had to clean the latrine [head] for a week or two weeks when I was getting my commission. I had to do that until I got my commission.

I could have made it as a flyer, but I was too dangerous. Others washed out too, but I still had a chance to become an officer. Captain Callahan selected some of us "wash outs" for Operations duty.

Changing Uniforms

The point of this journey for me, I thought, was to get an understanding of what it was like to change from one uniform to another. I grew up hearing about the larger sense of community they had back in what Studs Terkel called the "Good War." I grew up in comparative affluence to these guys who were kids during the Great Depression. It sounded like another world, but a world I wish I'd lived in.

I was sure that ball players were angry about having to give up their careers. I'm sure they resented it. I sure would have had regret if it were me, even bitterness. My students asked me to ask players about this; they sensed an injustice there, too.

When I asked Johnny about this, I was once again awed by the sense of duty and selflessness from yet another veteran. I envy them that feeling; it's a trait I think every father should have. A sense I would like to be able to pass on to my kids, so our nation will prosper and grow in liberty.

Again I asked Johnny, "How come you weren't angry?"

Why should I get mad? Our country's survival was at stake. I think Bob Feller had the best answer for that. He said something like, "This [war] is a bigger job that we had to do and we were proud to be involved in it, and you accepted that." If you fought the draft, you might have gone to jail, so why not fight for your country and do something with your life as a human being? Resentment, you asked me? No. I wish I didn't have to go, of course. But I was like any other kid; everybody in my neighborhood was joining up, and players were going in left and right. I wasn't...angry. Nervous? Yes.

On my way to the Pacific I was able to stop by home. You know, say goodbye. The proudest day of my father's life was when I came home with my Navy commission. I told him, "Pop, I'd trade all this gold braid back to Uncle Sam in a minute for my Red Sox uniform."

I was very interested in this part of Johnny's story. His family was an example of our nation's attractiveness for immigrants and the pull that freedom and opportunity has on the rest of the world. I wanted to know how his dad took Johnny's becoming an officer in two years, when it took him 12 in Europe.

There's a story about that. When I got my commission, I got a leave. I was waiting for assignment. They gave me 14 days so I went back to Portland, and when I got there, we had four types of uniforms, khaki, green, dress blues, and white. I come in wearing the green uniform, and I came in late at night. I come in the door; of course my mother was there, my dad, and my older sister. My dad looked at me and says, "How come the green uniform, John? You're in the Navy; you're not a Marine." I said, "This is part of the many naval uniforms we were all required to have." "Well, where is your blue one? Your whites?" I had them all in my bag, and I had *this great khaki one that I paid $75.00 for and I thought I looked like Admiral Nimitz. But not Dad. I had the blues and my whites...which we usually wore...it happened to be in August, and the whites were the uniform of the day in summer. I wanted to wear the khaki uniform I liked, but Dad always got his way.*

We were going to Mass on Sunday and my dad wanted me to wear the whites 'cause it had the epaulettes on the shoulders and those stood out on the white uniform and the cap looked pretty good to him, too. So here we are all waiting to go in to Mass, and I was standing outside the church. Dad was standing there, too, with all of his cronies. It was late in the morning, and I said, "Let's go in, Pa, let's get a seat."

He says, "No, wait, wait, the church is starting to fill up." Finally we go in, he's on one side, my mother's on the other and I'm on my father's side, and we're going down the aisle. He went almost to the front of the church and he was looking over, he says, "My son, the officer. " He was more proud of that than when I played ball. He told me, he says, "Johnny, you're an officer, right?"

I said, "Yeah."

He says, "How long you been in the Navy?"

I said, "Well, almost two years."

"Do you know how long it would take to get what you got in my country? Eight, ten or twelve years."

I said, "But Pa, I'm not in your country. This is America."

Powerful stuff, I thought. My mind quickly went to conversations I have had with Del Crandall, Mickey Hatcher, and Mike Scioscia who all tell me about the passion and a deep work ethic that many foreign players and first generation families bring to the game. Del says he saw that in Pedro Martinez. "Todd, when you come from nothing, baseball can be very liberating."

I guess for Johnny's dad the military was a common experience he could share with his son. Baseball was never popular in Croatia. As I was thinking about all this, Johnny interjected...

I tell you, Todd, if you take a look at those kids that gave their lives for country and baseball, those are the players that I admire. A lot of them came back because they got hurt; a lot of kids got hurt and stayed in Veteran's hospitals. It was a tough thing. You know, I was taught by my immigrant parents that if you were born in this country it was a privilege; my parents taught us that. When they came over from the old country, they had to work very hard to make a living. So we learned to appreciate everything. Those were our guidelines in a sense... appreciation, but sure I had to adjust to military life.

I mean, you had to have respect for the uniform no matter what jerk wore it and you went through indoctrination periods of common courtesy to gold braid officers. Officers and rank!

I tell you in some ways, I think that rank is overrated. Let me tell you, the war was run by the Navy Chiefs. Every Navy Chief that I ever knew was a class guy. They took their jobs seriously, and when your life is on the line, you go on the straight and narrow and you try to stay out of trouble. It all came down to discipline. The discipline instilled in me was a result of my parents of course, but also... baseball. I didn't really have adjustment problems... I was just a kid just like anybody else. I took my chances and God was good. He was looking over my shoulder.

Of course, this thing came up when Callahan called me to go to this operation school. I never left the base, and I studied everything. I was in the class of '44, but I always hung around with the smartest kid in the class. He was a kid from the University of Buffalo, a kid named Adam Sachet. We went everywhere together. Even when we had a little time we would go watch the Atlanta Crackers play. In the meantime, I met the girl that I married, and we got married in January '45, January 10th to be exact. Then we went back to the base and two weeks later I'm sent to Pearl Harbor, Hawaii and I said, "Oh boy, I won't have a wife when I get out of this." It was hard to tell her she couldn't come.

At Pearl Harbor, I was a station officer and many of the guys like me took care of certain things, learned about aircraft maintenance routines. Studied all those enemy aircraft charts and played on a service ball team. Then we were told to get ready for overseas. My group was headed for the big buildup in Okinawa to invade Japan. As I was in our living quarters packing, there was about 45 of us in there: Ensigns, JGs, lieutenants, full lieutenants and so on... and they told us to get ready to go. I was getting *nervous. This war business was becoming pretty real. Then...they dropped the big bomb and that ended everything, then we were searching for points to get out.*

You asked about regrets. There was a lot at stake for America in World War II. Hitler was killing all those people. Tojo was killing everybody out in the Pacific. I especially remember the Marianas, and I finally learned some new names for some of those islands I had never heard of before. Then I met some kids that I knew from baseball who were in the Army. As a matter of fact, a kid that I played ball with, Donny Kirsch was his name, and he was a better player then I was. He was a second baseman and I was a shortstop; we played together for about three years in semipro. He served in the Battle of the Bulge in 1944. I later found out that he was shot up pretty good. There was a lot of Americans lying on the ground. He told me the Germans left [him] for dead, but a medic come by and Donny happened to twitch, and they got him back to the hospital. He had shrapnel all through his body; he had maybe 15 operations to get that stuff out of his system.

He was a great player and he was a great kid. He gave it all up for you and for me. Makes you feel a little bit guilty at times. We had lived together as kids in Silverton, Oregon. Just kids....

I could see Johnny looking out into the expansive green field of Fenway Park, but he was far away, back in time seeing faces and memories as if they were there. Chewing on his tobacco and spitting in to his paper cup, Johnny brought up many experiences and opinions. He leaned back, crossed his legs, and I just listened. I kept thinking how amazing it was, the journeys all these men have taken to get here. Johnny, Bob Feller, Jerry Coleman, and so on—I realized the different paths to greatness began humbly. Whether baseball stars or not, all these men were humbled by the country's call. Where do we find such men? Lost in thought I came back to Johnny's voice...

I think Mr. Truman did a very wise thing in using the A-bomb. He saved a lot of lives. MINE! That's why it was the right thing to do. It saved American lives. When we dropped the A-bomb, the Japanese realized what this could mean for them! They gave up. It saved a lot of people in Japan, too.

But when I think about that war…it cost us so much. I don't know what the count was that we lost in the Pacific, but it was big. BIG!…I don't know how much they even lost in Europe. I read all those figures and it was astronomical, but I was very fortunate in that respect. I didn't get to see any live action, but my brother did. He was on Guam, the Japs were still over there, he was hiding, having to duck, but…we made it home. Safely. Thank God.

I thought President Roosevelt and Truman were great leaders. I thought they were the right guys…and I'm not even a Democrat. But even these great leaders didn't inspire me. Not at all. You get inspiration from the people you associate with.

I wanted to get home. I missed baseball. I kept up on baseball overseas. You bet! Everyday, the games were all over by the time we got the papers, and I'm watching the papers every day. When we could, we listened to the radio. I made it back home and loved playing ball again. Putting on that Red Sox uniform…wow, it felt good to be home. 1946 was a great year.

First Pitch

Johnny had to go hit grounders to his infielders using his fungo bat. My timing to see Johnny at Fenway was perfect. The Red Sox were observing Memorial Day and were having Johnny throw out the first pitch honoring his service. Johnny had to go, but he kept on talking, talking about the honor of this moment. He was saying that he was representing all veterans, not just himself.

Pesky Pole

Regrettably it was time for my last game at Fenway. Bill, Morgan, and I sat down by the foul pole in right field. I was more relaxed having completed my interview with Johnny the day before. We weren't too far away from the foul pole in right field. I looked at this foul pole and there was graffiti all over it. It was full of names and sayings. I asked Bill about it and he said, "Well, that is called 'the Pesky Pole.' Johnny Pesky hit a very few home runs around here."

I had a marker. I brought some baseballs to have Johnny Pesky sign. They read: "Ensign Johnny Pesky United States Navy" and I love that.

So I thought, well why not? I had my Boston hat on, so I wouldn't get yelled at anymore for being a Daaaadger fan and I went over and I thought—what do I want to write? To say I was here?

No, the only thing that seemed natural to me to write, and the only reason I was there, made the decision simple.... I wrote on that foul pole, "Wally Anton...Dad we made it."

11

Dom DiMaggio, Boston Red Sox, USN

I Want to Be in the Navy

The Professor

How does a public school teacher end up talking to Dom DiMaggio and all these guys? Sometimes I sit back and marvel. I think it comes from being passionate about my research. People know if you are sincere or not. People know if what you are doing is all about you or the subject you are trying to honor. I am not, or was not a professional player, nor was I ever a professional interviewer. I was neither a journalist nor, as those who know me would testify, even a good listener. But I was passionate about this journey to honor my dad, America, baseball, and veterans.

Maybe the America I was taught about only existed in my father's memory, or in the writings of those who lived it. It seemed to me as I grew up that everyone that served in W.W. II was some sort of hero. As a kid and even now, I am in awe of them, but why? All their stories and descriptions of life in America made me long for a simpler time that seemed to exist. Was the *Andy Griffith Show* or *Leave It to Beaver* a microcosm of all America? No. Why do we always seem to revisit our past and look for only the good things? Comfort, I guess. When many of these men I interviewed started talking about this idyllic past, it brought up these shows in my mind. "Dad," I would say, "Nobody, and no time period in America, was ever this good. June Cleaver was never dirty cleaning the kitchen; Ward never cussed, and who watched Opie after Aunt Bea left the show? Opie was a latch-key kid, Dad. How's that good parenting?"

Being the smartass I am, I was reminded by these guys that it wasn't the details of these shows that mattered, it was the values they reflected that were desired or upheld as virtuous. "Sure, maybe not everyone lived in Mayberry, Todd," Dad would say, "But I can tell you, son, everyone still wants to go there."

He's right.

There was a time when it mattered how you lived your life, not how much money you made. There was a time when it mattered how you treated others, not how you manipulated them to your ends. There was a time when friends and family stuck together, and didn't sacrifice those relationships for personal gain or agendas.

Talking with a player like Johnny Pesky, the character and integrity of yet another veteran resonated within me. It wasn't too much of a stretch to see Dad's point: a bit of Mayberry lives in each of us.

Dominic DiMaggio wore eyeglasses, a rarity in professional baseball and more so in those days. This fellow outfielder was dubbed "The Little Professor" by none other than Ted Williams.

When I talked to Dom DiMaggio, the great Red Sox center fielder, I learned about a man of tremendous accomplishments and character and also about a man who achieved much on his own despite growing up in the shadow of his brother Joe's celebrity. Mr. DiMaggio and I had something in common.

Your Name Seems Familiar...

I gathered up my courage—still feeling those same pangs of nervousness—and telephoned Mr. DiMaggio from a back bedroom in my house.

Nobody was home. I left a message.

The very next day he called back and left a message on my machine.

I couldn't ever call him Dominic or Dom. I haven't earned that right. In thinking about him, I felt a sense of deference. Was it his name and the reverence so many hold for it that made me feel this? I don't know. But I placed a return call.

I was anxious, but when he answered, I could instantly tell by the tone in his voice I had nothing to fear.

"Hello, Todd, I'm glad to help you. Tell me exactly what you are doing." I explained. He liked my idea and told me that he really

Baseball at war: Joe DiMaggio of the U.S. Army 7th Air Force (left) and future Brooklyn Dodgers captain Pee Wee Reese of the U.S. Navy (right) sign baseballs for the brass. Courtesy Bill Swank.

thought Ted would have liked this, too. "This was right up Ted's alley, Todd. I think this is great that a teacher is doing this; you guys really do a lot for so many. Please go on and tell me more."

I told him all about the military and baseball veterans I had talked to and about my attempt to remind all of us that there are larger things to celebrate in life and baseball than contracts and superstardom. Family still matters.

"You are right, Todd; there is a lost sense of courtesy in our current society and in baseball. People are forgetting about the better things in life. It's all about the almighty dollar. Yes, Todd, there was a time when people were more important than profit."

I thought of Mayberry again.

We were making small talk and he asked me a question I was familiar with. "Todd, your last name seems familiar. Is your sister Susan Anton, the singer?"

"Yes, she is, Mr. DiMaggio." I saw an opening, and I asked him in jest, "Aren't you related to Joe DiMaggio?"

"Yes, but you forgot Vince! I am related to him, too." We both laughed a little. "Well, Todd, I guess we do have something in common, don't we?"

Sure, I loved my brothers. But we were brothers! It isn't always smooth or perfect. You know, people are always looking for controversy about all that and all I will say about Joe is that I loved him very much and he was a great player. No doubt about that. I wanted all the best for him. His pressure was nothing like mine. I wouldn't have changed places with him for anything. I was happy to be just where I was, playing center field in Boston with men I loved very much, raising my family whom I loved even more. But you want to talk military, not family, right?

I sensed that he was ready to move on. I respected that. I told him I had no agenda, but was just curious about his feelings as a sibling of a star. "You know, Mr. DiMaggio, I remember how, when I was growing up many of my achievements were quickly brushed aside with a comment like, 'Oh, his sister must have done it for him.' Even in my high school basketball days, when I scored 15 points, and had 8 rebounds, the local sportswriter commented in the paper that the brother of actress/singer Susan Anton had 15 points and 8 rebounds. He didn't mention my name or anything. I was anonymous. I was used to it."

"Well, Todd, you just have to embrace it. You can't ever change it. Don't fight it. Embrace it and you'll be happy."

Then my thoughts turned to the task at hand—trying to better comprehend the sense of duty that so many of these veterans embraced.

Changing Uniforms

What was it like to change uniforms? Dom DiMaggio was no different from the others I'd interviewed. There was no sense of anger or resentment.

I didn't have any regrets about changing uniforms. None whatsoever. I had to fight my way to get into the Navy to begin with. It was my eyesight. They didn't want to take me. I pleaded with them and I talked with the optometrist who checked me and he said, "I'm sorry, they won't take you."

I said, "What are my chances in the Army?" My chances were forty percent, they said, "Well, if there's any chance, I want to be in the Navy."

Finally, after the longest time, he said, "I may be able to do one thing. Mr. DiMaggio, I could have you draft a letter and have all of the people here at the Federal building on the staff, countersign your signature and we'll send it to the War Department and recommend that you be accepted. We will tell them that your 'athletic ability will offset your deficiency in eyesight.' So, you want me to do that?"

"Absolutely," I said—and so that's how I got into the Navy.

I wanted to be on the water. I love the water, I live near the water here in Massachusetts, I live near the water, or close

Dom DiMaggio takes off his Red Sox jersey in favor of a Navy uniform. Courtesy of Bill Swank.

to the water in Florida; everywhere I've ever lived, I've always been close to the water and the sea. I love it. I guess that comes from being raised in San Francisco.

I went in and did my duty. I served in Hawaii, played Service ball for the Navy, too.

I just didn't want to be at home playing baseball while all my fellow countrymen were out fighting and serving the country. I wouldn't have felt right about it.

This was the attitude I was trying to understand. It seems to me today's athlete might just not be as eager as Mr. DiMaggio was. I suspect I would not have been, either. I asked him why he thought that was.

Todd, Pearl Harbor changed everything. In World War II, all America was on the same team. We were so angry, it was not all that different than 9/11, but we knew what we were fighting for and who we were fighting against! Nobody wanted to be left out. The Depression taught us a lot. We as a nation had a sense that we had survived some sort of test and now we were getting another one. At least that's how I see it today.

I didn't think anything different about guys who stayed home and played ball. That is their business. I wanted to be able to look at myself in the mirror and know I did the right thing.

I feel that way even today. Self-respect is an important attribute that can easily be lost. I hope you teach that in class, Todd.

My Great Objective Was to Not Be Left Out!

The majority of professional baseball players in World War II served in the U.S. Navy. I found this interesting because the draft was taking all men across America into all branches. I wasn't aware of any arrangement between Major League baseball and the military, or the players colluding to join the Navy. But with all the interviews and reading I have done many, many ballplayers are veterans of the USN. Was there a wink of the eye to take care of players...you know, preferential treatment? So I discussed this with Mr. DiMaggio.

Todd, I never ever had any suggestion in any way, shape, or form from management as to whether or not I should try to get in or enter the services, or that I would be protected. Like I said I had to fight to get in. It mattered to me as a man, that I serve and do my part. I wasn't going to be left out. I would not allow that. I would not have wanted to be the one player who did not serve. That's why I tried so very, very hard to made sure I got in and to get in to where I wanted to be. My great objective was not to be left out, let me put it that way.

One might think the war changed everything for me. In some ways it did, but it did not change my outlook on baseball in the least. I entered, I did what I wanted to do at the time and completed my service to the Navy and waited for my regular discharge, and fortunately it was in time for me to come back and play in the 1946 season. I had absolutely no regrets. None whatsoever, I'm very pleased and proud I made the effort to join the service.

I wouldn't have it any other way; I learned a great deal, being in the service. I think I was a better man coming out of the service than I was when I went in it. You're confronted with a lot of different things that you would not have confronted if not in the services.

We were part of a team. You just joined another team—that was all that happened in World War II. I do believe that anyone who went into the service for even a short period of time, picks up a lot more for their future as far as living and understanding things a [great] deal better; a maturity, so to speak. It teaches you, yes. It's another avenue of learning.

A Common Goal

I wanted to see if President Franklin D. Roosevelt's leadership inspired him. I asked: Did he inspire you? Did he give you a sense of confidence and reassurance at such a difficult time?

Oh, I don't know if it could call it inspirational. He was the President of the United States; he did what he felt he had to do. I'm sure the pressure was enormous.

As a war time president, I think [FDR] did a fabulous job. I can't recall any presidents off the top of my head that could have done better. He was the right man at the right time. He had a tough job. The man was crippled, but taught America to stand again. He started the WPA, and CCC, did many other things. He put people to work, not on welfare.

FDR was on a whole different level than me. I was too busy to be inspired. I had a job to do. You know, the best thing I remember about what President Roosevelt did was the GI Bill. But all of Congress did that, Todd, not just him. That did a lot of good for many people. I saw this when I went into business after baseball.

I guess, all in all, World War II taught me we're all on the same team working for a common goal and hoping somehow that we could all get back to where we were. I understood that, being a player. I understood it even better in 1946 when, in my first year back with the Red Sox, we made it to the World Series. That was to be my only trip there, but the war gave me a heightened sense of discipline, maturity and even freedom.

I asked Mr. DiMaggio what freedom meant to him. His response was short, but passionate.

What does freedom mean to me, Todd? Oh my! Thank God I was born here. Thank God my folks migrated here.... Look at what America has done for the DiMaggios! How do you expand on that?

12

Sergeant Ken Coleman

US Army—China, Burma, India;
Hall of Fame Broadcaster

Both Jeff Idelson and Bill Nowlin suggested that I interview Hall of Fame sports announcer Ken Coleman. Not being that well versed in the baseball community, I didn't know Ken Coleman. I asked Jeff and Bill what Ken Coleman would bring to this project. I was writing about players. Bill told me to ask Ken that very question when I talked to him. The tone in his voice told me I'd get an interesting answer.

Another trip to Boston was out of the question. A phone call would have to be good enough. I told him about my journey, my success and failures, and I admitted my nervousness. He appreciated the honesty and told me that this 78-year-old man would do whatever he could for me. He said he thought so much of my desire to say "thanks" to baseball veterans that he knew his good friend Joe Morgan would be interested and could help in some way.

Wait a second, I thought, did he just say Joe Morgan? Who was one of the best second basemen in the history of the game? Yes, he did. "Todd, I have to believe this story of yours would make a great ESPN segment or something. What you are doing is restoring some sort of purity about the game and the fact that it is being done by a school teacher, wow that makes it all that much better. Todd, this is a good story."

I was pleased. Ken had validated my profession, one so often trashed. He said I was indeed "on to something." I liked this guy. And, being an experienced interviewer himself, Ken knew what I needed from him as a interviewee. He was a very generous man, much like Ernie Harwell who took the time to make a difference.

Baseball is bigger than just the players!

Without trying to sound disrespectful, I pleaded my ignorance when I asked, "Mr. Coleman, what can you bring to this project? Just who are you?" I said a quiet prayer asking God to let him understand what I meant. He did.

Actually, Todd, that is a good place to start. What can I bring to your project and who am I? Well, as a person who has broadcasted thousands of games over the years, I have been witness to America's and baseball's best and worst moments. I've worked for the Cleveland Indians, Boston Red Sox, and the Cincinnati Reds. My first job was not in baseball, however. It was broadcasting the great Cleveland Browns football teams in the 1950s.

But, not to sound presumptuous, without us up in the box broadcasting the games I doubt that it would become the popular pastime it has. Baseball is bigger than just the players. There is more to the game than people know. Of course we do not hit the ball, pitch the ball, but we put the game in the hearts and ears of the people and that is a powerful influence. I saw a lot of great moments on those fields, but they do not even compare to what I saw young men do on fields of battle in World War II.

Pearl Harbor Day and World War II

When you're 16, 17 years old, you think you own the world. You know, the world revolves around you. You're invincible. Then the Japanese bombed Pearl Harbor in '41 and those feelings all change. You know everybody was excited, angry and we were all anxious to get in and do our part. This was an invasion! The Japanese had come over and bombed Pearl Harbor and we had to respond in a very strong way. Then we saw those films about the American surrender in the Philippines. It made me sick. You know those Japanese soldiers just throwing our flag around. It hurt me. Why? I didn't know. But it did. When I see someone burn the flag now, I just tear up. My buddies and mates died for that flag and it is as if you are burning them. Anyway, as for us kids then we were caught up into the romantic view of war. I think most of us pictured the war from the movies we might have seen where, you know, you go to a camp and you meet the colonel's daughter and dance with her and you know that kind of thing. It wasn't a realistic kind of a view, but anyway an adventure is what we expected. I remembered those feelings very well. It seems like yesterday. But then what happened was when we graduated in June of '43, every, every male in my class went in the military. I remember some of the other guys. There was this other fellow from school, John, who subsequently went in the hospital immediately because when he took his test, his urine test, it looked like Coca-Cola. He didn't know anything about a health problem. He was scared. He had sugar in his urine, and as a result they kept him out and [he] was classified "4-F" which is a term which declared a man unfit for service. He left and went home and swore he would get into the service. He was very distraught. Guys across America were committing suicide for not making the service. They felt that they were some how less than a man. It was a different world then. A man's honor was everything. John eventually served in the Marines, I believe.

Shortly after that, I went in for my physical. In my case I had eye issues. I was worried about being declared 4-F, too. When I had been in the eighth grade I had been shot in the eye with a BB gun and was blinded, I continued to play baseball and so forth as a kid, but they wouldn't accept me in the military. I was on the road to 4-F in my initial physical. And I couldn't accept that. I was going up to the draft board every month saying "How come?" You know? "Sir... I want to be in this thing. All my friends are in, my buddies are in and I want to be there too." So finally they put me on what they call "limited service" and, finally, I went into the military. Initially, I went to Fort Devens, Massachusetts where everybody from this area in Massachusetts went and then I was shipped down to Camp Lee, Virginia. When I went down there I took infantry basic training just like everybody else did. So much for "limited training." This training was tough. Real tough. I probably was in the best shape of my life when I got through infantry basic. My teacher was a very rugged man but, all in all, it was an experience... I guess I grew up. I didn't mind. I was serving my country. I felt that pride then and now. People today might find that hard to believe, you know, patriotism. After this training period, I was put on staff at Camp Lee for three or four months. But I kept on writing my friends who were over in Europe and the Pacific and here I am, over here. I felt guilty. It was a terrible feeling for me. I wanted to go overseas so I kept asking, applying, and it was granted. So finally I went "Over There." I left on Christmas day to go by military transport train all the way to California.

Ken Coleman, standing front left, on a truck in Burma. Courtesy of Susan Coleman.

So by going this direction, I knew I was going to be fighting and helping to defeat the Japanese Fascists. I kind of wanted it that way. They bombed Pearl Harbor, not the Germans.

After a few days in California, we shipped out for "somewhere" in the Pacific on January 11, 1945. You know, the Army staff officers didn't tell us anything except that we weren't supposed to refer in any letters [to] information that would indicate where we were going. But as a matter of fact we didn't know where we were going at the time ourselves other than they had put us in some ship which had some tropical camouflage clothes for us to wear. So the secret was safe. In reality I was on the first troop ship which was going to land in Calcutta, India. The GIs had been going to another port for some time, so this was the first one to go into Calcutta and from that point forward, I went up in to the country of India. I was stationed in a province of Assam near the town of Myitkyina on the Ledo-Burma Road, which is on the border of India and Burma, and was with the 472

Quartermaster Truck Regiment. My HQ [Headquarters] company was also known as the "Shamrock Regiment" because of our commander Col. Ireland.

The job of a truck regiment was to drive supplies up the Burma Road and take supplies over to the many airfields in the area. Of course the thing I learned about war in the China, Burma, India Theater was that for every GI going in the front lines it takes twelve men to support him up in the front lines. And I was proud to be one of those twelve men. Actually I wasn't even supposed to be there with my eye injury to begin with, but there I was. I am very proud of my service.

I worked in the Army postal unit in HQ Company and sometimes, to get over the boredom, I accompanied the trucks. Sometimes they were not even in our unit. It just got so monotonous at times I went as often [as I could]. I felt it a privilege to deliver the mail to some of these kids. Even though I did not see combat, I saw an awful lot of people who did. You know...the results of war. These fellows who were my age and came back down that Burma Road, and shared their stories with us. My God, it was incredible what some of those men went through. The China, Burma, India Theater of Operations is largely forgotten or ignored. People didn't know how bad that war was.

Ken and I went on talking about his service as you will read, but I could sense he was holding something back. I asked him, "What did you see that was so bad or made it stand out for you?"

"Well, Todd, there are some things you just do not want to talk about and I'd like to leave it at that."

I knew better than to press such a sensitive issue. But I did know something happened. Ken kept asking me how old I was and how old my students were. He went on to talk about the preciousness of youth and how lucky I was to be surrounded by all that youth, energy, and innocence. But I could tell there was something more behind it than a polite interest in my students. A little bit later he let me in.

Finally, Todd, we knew the war would be ending. We dropped the A-bomb.

A schoolmate of mine, not a classmate but a schoolmate, named

Charles Sweeney, General Charles Sweeney, who was in the class of '37 or '38 at North Quincy High School, eight miles from Fenway Park. He was the man who dropped the atomic bomb on Nagasaki. Tibbets dropped the first A-Bomb from the Enola Gay on Hiroshima and Chuck did the second one which was the bomb that actually forced the surrender. I found these missions to be very interesting reading material after the war—a number of those fellas who were involved in those A-bomb missions had some severe mental problems afterwards. You know . . . survivor's guilt. I understood that after my time in Burma.

But Charlie Sweeney, who lives near me, on Cape Cod, these days didn't have any qualms at all, because he recognized that he saved God knows how many thousands of American lives, including mine by going on this mission. Absolutely. His conviction and confidence in the mission helped me to heal too. I think our unit would have been one of those who might have been called upon to support the invasion of Japan. But the bomb saved us, so we just sat and continued our mission. Just because we knew the news on the radio didn't mean the Japanese in the bush knew. So we kept on our toes. There was no real celebration. No sense of relief.

So I did my postal duties and learned about the Burmese and Chinese culture and their people, but I missed home and to be honest, when you are overseas who you were when you went in to the war changes. You look at yourself in the mirror and wonder just who it is that you are or better yet . . . were.

I knew I was changing and I didn't like it. Some guys drank, there were even some deserters who went into the hills with their 16 year old Chinese girlfriends. As for me, I just did my job and diverted my boredom by listening to Armed Forces Network's baseball games. You know that helped me. It helped me a lot. I knew I wanted to be around the game and sports in general when I got home. We had sports on base too; a pretty sad group of guys who played ball for the 472. Some were pretty good. We just didn't look all that good. But it was a healthier diversion than others were doing. I just went and watched most of the time. I guess the competition of sports and being around so many young kids who were healthy, active and the innocence of sports made me feel better.

But our small little truck company has one claim to baseball fame. We had some visiting pro players in to play against our team. The two guys that stood out on that team were Dixie Walker and Luke Sewell. We had this young kid who just threw lights out. He was hard and mean. He struck out 12 guys that day! Impressed, Walker and Sewell went home and told them of this kid. Thus the legend of "Bubba" Church was born. He was quickly signed by the Phillies as soon as he was discharged. Bubba never played one day in minor ball. He went right to the majors. In his first year he won 20 games. I think he was beaned by a comeback line drive and was never the same again the following year.

Even later in my career, I didn't care if I was talking to a current player or someone who became a Hall of Fame member later on, they were all kids to me, untouched by war and that made them young to me so long as they played ball. Age isn't important. Baseball keeps us young—tired, but young.

I don't mean to demean anybody by saying this but when the professional athletes got into World War II a lot of them were playing baseball in the service and for the service you know. They were protected somewhat willingly and unwillingly. Playing ball was all many of them did. Some guys like Greenberg, Birdie Tebbetts, Feller, Spahn, Houk, and Jerry Coleman and others were the exception, but some players who wanted to serve never got the chance. One case in point was Dominic DiMaggio. He told me as he was going overseas to the South Pacific to serve, he was a considerable distance from Pearl Harbor or Hawaii, and they brought him back to play in what they called the Armed Services World Series or some such thing like that. So he did as ordered. But I get the feeling he wanted to do more that he did. Just like me we had to fight to get in the service to begin with!

Recognizing the fact that I would never be a major leaguer, I decided when I was overseas, I would become a major league broadcaster.

Indians, Red Sox, and the Big Red Machine

Ken enrolled at Curry College in Boston, using the GI Bill to get into school, and took courses in broadcasting and English composition. He learned what he needed to do and how to function behind the mic. After a year, he landed his first position, broadcasting from a Rutland, Vermont radio station. He took some pride in overcoming his fear of the mic, and he expressed gratitude for the GI Bill.

Ken's big break came when he received a job in Cleveland broadcasting Cleveland Browns football and Cleveland Indians baseball;
his heart was always more with baseball. He worked in Ohio broadcasting from 1952 to 1965.

In 1966, he came back home to become the voice of the Boston
Red Sox, working out of Fenway Park with Ned Martin and Mel Par-
nell, the three of them rotating in shifts through both radio and television broadcasting.

*I saw it all in Boston—highs, lows, unmet expectations, and heroes too.
Some of my fondest memories were of that 1967 "Impossible Dream" season, at least that is what some call it. That was when we put together a remarkable run to win the AL pennant. We lost to the Cardinals in the World
Series. I broadcasted that Series with the former Red Sox broadcaster Curt
Gowdy, whom I replaced, along with Harry Caray. In 1974 a new station
bought the rights to broadcast Red Sox games and let's just say we parted
ways. I was hired by the Cincinnati Reds.*

Ken had spent 19 years broadcasting in the American League, but
now found work as broadcaster during the glory years of Cincinnati's
"Big Red Machine." It was there that Ken got to know Joe Morgan—
and got himself two championship rings.

Five years later, he returned to work broadcasting the Red Sox, and
suffered with fans through the crushing defeat in the 1986 World Series. Ken was inducted into the Red Sox Hall of Fame in 2000.

The Love of the Game...

*One thing that was very interesting over where I was in India, was the thrill
we used to get listening to the Armed Forces Radio Service. Like I said, those
baseball broadcasts were such a thrill for us homesick guys. You know we're
about as far away as you can get from Massachusetts to the Province of
Assam on the border of Burma, and to be able to hear the games. It was
special. But when the announcer said, "This game goes out to all our troops
across the globe...," it let us know we were not forgotten..., but I am repeating myself. Let me tell you about my moment of truth—the day when
the war ended for me. It wasn't 1945 or 1946. It was 1954.*

One of my first times on the air doing play-by-play for an Indians base-ball game, I was doing the play-by-play. I'm still learning of course as I go. You know, while you are working during the broadcasts your crew was handing you papers with stats on them and advertising to read over the air, you know...commercials. So you get the paper, read it and throw it away and get back to the game. So I guess it was about the third or fourth in-ning, in a game against the Tigers. When I started to read this piece of paper with a message... "This game goes out to our troops over the globe on Armed Forces Radio Network," I knew what that meant. I cried, because of all those emotions from the war coming back to me: seeing the severely wounded boys on a plane, and a burn victim who was just a kid in Burma, it all came back and I wept. I had to take a few minutes to compose myself and I realized something was different. I was home. The war was over. I had overcome my fears.

After we concluded our talk and I hung up, I was happy with what I had, but I knew Ken was holding back. I turned the recorder off and went to talk to my wife about how it went. As we were talking in our kitchen the phone rang. I picked it up and it was Ken Coleman calling me back. I didn't have time to get to the back room to record, so I grabbed my note pad. You know, one of those yellow legal pads, and hurriedly made notes.

OK, Todd, let me share something with you that I really don't like talk-ing about it. You asked and I'll tell you. Most of the time we just ran sup-plies around. Although we didn't know it, we were nearly surrounded many times by Japanese units to the north, east, and south of us. It was our job to get supplies out to the C-47 cargo planes so they could fly supplies over "The Hump" to Chinese troops in combat with the Japanese. That base was running 24/7, unless it was too foggy. Our base was keeping China in the war!

The Japanese were very close to our base a few times. One such memory of fear that I had was when late one night somebody, most likely a Japan-ese soldier or Japanese collaborator got on to our base and burned down our supply warehouses. As people ran about to put out this fire we came under sniper fire. That was scary and you just felt as if any moment was your last. I kept thinking about the randomness of it all. One guy I knew got burned pretty badly. He had a letter in his pocket and asked me to read it to him. I took it out very carefully. Oh God, it smelled so bad, you know burnt flesh, but I read him his letter. The medics came up to help and I looked up at them. Then I looked over at this kid next to me and he was either passed out or dead, I didn't stay to find out. Why I didn't ever ask I don't know. But that smell—whew! When they drove away, his body hung limp. A few times we were under Japanese air attacks. It is the fear that wells up inside of you. Sometimes it got pretty close. But I guess what I am telling you, Todd, is I am admitting to my fear...you know...being afraid. I don't like saying that, but tell your students, especially the young men you teach, that it is okay to be afraid. It is a part of life. Life is facing your fears and overcoming them. That leads to wisdom, integrity, and most importantly of all...character.

One other vivid memory I have was at the airport. We would run mail and pick up mail sacks out there on the flight line. One such time there was a medical C-47 full of wounded GIs or British troops, I don't remember, but again it was a very sad sight. Good brave young men obviously hurt and needing attention. There were ladies...nurses...aboard. Just to see an American girl was something, let me tell you. But seeing those guys looking at me was a real lonely experience. I loaded what I needed to on that plane then I went back to work at the post office, handling some of the letters. Some of those letters were marked "Returned...Deceased." I hated that. I tried to escape that misery that was haunting me by listening to the radio, by listening to AFN's broadcasts of Major League baseball.

That is enough of that. I do not want to talk about that anymore. I've never shared anything about those memories publicly. I've got to go. Good luck to you.

I was in tears. I knew I had been given a gift. I still to this day try to figure out why Ken shared this with me. My guess is it has to do with my youth and the youth of my students. I really think we reminded him of those kids in Burma. Maybe I'm wrong, but it's all I can come up with.

Thinking about our conversation today still makes me realize how lucky I was. Ken had a remarkable life. He was surrounded by history. He shared about the last few days of World War II and couldn't get over this remarkable era that he and my dad lived in, and through... thankfully!

"Goodbye, Todd.
Let's Meet in Cooperstown Someday."

I was speechless as I hung up the phone. Ken Coleman had indeed brought a lot to this journey. I was emotionally drained, but thrilled too. I considered it the most remarkable phone call I have ever had. As we hung up Ken was asking me to attend the Induction Ceremonies at the Hall of Fame...as his guest! "Of course!" I said, but I couldn't do it, as my funds for traveling were rapidly being depleted. I had a mortgage; I had a family depending on me. I had to be very careful about where the money went. Even though I was a school teacher on a mission, I was still broke. I had to be responsible. So, regrettably, I told Ken, "No." I asked him if it would be all right, however, to send him a ball to sign, as I have tried to get a ball from each person in this book. Of course! He said, "I would be delighted. Goodbye, Todd. Let's meet in Cooperstown someday. Bye." So I got this ball into the mail to Ken a few days later. Actually over the next few weeks I forgot about it. Then, as God has his timing for everything, I got an e-mail from Bill Nowlin in late August of 2003, telling me that Ken Coleman had passed away that day from bacterial meningitis. No! It wasn't true. I was going to see him in Cooperstown after this book came out. He said he would introduce me to Joe Morgan. He'd even attend a signing session with me to help promote the book. I had a new friend. Ken told me he believed in me during that phone call. The way he talked at times, it was just like listening to my dad and now they were both gone.

I went on a walk to compose myself, gather my emotions, and focus on how special it was that I probably had one of the last interviews with this great man. I knew, whether this book made it or not, I had been blessed. I walked down the sidewalk to my home. It was twilight time. The windows to my house were open and I saw my son

Jason jumping on his bed. That made me smile, I stopped to get the mail, opened the mailbox and in it was a returned autographed baseball that read: "To Todd...Best Wishes. Ken Coleman China, Burma, India."

God has a timing I will never understand.

13

Del Crandall, Boston/Milwaukee Braves, Sergeant US Army

Almost Like Home

My Moment as a Dodgers Pitching Coach

Let's get started at an unusual place, Mavericks Stadium in Adelanto, California, home of the High Desert Mavericks, a single A baseball club, an affiliate of the Arizona Diamondbacks at the time. Adelanto is 10 minutes down Highway 395 from my Victorville home. The talent isn't major league level, but I've seen future All-Stars and Hall of Famers play in the California League: Ken Griffey Jr., Mike Piazza, and the list goes on.

Dodger Stadium is almost two hours away. So is Anaheim. It's not bad going to my favorite places. The drive down seems to go quick, but those midnight or 1:30 a.m. drives home get old. But this year the California League was fun for me. The Dodgers had a minor league club in San Bernardino called the "Stampede" and a new manager ...Mickey Hatcher.

Mickey had managed rookie level ball for the Dodgers in Great Falls, Montana. Then he coached first base for the Texas Rangers. When the Dodgers offered him a managing job, he took it. Neither my dad nor I had seen Mickey for some time.

Not only was Mickey back with the Dodgers, he was right here in my hometown area. I couldn't have been more thrilled. I called my dad to see if he wanted to come up to a game and give Mickey a hard time. He said he'd already been to a Stampede game and done just that, so I went to the game by myself. I didn't tell Mickey I was going to be there, but I got a front row ticket right by his dugout. Sitting next to me was a middle-aged man with notebooks, clip boards and a program from the Mavericks, obviously a scout. We made some small talk and he introduced himself as Del Crandall.

"Your name is familiar to me," I said to him.

As if done by rote or habit, he said, "Oh, you probably heard of me in baseball, I was a catcher for a number of seasons."

I said to him "No, I haven't heard of you, but it is your last name. Oh, I know! The music director at my church (High Desert Church) is a Jeff Crandall; that's probably why I noticed the name."

Del chuckled, "Well, that is my son. That's what he does for a living." Small world, I thought. Little did I know it was going to get much smaller.

Mickey finally stepped out of the dugout and I smiled. What can I say to get his attention in a way that would make my dad proud? So I shouted, "Hey, the Dodgers must be pretty hard up to hire some broken-down old college football player." I kept it clean. Breaking out into that smile of his, with that glint in his eye, Mickey turned around and said, "Asshole"—and came over. We talked and caught up. I was so happy. Mickey noticed Mr. Crandall next to me and asked him if he wanted a new seat, away from "this moron" (me).

"No, I'm fine. Actually, Mickey, I'm here to evaluate you, not the players this time." Del was Mickey's manager when Mickey played Triple A ball for the Albuquerque Dukes back in the late 1970s and he knew how to pull Mickey's chain. Del was kidding, but I enjoyed Mickey's discomfort.

It was a hot day, at least 105, and sitting in the dugout can be very hot, so Mickey pulled out a plastic chair and put it right in front of us near the dugout. It wasn't the Stampede's day. They were getting pummeled and, being the sensitive one, I kept yelling at Mickey, "It isn't the players fault. You're calling crappy pitches." Del was laughing pretty hard, but my teasing didn't bother him. He was working, watching, writing and evaluating players—not Mickey—"but Hat~¹ doesn't need to know that," he told me.

Finally, Mickey said... "OK, smartass, think you c~

I said, "Sure." So he asked Del if it was ⌐

pitches.

"Hell, Mick, he couldn't do any worse."

So Mickey gave me the bottom of the seve

to call! I thought he was kidding, but no. He walked out, made a pitching change, and told the catcher, as the new pitcher was coming in, to look at him. He was calling these pitches…as directed by me, of course—but only Mickey, Del, and I knew about this arrangement. The players just thought the boss was in charge. How wrong they were.

I knew these Mavericks hitters. So, I thought, why not? Here we go. I called for a curve and it was shaken off, change-up and…it was shaken off again. This kid wanted to throw a fastball and I knew it would get sent out of here. There were two runners on base. So he threw his fastball…right down the middle of the plate. Although I was calling the pitches, this pitcher didn't know that; he thought he was shaking off his manager Mickey Hatcher. Mick asks me, "Hey, you called for a curve, didn't you?"

I said "Yeah, Mick. I thought I'd work this hitter backwards." That means go with the off-speed pitches and then show them the fast stuff. Throw their timing off.

Now Mickey was pissed. Not for my sake; his leadership was being challenged by this kid shaking off his directions. It only took one pitch and boom! A three-run homer. I was laughing so hard. Del was laughing too. One pitch and Mickey went right out to the mound. I could tell he was mad; he's got this duck kind of walk when he's mad. It's funny to watch. He gets to the mound and tells them a story and points over at me! I'm not sure what he said, but when the pitcher comes off the mound, he looks at me and flips me off!

Mercifully, the game ended and Mickey called me up to meet him in the visiting clubhouse, spartan to say the least. A table with some oranges on it, packaged lunch meat and a squeezed mustard bottle lying on its side was the board of fare. Mickey takes me right over to this pitcher and says, "Hey, Einstein, here is that person you flipped off. Let me introduce you to the Dodgers' new minor league pitching coach, Todd Anton." Let me tell you, *that* was a great joke!

That kid looked so scared. He apologized effusively, "I'm so sorry. Anton. The other players told me you were just a friend calling es—and I am not going to let anyone get in my way."

I had to leave that room. Mickey and I were laughing so hard. I said goodbye to them all. When I saw Mickey the next week in San Bernardino, he was in his office packing up. "Big changes were in the works in the Dodgers organization," he said. Manager Bill Russell had been fired and Glenn Hoffman had been appointed manager. "Glenn asked me to be his hitting coach." Mickey was heading back to L.A., back to my "Blue Heaven." Perfect.

Years have passed and my dad has passed on since my coaching debut for the Dodgers. Mickey now coaches for the Anaheim Angels and we often talked about my pitch selection that day. I could tell how much Mickey liked and respected Del. When I learned how old Del was, I knew he had to have been in the service at some point. At church, I asked Del's son Jeff about his father and I was right. Del is a veteran. Jeff set up a time for us to get together.

'Hey, Kid, You Want to Catch?'

I drove down to Del's home which is in an upscale mobile home park not too far from Anaheim Stadium. I was happy to be interviewing somebody so close to my home and somebody I had previously met. I thought it would be easier. I wasn't as nervous as I had been with other players. I pulled in and walked up to his door and rang the bell. Expecting to be expected . . . I was ready to get to work. Del opened the door and I could tell he had had a long night or had just awoken. I felt bad, embarrassed. Did I come on the wrong day? I could see myself doing that. No, Del had just forgotten. He was caring for his wife who was ill and had hurt her hip. She was bedridden at the time and he was serving her, caring for her. I told him I could reschedule, but he said no, but could you come back in an hour or two?

Perpetually hungry, I found a California Pizza Kitchen in a local mall, got a table outside, and sat down to read and prepare for my next interview. I hoped to talk with Duke Snider, who also lived nearby. It was one interview I really, really wanted, not because he is a Dodgers icon, but because he served in World War II alongside his father. As far as I know, Duke Snider is the only member of the Hall of Fame to have fought alongside his father in warfare. I couldn't imagine what his mom, Mrs. Snider, felt seeing both her husband and son go overseas. Worse yet, Mr. Snider was deployed in a Marines assault battalion while his son Duke served on a submarine tender called the USS *Sperry.* "What a compelling story," I thought. I saw it as a great chance for Duke to honor his dad and his mom's courage, as a W.W. II family. But for some reason it wasn't to be…yet. I still hope and pray for that opportunity.

Looking at my watch, I noticed it had been almost two hours. I ordered a chef's salad for Del. I figured he would be hungry, he was so busy. I knew he wasn't eating enough.

This time I was expected, but I felt out of place. I knew Del's mind was on caring for Fran, his loyal wife of 53 years, so I got right to the point.

Del looked at me and said, "OK Todd, I'm all yours"…

I was raised right here in Southern California, born in Ontario and raised in Fullerton. I lived on what they call "the other side of the tracks." That was a great experience. Whatever few blacks we had in town went to my school and quite a few Mexican kids did, too, I learned a lot. I can remember being in the fifth grade; I was a very, very timid kid, but I liked to play sports. I was very timid, and I can remember the coach going down the line of fifth graders with a catcher's glove and a mask in his hand. The best athlete was down at the far end of this line and I was at the other end. I was one of the last kids chosen because I was small. I didn't grow until I was a freshman in high school. Art Johnson—the coach—approached this top athlete who fought, who could run. He could leap and he could throw. Art had a mask and glove in hand and asked, "You want to catch?" The kid said, "No, I want to play the ump"—being a smart ass. So, he went down boom, boom, boom. The coach knocked him on his tail! All the athletes that I knew were tough kids, and they fought when they could. The coach walked all the way down to me. I looked at him, and he said, "You can catch."

That's really how all that started. Those tough guys didn't want it, but I'd show them I can beat them. I had no right to do that really, because I was so small and a little on the chubby side. I was scared of my own shadow, but that was the beginning of my life as a catcher. Every time I'd get hit with a foul tip, I wore that bruise proudly. I wouldn't flinch; that was a very, very big motivation.

My parents were poor. We never had any money, yet they always seemed to be able to let me go to the baseball park when I wanted to. I always had to work, but I worked for bosses who always asked, "Do you have a game today? Well, you need to do this amount of work and then you go play." They were determined to help us kids, wanted to give me an opportunity to do whatever I wanted to do. People who took the time to help kids saved a lot of futures. There are many unsung heroes in communities these days doing the same thing for kids.

One such hero in my life was Pat Lemon, the Fullerton youth sports leader back when we didn't have a recreation department. But he gave all of us kids an opportunity to play baseball. It cost him his own money at times, but he was there every day and he did a little catching professionally with the Cubs too. When I went into professional baseball, I found I already knew basic fundamental catching. He had taken care of that when I was a boy of 14, 15, 16, and 17 years old. I was ready for my opportunity when it came.

I loved this part of Del's story. As a teacher you sometimes wonder if you have an impact on kids and you could still see Pat's lasting impact on Del.

I wasn't too far removed from high school when I went into professional baseball. My first year was 1948. Then I went to Class B League in 1949, and then in June of 1949 I went to the big leagues, I joined the Boston Braves. I was there half of 1949 and all of 1950. I played almost as much in 1949 as I did in 1950, and they got Walker Cooper in 1950 and he was a veteran catcher of course. They weren't sure that I could do the job there in Boston, which is understandable being that in 1948 they had won the National League Championship, so they were hoping to get back to that.

I went to spring training in 1951 and in early March I received my draft notice. Johnny Antonelli received his just about the same time. So, we were the same age and both of us had our careers interrupted.

I asked Del whether he was angry at this military intrusion and interruption in his career. I tried to bait him, tried to get him to give me some anger, to give me a response I could understand or relate to. I couldn't ever get this response. But as it always is with this "Greatest Generation" the answer was the opposite of what my selfish response would be if it was me. Del said... "What am I supposed to do? Not serve? I grew up seeing World War II and the price paid by so many. I just figured it was my turn. That's all."

I couldn't just accept that response so again I asked him... "You were not the least bit angry?"... and he looked right at me and said ... "Do I have to draw you a picture? For the last time...no!"

The G.I. Jive

I went into the service, and then I came home on furlough, and spent a little time. Actually, I got married during that time I was home, to Fran. I then went to Fort Ord, reported for duty, and I went to spring training and was able to stay in the states. All of 1951 I played baseball. I didn't really do much else, except play baseball. I did play some basketball, also in the service. Then in late 1951, we had just formed our post club up in Fort Ord, and it looked like all of us were going to be able to stay there for a while, but I got orders to go overseas.

Initially, I was stationed and did my basic at Fort Ord, California. I was a clerk in D Company of the 63rd Regiment. It looked like we were all going to be able to stay, but the rich, influential people in Monterey, people that had kids who were overseas, got a little bit upset that athletes were being stationed at Fort Ord and not their kids. I understood that feeling. I wasn't treated differently because I was a baseball player. No. Outside of just knowing whom I was and what I did...no. The N.C.O.s [non-commissioned officers] didn't treat me any differently. No, I did not knowingly have that experience. Now, I can't say that about the officers because I was put on orders a few times, and because I was an athlete, and because they wanted to keep me there to play baseball and basketball, I was taken off of orders quite a few months before. Finally the general said, "I can't help you anymore, you have to go overseas." I didn't ask for the help. I wasn't like that. I don't know what he was thinking. Also I am not aware of any pres-

sure on the services that I know of to take care of its players. Oh no. No. I have no idea that a conversation like that ever took place on behalf of major league baseball and the military. When I left spring training with the Braves to report for induction into military service, I got the feeling that I was out-of-sight out-of-mind, which is okay. I mean, I'm just another guy. I just happen to have talent to play baseball, but I'm really no different from anybody else. I never considered myself someone who deserved favors and deserved to be treated differently. I have never looked at my life that way. I am also realistic enough to know that those things happen, the favoritism, but that's not how I live.

But my turn came. I got my orders to go overseas, and so I went, and got over to the Pacific in about June of 1952. Of course, they were looking for baseball players. I never did get to Korea, but I did spend about 8 months in Japan, and played baseball all during that year, and I had a sore arm; I hurt my arm in the States. We were playing against Stanford while I was with the Fort Ord team. They had been working out for a long time. This was about our second day with a baseball in our hand, and Stanford players were running, and I was throwing, and I came up with a sore arm. Then I went to Japan.

Playing in Japan was painful. I did some catching, but I also played a lot of first base because I really couldn't throw. This was the early part of February in 1953. While I was in Japan, I was in Special Services and I played baseball, but then after baseball season was over we had to do something. I was in a very small four-year Triple-A headquarters in Haiyoshi, Japan, and we had to do something else to pass the time besides just hang around. We didn't have a basketball team. So, I went to work in the mess hall, and I was in charge of going into Yokohama in Tokyo and getting supplies. We were kind of in between those two big cities. It was my job to go out and pick up rations and bring them back. I did that five days a week. Three days a week I think I went to Tokyo and two days a week to Yokohama. Also, worked at the service club; at that time Army pay was a little lean, so I was able to earn a few dollars at the service club to send home to my wife and baby.

It was not too soon after World War II had ended in 1945, that I was over there in 1952. Americans weren't all that popular over there. I had

Del Crandall in Japan. Courtesy of Del Crandall.

probably four or five former Japanese soldiers who worked under me to get the supplies picked up and get them loaded and unloaded, and I had a Japanese driver that drove the truck. It wasn't easy for them you know. I guess you can appreciate it. We were in such a mindset about what they did to us at Pearl Harbor, we didn't feel too sorry for them, but when it was all said and done the Japanese seemed to do their work, they didn't really cause a lot of trouble. There wasn't a lot of animosity over there. We just knew that they weren't dependable. The way they did their job you could tell they would rather not do it. They liked to see if they could get away with supplies and that sort of thing, but it wasn't really all that bad.

So I was able to play ball and actually, I think that time in the service did me an awful lot of good. It's hard to leave major league baseball. I got my opportunity, actually I got my opportunity probably sooner then I should have; I was only 19 years old, and that was a little bit young to be going to the big leagues, but Uncle Sam said "go," so I didn't argue too much. While I was over there, I think I had a chance to grow. I had a chance to mature. I got stronger. The only problem was I had a sore arm, and I couldn't throw, and when I got back to the States I still couldn't throw, and of course, nobody knew what to do in those days. Dr. Jobe wasn't around doing his "Tommy John surgery" yet. I got a chance to hit; I got a chance to play; I got a chance once again, to get bigger and stronger. So, when I came out of the service I was a little bit better prepared outside of not being able to throw, which was kind of important. But I was a lot more prepared to face what I had to face in trying to become a major league baseball player; as somebody that could have a career and could stay around a while. It also, I think, gave me the maturity to look at this sore arm thing in a better light. I think if that would have happened earlier, and I had not had the service in my background I don't know if I would have had the strength or the will to beat it because I knew that what I went through in the Army was not what I wanted to do as a career. So, I think from that standpoint it really did help me become mentally stronger, and I think you really have to be mentally strong in order to compete with anything, whether it's sports or whether it's any other endeavor. A reference point is a beautiful thing.

I believe the Army afforded me that opportunity to grow, and I think I have used that time well; I didn't waste it. I didn't sit around moping and worrying about what it was going to do to my career. I tried to do the best I could for what I was called upon to do, and probably if I would have been called upon to go to Korea, I would have approached it in the same manner, but fortunately I wasn't. There were some other guys that I had went to spring training with in Fort Ord that went to Korea and did not come back from Korea. These were guys that you get thrown into a platoon with and into a company with. You know that is what the military does. They treated me just fine, we talked a little baseball. They were shipped out and never made it home.

Japan

There weren't too many American big leaguers over there. They were mostly in the minors. Nelson Howard was in Japan. There were a couple of guys who had played Pacific Coast League baseball, and I can remember a kid by the name of Olson, who was with the Red Sox at one time, but it was so long ago that it's so hard for me to remember.

We had our team. The 40th Triple-A Brigade had our team, and then we would play colleges, and then we would play what would be considered semi-pro over here.

I think in Japan the thing that stands out, outside of getting out of the service, was the people that I was around when I was in Japan. I can remember the Toso twins that were baseball players, and just real neat guys. I met one of my best friends over there, Morrey Rio, who passed away three or four years ago. He was a teacher in the Triple-A Brigade Headquarters. I just remember the people who came in there were just great people. You're all by yourself. You're over there all alone. My lifestyle was very dull, and you know to leave the base was a hard thing for me to do, and it's the people that made that time enjoyable, if you can say that.

Outside of being able to play baseball, which was enjoyable most of the time, the guys made the difference. I wasn't always on the baseball field and the guys made time pass and gave me something to feel good about. We were helping each other, letting each other know that we weren't wasting our time. They had a good frame of mind.

I don't think any American can believe what they saw in Japan in those days. I mean, if you had a pretty good bicycle you were in business. I mean they had no automobiles, three-wheelers they had. Once in a while you would see some form of a truck, but their houses were made of what looked like, made out of paper. I mean it was just a third world country, as we know of those countries today.

Like I said, I played in Yokohama. We also played in Tokyo. But I played a lot in Yokohama. They had an base there, I think in Yokohama, called Kalkodie Barracks. I think that's where we played, and there was another service club that we played there. We did play a lot of service clubs. Mostly Army teams. There was this field. It was just beautiful. It had ivy on the walls. Just like Wrigley Field.

Coincidence? I Don't Think So

It was at this moment my heart and jaw just dropped in shock and I knew why I was there with Del. My father was a proud veteran of

World War II of course, but he was even more proud of his service in Korea. I asked him why numerous times, because World War II is so popular, even called the "Good War" and Korea is largely ignored or "forgotten" in America. But it's not forgotten by my dad or my mother. I can still hear his answer . . .

Todd, you see, in Korea, I was an officer in charge of many men and their welfare, as the Lieutenant commanding the 715th Transportation Truck Company in main combat zones. It was up to me to take charge. I did. Also I had a wife and kids who depended on me. So much was at stake for me in Korea. In W.W. II I was just a snot-nosed kid sergeant following orders, responsible for very few men, or anyone at home. Korea was different. I kind of felt grown up myself. You know what I mean now don't you, Son? You have your own kids and have taught thousands of kids in school. That is a lot of responsibility, not like it was to be a student. That's kind of what it was like for me in Korea.

Dad saw a lot of combat again in Korea, but what he fondly spoke of was his time in Yokohama, Japan. This was a family experience. My mom flew to Japan with two children: Greg who was five and Susan who was four years of age. Here is this woman, my mom, and two kids boarding a DC-9 to fly all the way to Japan to be together. My mom boarded this plane with fear. A DC-9 is a rather small plane compared to today's 747 behemoths; Mom was praying to just get there safely. Her fear increased as there were storms over the Pacific and they set down to refuel on Wake Island. "My God, Todd, it looked like a postage stamp, how were we going to land? I thought we were coming in for a water landing" she said. I was amazed by my mom. Here were my mom and my dad wanting to be together, pushed by love, tempered by fear, being a "Citizen Family" in the foreign land of a recent enemy. Obviously pleased at being together, Mom and Dad had some catching up to do. Which they did as evidenced by the birth of my brother Brent 9 months to the day of mom's arrival in Japan.

Dad was the commanding Army officer of the Second "T" Major (Transportation) Port of Yokohama. He had many men serving under him. These men were young and full of youthful energy and this led to many problems in town. Drinking, fighting, and prostitution were powerful attractions for young men. It was becoming an issue and it was dealt with by the commanding officer, Lieutenant Wallace Peter Anton, my dad. He believed that if these men had so much energy they needed productive things to do. So he put them on a full scale construction project…building a baseball field near the Kalkodie Barracks. Building the stands, and the initial landscaping was all done by hand. Even though they had all the machinery available, my dad ordered it done by hand. The purpose was to tire his men out. It did, but this wasn't the end of his efforts at discipline, or of the building of the field. Now it was time for the Japanese touch.

My dad knew that many men in Japan had a passion for gardening and he knew of a man who would make this field look just like one back home he so revered and wanted to see…Wrigley Field. Dad never made it to Wrigley, but his new found gardener, Mr. Koniko, made him feel as if he was there. First thing Mr. Koniko did was to place newspapers all over this expansive field. Then he and his Japanese coworkers layered grass seed evenly all over the field on top of the newspapers. Then Mr. Koniko spread manure and water over the top of this to form a mixture which would grow very quickly. It did. Then Mr. Koniko went to work on the wall. He got some aluminum fencing and painted it green all along the outfield. At the base of the wall, ivy was planted. It wasn't baseball season yet, but the field would be ready for the next season.

It was.

"It was amazing to see," Dad said, "to see these Japanese and GIs set up the infield and base paths. The grass grew in very nicely and thickly. Now the guys went in and cut out the grass revealing dirt pathways of about four feet in width and richly brown. These were the base paths for first and third base. The infield was also cut out, which revealed a rich dark brown field. "This way," Koniko said "no clay was needed and [it] was beautiful. Just like Wrigley Field, Mr. Lieutenant Anton." Dad was thrilled and opening day was scheduled by his order.

The grass just needed to be mowed. It stood about 1–2 feet high.

On opening day Mr. Koniko showed up to cut the field with his crew. About 15 men showed up, wearing ancient traditional Japanese colorful kimonos, wearing haitchimakees [sic] around their heads and all holding large sickles to cut the grass. This they did. My mom remembers seeing these guys all out there cutting the grass and it appeared to be as short as if a mower and gone through it. "It was quite beautiful," Mom remembered, "to see all these men working together. It looked like poetry."

Now Dad ordered his men to play at least three games a week to gain a much desired "Liberty Pass." Thus the drinking, whoring and fighting all but disappeared. Dad handled this issue in a proactive way using baseball as the medicine for homesick men. The attractions of Yokohama were still strong, but guys wanted to play and remain eligible, so they behaved. Now all those emotions were coming back to me again through Del Crandall. It was a small world.

Interrupting my daydreaming, Del looked at me and said... "Yes Todd, that field was my favorite to play on. In fact we played many games there." To think that one of the greatest catchers who played was on this field built by Dad was something else. Del appreciated the moment too. "Wow Todd, this is remarkable, really something. A small world indeed! I, too, loved Japan."

I wanted Dad to be alive, to hear this validation of this, his "Field of Dreams," not the one in Iowa, but the one in Japan. I'm sure somehow he is a part of this journey, this project and my meeting with Del Crandall. Somehow I felt I was indeed... "Going the distance."

Back... Safe at Home

I was discharged a little bit early as they were doing in those days. I was discharged maybe a month-and-a-half early. So anyway, I flew home to Fort Ord again, and was discharged just in time to say hello to my newborn baby, who was four months old. He was born while I was over in Japan, and then my wife and I and the baby got in the car and drove back to Florida. Back to baseball.

I got out of the service in 1953. I drove to spring training and arrived in Bradenton, Florida pretty much on time. When I got there I could not throw. There were lots of rumors about how I hurt my arm, that I had fallen out of a jeep, you know. I had just hurt it throwing against Stanford and there were no accidents. But once again, people like to make up stories to make it more interesting I guess. But I was not able to throw at all through spring training. Finally I went to a doctor and once again, they had no idea. You could either throw or couldn't throw. Whatever they did and whatever was wrong with me, all I knew is when I would throw, it would hurt. But I did not know that each time it hurt it was actually doing some good because it was breaking down scar tissue that had formed in the shoulder. So anyway, I was able to throw later, about August. I threw just as well, but without the arm strength, but I did not have any pain, and was able to do my job. I could build up strength. I just worked through it and went on with the rest of my career.

What a career it was. Gold Glove Awards for being the best at his position. An eight-time All Star. These are no small achievements. Del didn't seem to want to talk about it too much. Baseball was more of a means to an end. Of course Del knew he was fortunate to be a member of the World Champion Milwaukee Braves of 1957, as well as other great teams. I reminded him of just how big that World Series was to the people in Wisconsin. I told him my mother-in-law Beverly grew up on a dairy farm in Marion, Wisconsin and Braves games were a big part of her daily routine. She was a Del Crandall fan. "Well Todd, you run into those gals every now and then. Of course I know how much that championship meant, but after the service you just learn to place things in perspective."

Del Crandall caught one of the best pitching staffs in history with Warren Spahn and Johnny Sain. Also, all of these men were war veterans. Warren Spahn was a hero during the Battle of the Bulge and he somehow survived the collapse of the Bridge at Remagen. In fact, Spahn received a battle field promotion for his heroism and as a result of his new found officer status he had to stay overseas almost 10 more months. This cost him another season in baseball.

With pitchers and catchers being so close, I thought Del and Spahn would have talked about it.

I never did ask "Spawney" about the war. I think Spawney, you know,

Del Crandall with Milwaukee. Courtesy of Del Crandall.

got the Purple Heart and was at the Battle of the Bulge and had some se-
rious time over there, but I never heard any of his stories. I never heard any
of it, so I don't think that was something that he would bring up and talk
about, but I'm sure in the right circles...you know there are times when
you know not to talk about it. I kept my distance on this. Actually he was
a very funny man and that says something, to have gone through all that
combat and still be happy...that says something about him.

Then Del told me not a Warren Spahn war story, but a story about
perspective.

Todd, I guess before the war Warren got pretty upset when things went awry on the mound. Then after the war he said, you know if I give up a few runs and come out, it's no big deal. I've got some help coming in. It's not like somebody is shooting at you.

Del went on to become a successful member of the Los Angeles Dodgers organization as a scout and minor league manager. He is respected, and his experience is valued. I know that personally, as Mickey Hatcher has told me, "I'm lucky to say I have played for Del Crandall."

What I Learned

My conversation was drawing to a close as his wife was awaking from her nap. Obviously Del was distracted as I asked my last question. Del, how did your military service affect the way you raised your kids and played the game? He blanched, "Wow, why are you asking that?"

"Del, I've asked that question in all of my interviews with veterans and it is a question they do not like. Usually I get asked 'Why are you asking me that?' I always tell them it is for your kids to know you better, to see you better, and to understand you more completely."

Well as a father I probably would fall in the category of a strict father, but you see I was gone so much on the road. My wife was the mother and at times, the father of the kids. Since I was gone so much when I came home it was probably very hard for the kids because I was strict. I liked discipline; I liked order. Whether that was military or not, I don't know. My wife did the job and supported me and our kids. Always.

I could sense an emotional tone in Del's voice.

You know the Dodgers gave me a leave so I could be here to take care of her and show her I love her by being by her side for a change. She is everything to me....

Del drifted off in loving thought, but he went on to answer the other part of my question about how his military experiences shaped him as a player and as an American.

Well, I don't know how to describe being an American in any other way, but just one word...freedom. There's nobody hitting you over the head saying "you can't do this, you can't do that." I know we have to obey laws, and we have to respect all individuals. But freedom is really up to us to define. I think America was originally based on that approach. I think that maybe we have gotten away from those ideals a little bit. Also I think America is really all the things we take for granted; that is what makes this country great. I think that it's just too bad that we don't stop and reflect once and a while. That is why I like what you are doing, Todd. You are getting us, and hopefully the readers, to appreciate those values again. I hope the players read this and are reminded how lucky they are not only to be playing baseball, but to be Americans.

I've been to the Dominican Republic, Mexico and I've been to Japan. I have done a lot of traveling. I've been to Puerto Rico. I've seen what the "American Dream" and baseball has done for these kids like Ramon and Pedro Martinez, Fernando Valenzuela...all those people. I have seen the opportunities our country provides for them and our own citizens, albeit it took too long, for great men like Jackie Robinson, Don Newcombe, Roy Campanella. I've gotten to see what the American Dream has done for all races and nationalities. I think baseball is a perfect example of that dream ...freedom.

That was about it. Del thanked me for the chef's salad I brought him from the California Pizza Kitchen. He signed a ball for me, which of course, I treasure. For it wasn't just the afternoon that I spent with the man Henry Aaron called "the best catcher I have ever seen," or a four-time Gold Glove winner of the Braves. I had spent some time with a man who played on my Dad's field of dreams as a soldier of the United States Army in Japan. Remarkable. A small world indeed.

14

My Blue Heaven—Dodgers All

Vin Scully USN
Don Newcombe US Army
Tommy Lasorda US Army

Vin Scully. His voice conjures up for me memories not only of baseball, but of boyhood. Watching my dad work out in the garage with the radio tuned to the game, the summer wind gently moving the American flag in the front yard, twilight nights seeing Mom and Dad sitting on the front steps of our home sharing a cup of coffee, a cigarette, the ball game, and the love of just being together. Vin Scully's voice is a part of who I am. Reassuring. This story wouldn't be right without him.

Vin Scully is a veteran of the United States Navy. He doesn't talk about his service time because it was a short stint. It wasn't glamorous, but it was service nonetheless and I was taught to honor service of any sort.

Getting to him wasn't as easy as one might think. I didn't get help from anyone in baseball. Through my sister's business relationship with a well-connected man, I got the chance to meet "Vinny."

The day approached and I went to Dodger Stadium early. My thoughts drifted back to that momentous Flag Day at Dodger Stadium when I took Dad's ashes to center field. This was my first time back to Chavez Ravine and it was emotional for me. I looked out towards center field and I smiled thinking back at the love and care the Angels, Mike, Mickey, and Ron had shown me. I remembered special moments over the years with my dad, my friends, and my wife at this—my Blue Heaven. Time goes by so fast.

Vin Scully—Dad, Are You Listening?

I went to Vin Scully's box on the press level and waited, watching batting practice and listening to the crack of the bat. I heard a familiar sound that seemed out of the past, only this time it was Vin Scully in person. He could only spare about 15 minutes, but it seemed like all my thoughts and questions left me at that very moment. The first thing I thought of was my brothers, how they would love to be there. I wanted to be an interviewer, but in reality I was a fan. Who isn't a fan of Vin Scully?

Vinny often alludes to American history and our heroes in the armed forces in his broadcasts. It was his Fenway Park Father's Day story broadcast on Father's Day eve 2002, which helped prompt me to start this trek. His ability to tie together history, baseball, and patriotism without sounding like a preacher is a real gift.

So I asked a few questions: "You certainly have a deep respect for our nation's history, remembering those in the service. Where did you learn that respect and why is it a part of your broadcast?"

Todd, I think patriotism is part of my life. World War II was an absolute major part of my life. The impact of Pearl Harbor, even though I was relatively young...the loss of neighbors and friends growing up in New York. If you were a parent or a wife, and you had someone in the service, you would get a little flag with a blue star on it, and hang it in your window, telling everybody you had a loved one in the service. I vividly remember watching those blue stars change to gold stars meaning someone had made the ultimate sacrifice, hearing screams when the Western Union telegrapher or the Western Union boy arrived on the bike.

I was listening to a football game and I was underneath the radio, which is my favorite spot, when I was a little boy, and they interrupted the broadcast of the Giants football game. The Japanese had bombed Pearl Harbor. I had no idea what that meant. I assumed Pearl Harbor was in China, because the Chinese and Japanese were fighting each other. When there was a timeout, I vividly remember going in and saying to my mother and father, who were having lunch, "They just said on the radio that the Japanese bombed Pearl Harbor," and my father said, "Oh, my God that means war."

Then I asked him, "In your career with the Dodgers, did you notice a difference in character among service veterans (ball players) as opposed to other players?"

Maybe they were a little more mature than some of the others. We had one player, a marvelous third baseman named Billy Cox, and although I wasn't there, they said that when Billy first joined the Dodgers, they were on the road somewhere. He apparently had seen a lot of action. It was July 4th; that usually meant a doubleheader. Before the second game, somebody set off a bunch of fire crackers and they said Billy immediately dived for cover under the bench. It was a reflex action. Warren Spahn, the famous Braves pitcher, was on the Remagen Bridge in Germany. There were a lot of returning kids, but as a young man, my only military experience was a little time in the Navy. I didn't see any action. Thank God! I was just not quite old enough.

I still had time, although it was running out. "The last question for you, Vinny—what was the story about that baseball and the Red Sox?"

I remember reading this story and I was so impressed that I told it on the air. The idea of a ball that was given to a pilot to be dropped on Germany, like so many other things I guess they tried to drop it on them, and he decided to hold onto it, and brought it home. Eventually, on Father's Day in Fenway Park, the fathers were encouraged to go out on the field and play catch with their sons, and the father and his son went out in the outfield, they played catch with that ball that otherwise would have been dropped on Nazi Germany.

He signed a ball for me: "Vin Scully U.S.N." I was told by the Fox Sports West TV crew, "Wait. Don't make a sound or move." Vinny was going to film his quick pre-game introduction to be broadcast on TV about an hour later. I was in rapture. I was in Vin Scully's press box and I got to watch and hear him say the best sentence in the world. …"It's tiiiiiiiiiiime for Dodger baseball."

Watching batting practice, I noted an older African American man in a nice suit and stylish hat behind the cage. Could it be? Am I this lucky? Indeed; it was Don Newcombe. I was able to get down to the field. Don Newcombe was gracious enough to talk to me.

Don Newcombe—United States Army

I mentioned to Don Newcombe how his insight would add to this story. His perspective is valuable I told him. Taking my hand and firmly shaking it, he said, "I only have a few moments." I wanted to make it count. I asked him a question that I had been thinking about for quite some time. I knew about the injustices that African Americans had been subject to not only in our history, but in baseball and in the service. To say I understood this injustice is another thing altogether. I can never understand. To even say I do is disrespectful. I can only honor that which I have not experienced by doing a simple thing: listening.

My Dad's Men

My dad fought in two wars: W.W. II and Korea. Sometimes he said he fought in three wars, since he had to deal with red tape and the politics of leadership. Nonetheless, he was a leader and as a leader he believed that the essence of leadership directly reflected the conviction that your men came first. Not their feelings. "Who cares about that?" he would say. "But, Todd, you provided for their basic needs—food and shelter and orders given in a manner that allowed them to understand their overall relationship to a bigger picture. Didn't you hate the response you got from me, or your mother, when you asked us 'why?' after we asked you to do something? We gave you the answer, 'It doesn't matter why because we are your parents and told you to do something. Just do it! It was no different with my men, Son."

He was right. I hated that typical parent "because I say so" approach. I always want to know why. Once I did know, I felt I was a part of a larger team and I had value and... I worked harder. It was no different for my dad in Korea.

By Executive Order, President Truman had integrated the Armed Services and the 715th Truck Company was among the first to be integrated. It had many men from Alabama in its ranks. Many white, more black.

It made no difference to the Army. White and black were all going overseas together: to Korea to serve—and perhaps to die. The commanding officers had their fill of racism in Virginia. For my dad racism was something he had neither seen nor experienced. One time driving in a convoy of about thirteen $2^1/_2$ ton trucks from North Carolina to Virginia, Dad ordered a halt to the convoy and pulled in to a local cafe for lunch and, well, he tells it better...

I was greeted with open arms by the owner who says all the white officers are welcome, but your niggers will have to eat in the trucks.

I was stunned. Niggers?

Todd, it was the first time I had heard that word used in my life! It made me angry.

"Sir," I said, "they seem perfectly willing to fight and die for your sorry ass and I order you to feed them at your counters."

"An order? Listen, sonny, Truman may have integrated the Army, but he hasn't ordered me to do a damn thing!" Todd, I wanted to fight right then. I had seen many blacks on artillery units in Europe. I had seen some even die. Somehow he didn't give a shit about any of that. So I thought up something on the spot.

I told him as an officer I could commandeer any local establishments in the name of the Army if a dangerous situation warrants [it] and the US Government would repay. So I told him if he would not comply with our request for lunch...inside...I would simply commandeer his restaurant. Of course [this] explanation was all bullshit. But he believed it and went in and opened up everything and fed us. We continued to stop there as we brought up other trucks from Alabama over the few next weeks. It made him a lot of money and I heard he continued to serve local military units, white and black. Money talks, Son, money talks.

Dad's unit was getting ready to ship out to Korea.

Todd, once we got to Korea, we, the officers of the 715 Transportation Company, ordered the living quarters to be integrated; officers and enlisted men alike. I didn't care about skin color. We all had pride in our outfit and in each other. My job was to see that our conditions were the best they could be for all of us. Our base was located on the border between North and South Korea. This small town is called Ch'unch'on. We drove the Republic of Korea [ROK] soldiers up to the front. Many times we had to go up to the front to evacuate them, too.

Those moments were the worst. You know, you are driving ahead to meet men coming back pressed by an advancing enemy. They are not just going to let us stop and pick them up like some school bus. We drew fire many times. Once you hear those Chinese bugles blow you know you are in for some tough shit.

I heard those trumpets many times. I was never as scared for anything in my life as I was in Korea. I mean that. I've seen thousands of Chinese men pouring across mountains from a distance of two miles; swarms of ants heading straight for us. We just threw everyone in the back of our trucks and drove as fast as we could in daylight and in total darkness. I feared for everyone on those dark nights. We had these little black-out lights that barely lit up the ground in front of us. Combine that with a speed of 25 mph and total darkness, winding mountain Korean roads, covered roads, you're asking for disaster. Many times that is what we got. Accidents were common and we lost a few good men—black, white, and Korean.

Many of our black troops had never received adequate Army training on 50-cal. machine guns. Our trucks had untrained gunners on them. So one day I took them up to the 38th parallel and did some target shooting at North Korean territory. To our surprise over 100 North Korean and Chinese soldiers jumped up and surrendered.

What I saw next disturbed me.

We called Republic of Korea [South Korean] units nearby to come get these prisoners and they were there in less than one hour. I stood there with my men, mostly black, as we watched the South Koreans just beat the hell out these prisoners as they ordered them to strip naked and to stand at attention in the back of these trucks. The translator said they were told that if they even moved they would be shot.

Then as two ROK soldiers sat on the roof facing the herd of prisoners, the driver popped the clutch of the truck. Of course the prisoners moved, *men falling on each other. The machine guns blared and the slaughter was on. In seconds, over 50 North Korean and Chinese prisoners were shot by members of the Republic of Korea. It was a war crime.*

Although our trucks were not used in this transportation, we were witness to it. I had no love for the enemy. It was something that bothered me. It bothered my men. They were actually comforting me telling me that back in Alabama, "We niggers were hunted like that many times." I couldn't accept that. We went back to base and I reported what I had seen to my superiors. Nothing came of it. I was starting to become depressed. Lou Ellen's letters helped and hurt. News from home was great, but it also made the distance seem greater. Then, as usual, it became cold, snowed and then it rained. Fortunately, I was transferred out and sent to Japan to command the Second T-Major Port which received Army goods for the war in Korea.

Your mother, Greg, and Susan all joined me in Japan. Things became heaven as Army officers had a rather high life style. We even had a maid and a gardener. It was the best of times. I had even thought about making the service a career. I felt a degree of confidence in myself I had never known. Things were going great as evidenced nine months after Mom's arrival with the birth of Brent.

I felt Dad was changing the story a little abruptly. I stopped him and asked why he had been sent to Japan so quickly. He talked about some rotation schedule. I believed him. Even after his death, I believed him.

In researching his unit in Korea on the Internet, a year ago, I came across an e-mail message from someone in his unit, a Lt. Koppel. I wrote him and he responded with his phone number. I called him and we talked about their time in Korea. Much of his information was exactly what Dad said. That is, until I talked about Dad's transfer to Japan.

"Your dad was not transferred, Todd." Mr. Koppel said. "Wally was brought up on court-martial charges."

"My dad did something illegal?" I asked. "Yes he did, technically," Koppel said, "but it was all bullshit."

It was all politics. Everyone loved your dad, and even the black guys trusted him. *Then we got this new commanding officer who was also black and he just had it out for Wally and made things very difficult for him. He gave your dad all the worst jobs. I guess he felt that as a black officer he had something to prove and he demanded more from the black troops, too. I really think he resented Wally's relationship with the guys. He cut the liquor rations for the enlisted men, who were mostly black. So these guys started to make their own booze using radiator fluid drained from the trucks to get a buzz.*

That could be fatal. Wally knew this, so he took his own liquor rations and encouraged some of us to sell us our rations to him at cost, which we did. Dealings like this happened all the time. Not everyone drank. What your dad did was to take the liquor he purchased over to the black enlisted men and sold it to them at cost so they wouldn't get sick or die. Many guys had been getting very, very ill. He only got back the money he spent. He kept records of this for proof.

As an act of leadership and compassion, Wally looked out for the men. Somehow it got back to our new CO, who charged your Dad with insubordination and sought to have him court-martialed.

Your dad defended himself, explained the dangerous conditions these men were living under, and then showed his records. He was acquitted and transferred to Japan, promoted to First Lieutenant.

He left Korea as a hero to many men, mostly black, who told us that for the first time in their lives a white man cared for them as an equal. Todd, you have a great father to be proud of."

Indeed I do. Indeed I do.

Asking the Right Question

So with memories of Dad's experiences in Korea, remembering Jackie Robinson's truly heroic example of fighting intolerance and facing my own ignorance of the emotional impact of racism, I asked Don Newcombe a question I hoped he wouldn't take the wrong way. I asked him, a little apprehensively, "As an African American veteran, why fight for a country that was segregated, and for a sport that was segregated?"

Well, we did it for the most part because we're Americans. That's what we had to do. And, we knew that someday things would change. It had to change in baseball, it had to change in the military, and it had to change all over the country. I was only hoping that I would live long enough to see that change. I did. But when your country calls you, you listen.

This is the greatest country on earth and I always thought of it as being the greatest country on earth. I would never want to go to another country and not be able to express the words and opinions I can express here in the United States on this soil.

When I was put in the military during the Korean War in 1952 and 1953, I didn't want to go. I was only four months short of the age limit.

What were they going to do with an old man in the military, almost 26 years old? And, when I was being inducted in New Jersey at the induction station, an Army colonel came over from New York in his staff car with his chauffeur and pulled me off the bus because I was the oldest guy on the bus with all the other soldiers. I had all my necessary records. He pulled me off the bus and took me back into the induction station. I thought maybe I wouldn't have to go. He sat me down and said to me, "Don, if were not for the newspapers and public opinion, you wouldn't be going into the military."

I said, "Now, Colonel that makes me feel real good. I'm on the bus with the other soldiers and I'm going to Camp Kilmer like any other red-blooded American and that's what I'm obligated to do regardless of who I am or what my stature in life is. I'm going like any other red-blooded American, and you come and pull me off the bus and tell me this, at the peak of my baseball career."

I said, "Now I'm gonna try everything I can to get out of the Army, I'll tell you that. I don't know if I'm gonna be successful or not, but I'm gonna try to get out because I got no business being in the Army in the first place." Four months short of the age limit, which was 26, I was 25 plus eight months. Talk about bad luck!

I went. I didn't do very good at trying to get out of the Army, so I decided to be a soldier. And, I physically trained, trained new recruits in Camp Kilmer and then went to Camp Pickett, Virginia and trained new recruits there, and then was transferred to San Antonio, Texas where I trained new doctors.

Staff Sergeant Don Newcombe sheds his Brooklyn Dodgers flannels for the olive drab of the U.S. Army during the Korean War. Courtesy of Transcendental Graphics.

In my mind I liked the irony of this great African-American Dodger pitcher training mostly white recruits at a Virginia camp named after the famous Confederate General Pickett and then going into the deep south, Texas, with authority. America had come a long way.

When a doctor came in to camp, we physically trained those M*A*S*H units. Yes, we trained the doctors. My group was the demonstration group in San Antonio. That was a hard job, to try to get doctors to become soldiers and teach them how to, you know, field strip, clean up all the cigarettes and all that discipline stuff on the ground on base. They had to obey us.

We were the first experience they had coming into the military. We had a lot of fun and it was the most rewarding experience that I'll ever have in my life. Notwithstanding baseball, making history as one of the first black players with Jackie Robinson and Roy Campanella, the two years I spent in the service of my country were the most rewarding two years that I've ever spent in my lifetime. And I mean that very sincerely.

I had to go. It was game time. He shared a picture with me and signed a ball, and as I left he yelled over to me, "Hey Todd! Get it straight."

I hope I have.

As I left the field I ran into two men—Tommy Lasorda and former Dodgers broadcaster and local radio talk show host Stu Nahan, I'd met these guys before, and they asked me what I was up to. I told them about my quest to honor baseball's military veterans and my dad. Both men thought this was a fine idea. Tommy, not being shy, told me, "Turn on your damn recorder and talk to me! I was in the Army!"

Stu Nahan interjected, "Wow, Tommy I was in the Marines and we always thought A...R...M...Y stood for Aren't Ready for Marines Yet!"

"Shut up, Nahan!" Tommy yelled back.

Tommy Lasorda—U.S. Army

I don't know how much help I can be but I was in the Army. An Italian girl saved me from danger you know. She hid me in her basement. But it was in the Bronx! [laughing].

Off the cuff, I asked Tommy, "What does it mean to represent the USA as an Army veteran and as an Olympic champion?"

Good question, Todd. As a veteran, as with the Dodgers, I wore the uniform with pride. When you come from a family of many brothers, like me, we were competitive but our father would always tell us that we are blessed to live in a great country full of promise and opportunity. But that blessing comes with a cost. That might mean going into the service and perhaps dying if need be. It is kind of funny for a father to be saying this. But it is where I get my passion for our great country. I was glad to serve in the US Army. Something about the uniform means a lot to me. I haven't really thought much about my Army days, but what I do remember is the pride. The pride of being an American and seeing that flag, serving that flag. I'll tell you when I went to the Senate hearing on the protection of the American flag from burning/desecration, I told that Senator, who I won't name, that you know that flag means all of us, sir, and in times of danger and heroism it was that flag that stands for us and represents us. If you burn it you burn all of us. On Mount Suribachi, that flag was raised, triumphant in victory not just for the Marines, but for all Americans. You want to burn that? It is a precious symbol of who we are and what we are about. The flag. Our flag must be protected. Too many men have died so we can be free to do all that God has for us to do.

For me that opportunity was to be a manager of the greatest organiza-tion in baseball, the L.A. Dodgers. Somebody else paid the price so I can ful-fill my dreams. Protecting the flag is very, very special to me.

My time in the service was uneventful, but I still remember the pride. The pride of duty of service [to] the greatest country in the history of mankind. I challenge anybody to show me a country more dedicated to freedom than the US. You won't find it. You won't find it.

The Olympics? I reminded him.

Let me say when I took the job of being manager for the games in Aus-tralia, I called the team all together and told them that they needed to think in a new way. I told them I didn't really know any of them so what I had to say was this. I don't care about your school, or how much talent or achievements you have. As far as I am concerned we are all Americans here. You are putting on a uniform which bears the letters "USA" and with that comes the honor and pride and responsibility of representing your country. When you do so, remember wearing that uniform means that you are representing 200,000,000 people. It is not about you. It is about us as a country getting back that which is rightfully ours—the game of baseball.

Baseball is our sport. It belongs to America and not to any other coun-try—definitely not Cuba. Not Japan. Not Korea. Not Australia. Winning the Gold Medal and hearing the National Anthem is the greatest thrill I have ever had. Ever! I have won World Series championships, been to the White House, I have even been inducted into the Hall of Fame, but Todd, winning that Gold Medal was for all America. When we won the World Series not everyone in America was happy, not the Giants fans, nor the Cincinnati Reds fans, but when we won that Gold Medal, all America won.

It was a thrill to bring back on the world stage the game of baseball to the nation where it rightfully belongs. It is our game.

I could tell that pride was important to Tommy Lasorda. So I asked him about this thing called pride.

Pride is the confidence you have in yourself. You are nothing without pride. My father taught me that and the Army instilled it in me even more. Doing things right. The right thing to do. I have tremendous confidence and pride in our men and women in the service and so should all Americans. I had tremendous pride in all my players who ever played for me. But I really had pride when I wore the uniform of our nation in the Army and as an Olympic champion.

Spellbound by Lasorda's passion, I was walking away when Stu Nahan said, "Hey, Todd, I like what you are doing. The fact this is being done by a teacher is just great. You know this ol' Canadian [meaning himself] fought in the USMC in World War II."

Stu Nahan

So who is Stu Nahan? I knew who he was. He broadcasted many Dodgers pre-game shows on the radio, so I knew his voice. Many in the L.A. area knew his face as well. Stu was on TV in L.A. as sports reporter for KTLA's "News at Ten" broadcasts for years. Lastly, America might remember Stu the movie star, as the white-haired man wearing dark-rimmed glasses sitting ringside announcing the fight between Rocky Balboa and Apollo Creed in the blockbuster movie *Rocky*.

Stu wasn't a ball player; he was a broadcaster. Like Ernie Harwell, like Ken Coleman, like Vin Scully, Stu Nahan helped to bring the game to fans. These men, too, are essential for the success of baseball. The game is larger than just the players. I wasn't sure what Stu had to offer, but once he finished his story I appreciated yet another aspect of our great and magnetic nation and how the actions of a single man, joined with others, made a difference.

First let me explain how I got to the Marines. I am Canadian. I raised myself from the time I was all alone, at 14 years old. When I was 17, I wanted to join the war effort. I tried to enlist in the Canadian Army but was told I was too young for service in Canada, so I crossed the border into the United States and went to enlist in the U.S. Marines. When I was told I needed my parents' signature on the enlistment form, I told them my mom was out shopping and I'll get her to sign it and be right back. I went out and forged the papers and came back about an hour later. I was in!

The Marines was the family I never had. I learned a great deal which served me later in life. I learned things like discipline, duty, and honor. I really learned to love America when I saw what young men were doing in the Pacific. Although I didn't see combat, yet, I was around many who did. When I was shipped out to the Pacific, my first stop was Pearl Harbor. I was overcome with emotion to be at this sacred place. The USS Arizona was still sticking out of the water with all its jagged edges and all I could think of was about those poor kids down below who never got out. Never got a chance to fight back. After staying in Pearl for a brief time, my group and I were shipped out to many of the islands made famous by the Marines: Guam, Tinian, and others. I think we were being shipped to Okinawa. What I do know was we were going to be assault troops landing on the shores of Japan for the invasion. That all changed. We dropped the atomic bomb!

Thank God for that. I was fresh meat. I was going to be landing on those deadly shores. It really seemed like a death sentence. I felt like I had just been given a pardon by the governor. I was spared!

Funny that we are mentioning Tinian right now, I have my commercial pilot's license and do a great deal of flying. I flew to Tinian not all that long ago. That is where the B-29 bomber Enola Gay was loaded to drop the A-bomb back in 1945. To see this postage stamp-like island after all these years was something. I was struck about how this little place way out in the Pacific was a part of so much history. Of course, I know many see this bomb as horrific, and it was, but back in 1945 this bomb saved my life.

Standing up, Stu put his arm around my shoulder and said:

Todd, I like what you are doing. It is good for all of us especially us in baseball to be reminded how lucky we are to be doing what we do! I heard Tommy talking to you about pride. Tommy has it and so do I. I was a suc-

America's adopted son—USMC veteran Stu Nahan with Todd at Dodger Stadium.

cessful NHL player, and broadcaster for years with the Dodgers, but my time in the Marines brings me the greatest satisfaction, because as an adopted child of America I had a choice to serve a nation that wasn't even my home or asked for my service. Doesn't that say something about what America represents? Damn right it does!

Wow. What a story: unplanned and passionate. Just like life. My father knew what he was saying when he said, "Pal, you'll be surprised at what you'll learn."

15

Mickey Hatcher, 1988 World Series Hero, Los Angeles Dodgers

I Am My Father's Dream

September 11, 2002 was the first anniversary of the terrorist attacks on America. Ballparks across America were holding pre-game memorials and the Anaheim Angels were no different. Mickey had mentioned what I was doing with veterans and ball players to Steve Physioc and Rex Hudler, the Angels' popular and energetic TV broadcasters. Steve thought this would offer a perfect story for the pre-game show for Fox Sports on 9-11-02. So he called me a few days before and it all seemed ready to go, but there was a mix-up with his director who didn't understand what we were doing and it was nixed. Or was it? Steve was mad because he thought it was a done deal. He got to the park and found out it was all fouled up. Then the director said, "OK, let's go with it." Trouble is, I live an hour and a half away and Mickey had told me it wasn't going to happen. Then I get a call 45 minutes before the game from Mickey and Steve asking me to come. I can't make it, so Mickey is scheduled to be the "Angels in the Infield" pre-game guest and talk about this. He didn't want to do this. He is shy by nature.

"Todd, you get down here and do this. I don't even read books unless they have a lot of pictures. Besides this is about war, veterans, school stuff, not about hitting. I feel out of place." He gave in to all of us and agreed to the interview and he was the best promoter I could ever ask for. He sat alongside Bill MacDonald of Fox Sports and Rex Hudler and told a Southern California TV audience about what we were up to: Mickey, Wally, and me. We added one more veteran to this journey from the USS *Hornet:* Carpenters Mate Harold Hatcher U.S. Navy.

Angels in the Infield, September 11, 2002; Fox Sports West

I was so nervous, because my story hadn't been placed with anyone. I feared that someone would take the idea for themselves. I resigned myself to that. Other people have the means, connections, baseball knowledge, and the money to accomplish what I wanted to do. But this really wasn't about me. So long as the men I respect are recognized, I thought, it would be all right. I kept trying to tell myself that.

So I turned on the TV and watched Harold Hatcher's son Michael Vaughn Hatcher, a.k.a. "Mickey," turn on his charm to present our story...

My friend Todd and I were watching a commercial about baseball's greatest moments and he turned to me and said, "They still don't have baseball's greatest moment."

I asked, "What are you talking about?"

Todd said, "That moment was when they changed uniforms and went to fight for our country and saved the game of baseball."

"Wow," I said. "What a great story. You know, half of these ballplayers today don't understand what it is like to give up a game they love to go save the country, but that is what these guys did for us. Not only guys like Ted Williams, but other men as well: Warren Spahn, the DiMaggio brothers, Yogi Berra...there are a lot of veterans out there. Some we will never know or hear about. Todd, you need to correct that. We need to correct that."

Really, you know, for the game of baseball and the love of the game, there is a reason it is still going. It is a story demanding to be told. Especially after September 11, 2001. So many stories are told of guys who were pretty good ball players, went to war, and ended up with injuries and even amputated limbs. They never got to fulfill their dream. My father [Harold Hatcher] was one of those stories. He was a great ballplayer. I was his dream to become a ballplayer. I was his "footstep" to baseball. So it was a great thrill for him to watch me get there.

My dad served on the USS Hornet. In fact, he was aboard the USS Hornet for Doolittle's raid on Tokyo and he was also on the Hornet in the Battle of Santa Cruz where the Hornet was sunk.

And the bad part about serving on the Hornet was he was down un-

derneath, so when the Japanese were bombing the ship the
guys below didn't know what
was going on, especially at
Midway. It was really scary,
but he had a job to do. That
is what Todd's project is all
about. In spite of all the vio-
lence and fear, these guys like
my dad and Todd's veteran
dad, who I loved, faced it as
men regardless of the outcome.
We are better men for it. Our
country and baseball are better
because of men such as our
dads.

Harold Hatcher USN—Mickey's dad.

His face brightened up talking about his dad on the TV screen.
You could see the love and the pride telling how his dad saw him
make it to the majors as a rookie with the Los Angeles Dodgers.

I called him back to say a big thank you, and he and the Angels
went on to a remarkable run resulting in a World Championship. In
that off-season I tried to get Mickey to send me a picture of his dad
for this project. I finally got it during Spring Training in Arizona the
following March, 2003. I stayed with him at his house and as I looked
through his photo album, I was amazed at a life in pictures showing
a dream come true. I saw Mickey and Mike Scioscia standing among
many other players in what they told me was among the best teams
they've played for: the Albuquerque Dukes, managed by Del Crandall
in the 1970s.

Later that night at dinner, Mickey just started talking about his
dad. Stirring his drink and looking a million miles away, as though
seeking his dad in the crowd, he continued: "Dad survived the sinking, but was injured and hurt his back. He never really regained the
skill or talent that he had; when he came back home he had lost that

...he lost that extra step or whatever it was, but he never really quite regained that form. So he pushed me."

"Have Passion"—The Lessons of Harold Hatcher

I was a good athlete, but never a gifted one. I had to work at everything I did, both in football [Mickey played for college coaching legend Barry Switzer at Oklahoma] *and baseball. My dad would always say that I could never "slack off." So much is made about my passion and enthusiasm and joking nature throughout my career. Some might wonder how serious I am or was. I'm damn serious. Always have been. But it is OK to enjoy yourself. Have fun and enjoy the ride. Dad taught me that passion, but to enjoy the ride, too. Look, it's a game. A kids' game that we get to play and represent. Why shouldn't we honor these men who saved it by remembering how lucky we are to be doing this? So many never got the chance.*

My dad was a teacher in how he lived his life. His values still come through when I teach a player. I found I started sounding like my dad when I was manger of the Great Falls Dodgers in the 1990s at the instructional level. So in a way he still teaches today.

When I was a Dodgers player back in 1988, we were supposedly overmatched. Those Oakland A's were awesome. People told us they should beat us pretty easily. Those were the feelings out there. The more I heard it, the more it pissed me off. We were there because we were good.

Right before the playoffs, I started thinking about Dad and war, and his stories came back. My dad knew about being overmatched. Dad told me stories of how the Japanese dominated us. My whole life, he made me and my brothers watch all those W.W. II documentaries like Victory at Sea *and reminded us of the high stakes we as a nation faced. So I wasn't all that nervous in 1988. I drew from all those stories of men facing death and realized I was just facing pitching.*

But what Harold Hatcher taught his son was to have passion.

You know, Todd, in that '88 World Series against Oakland, they had a great pitcher, Dave Stewart. Stewart had his hat pulled down right over his eyes. He looked intimidating. But that didn't bother me. I was too nervous to notice. I got up there and hit a home run. It was such a surprise to me and everybody else.

I ran around the bases so fast, it looked like I never hit a home run in my life before. I really ran around those bases fast with my arms in the air and shouted. You know, it was just one of those magical moments. I'll remember it forever. I was shaking my arms and throwing my fists in the air, not only was I excited, but I understood what a special moment it was.

Dad taught me to do everything with a passion and... "remember those men in the service who sacrificed to give you this opportunity, and Son, when you run out a hit and when you run out a walk or when you run down a fly ball or when you run on a home run, you do that in honor of them, because there are a lot of guys who gave up everything so you could do that. You remember that when you play the game."

That moment so often shown on TV is misunderstood. It was in reality a moment between a father and a son.

So, Todd, I was relaxed for the entire World Series. It showed. I hit two home runs! We went on to win the Series... as a team. Again as a coach in 2002 for the Angels, I was a part of a team of destiny. Again I heard my dad's spirit in my teaching and coaching. Look what happened. We won it all. That spirit and passion still is here, although my dad is not. That is what makes that generation so great. People don't have to say they were a great generation; just look at the country they left us. I never get tired of baseball. Why should I?

I could tell Mickey was done talking. I got all I was going to get that night. We ate dinner; we all had meat dishes and Patty and Mickey were mad at me, because they were observing Lent and with all the talking, they just forgot and ate beef. Absolution? Hope they got it.

16

Pfc. Dutch Schultz, 82nd Airborne

War's Cost: My Chance with the Phillies

When World War II concluded, it was much more than the ending of a war. So often overlooked are the costs and burdens of war on the common citizen soldiers who fought, won, and eventually achieved the ultimate victory. Every returning veteran was a different man. All that many men wanted was to return and pick up their lives where they left off. That is easier said than done. For Arthur "Dutch" Schultz of the elite "C" Company of the 505th Parachute Infantry Regiment of the 82nd Airborne Division, his war continued. Many people have seen Dutch or maybe heard of him before, but might not know it. Hollywood shows us Dutch as the lost GI in the W.W. II classic *The Longest Day*, and the brilliant W.W. II historian Stephen Ambrose featured Dutch in his History Channel specials and his books. But one message is consistent: life was never easy for Arthur "Dutch" Schultz.

The Streets of Detroit

Growing up during the Great Depression in inner-city Detroit made you mature in many ways. Some call it street smarts. Others call it common sense. The streets were shaping me in ways my mother didn't like so she enrolled me in a Catholic School called St. Philips Neri. Let's just say I had trouble adjusting to their rules—too many rules. Rules for how you eat, how you pray, even how you dress. I was raised Catholic, but I had never seen it practiced like this before. I was a rebel. I liked to stir up the pot and challenge authority. Why? I am not sure; perhaps I was searching for more of a father role model since I was never all that close to my stepfather.

I played baseball for St. Philips and was seeing a lot of playing time. I dreamt of becoming a ball player. I'd go to then Navin Field [Tigers Stadium] to see the Yankees and Tigers play. I saw Babe Ruth and Lou Gehrig play. It was a doubleheader and I kept full by eating the spilled popcorn and food my brother and I found under the seats. Times were tough. You ate what you found.

My senior year in high school English class we were asked by the Sister teaching the class what we wanted to do with our lives after high school. As she went around the classroom, the kids were saying they wanted to go to college and so forth; when it was my turn I said, "I want to play baseball." Offended by my answer, the Sister said, "Any idiot can play baseball." I shot back, "Any idiot can teach English." I was expelled right then—two weeks before graduation! Then, my mother stepped in and reminded the staff that this meant I would be returning the following year. That did it. I was reinstated and was allowed to graduate. They made me walk last behind everyone else in the graduation ceremony. I didn't care. Most likely we all were getting drafted anyway. It was 1942.

World War II

My mother wanted me to go into a branch of service where I would learn a trade. Back in those days, with a school record like mine, you didn't think of going to college; you learned a trade. I let her and the enlistment sergeant discuss this back and forth. I had very little to say about it. They decided they were going to put me in Coast Artillery. That's a trade? I joined this artillery battery, and this is where the company commander gave me the nickname "Dutch" after the notorious gangster of that era with the same name. Finally I saw an announcement that the Army was seeking paratroopers and I volunteered.

I arrived at Fort Benning, Georgia for jump school not knowing what the hell I was getting myself into. I volunteered for several reasons. One, I wanted to be the best soldier possible. The best. Besides that, we got fifty dollars extra for jumping out of airplanes. I completed my initial jump training at Ft. Benning. On the last day we were to make our tenth and final overall jump, a very good friend of mine was sitting next to me in this C-47 and said, "Dutch I'm not going to jump." Well, we were taught if you don't jump you are dead meat. You are really dead meat. They warned us that in combat they could shoot you for disobeying an order.

In situations other than combat, they could make it so miserable for you that you would wish you were dead. They told us story after story about

Dutch Schultz. Courtesy of Gail Schultz.

what could happen to us if we refused to jump. So I was prepared and I did my best to try to tell this friend of mine, "C'mon, c'mon, let's jump, let's jump, c'mon," but I could have given him a million dollars and he still wouldn't have jumped. When it got time to stand up and hook up, we left him behind.

After I jumped, we were marched back to our company area in Camp McCall. We were told to put our fancy Class A uniform on and get ready for formation. We were then called into formation and they brought this buddy of mine out. They stood him in front of the entire company and then the company commander, executive officer, and the platoon leaders came out. They started berating and dehumanizing this guy like you can't believe. They cut off all of his buttons on his jacket, which was to signify a coward. They pulled off his jump wings. They slapped him around. With an open hand they slapped him in the face I don't know how many times. I was frightened to death for him. I was frightened for me too. I was sure I was never going to let this happen to me. I was never going to refuse to jump. Never! After this abuse was all over this company commander said to him, "If I give you another chance to jump, would you jump?" He said, very softly, "Yes." So he went up the next day by himself and he jumped. I couldn't believe it. He went up and jumped.

It was here that I started to realize a sense of duty and obligation. Our jump school was rough and I learned, number one, to be obedient. When the sergeant told me to give him 25 pushups, I gave him 25. If he wanted another 25, I gave him another 25. I didn't have any conscious sense of what was happening to me, except that I knew I was becoming different. When I graduated from jump school, it was the proudest moment in my life. This was a very important part of my life—becoming a paratrooper. I felt the esprit de corps. For the first time in my life I was proud of myself.

With his newfound dignity, my buddy and I went over to Europe together on a troop ship, joining the 82nd Airborne in Ireland. The 82nd had just come back from combat in Africa, Sicily, and Italy. They moved from Italy over to Ireland and that is where we joined them as replacement people just in time for Operation Overlord...later to become, as most people call it, D-Day.

"The Eyes of the World Are Upon You"

Dutch was a proud member of the 82nd Airborne and loved talking about it.

As I joined the 505 Parachute Infantry Regiment, I became more and more aware of my sense of duty. I must tell you, when I joined the 505 it was the first time I ever felt I was really in the Army. Why? Because, these guys had already seen combat, they already had two combat jumps, they were already battle-tested. They had a kind of maturity that I lacked. I had some adolescent ideas about what a solider was like that I picked up at Saturday afternoon matinees. Movie dreams...you become a hero without a price... that sort of thing. Maturity came much later, once I saw some of my buddies give their lives.

Before I went into Normandy, I got into a crap game. I shot crap as a high school kid behind a pool hall once in awhile, but that was for pennies. Anyway, I got in a crap game and I won almost twenty-five hundred dollars. *I couldn't believe I was winning all this money. In the movie* The Longest Day *they had me losing it all, though, to avoid bad luck. That wasn't exactly true. There was a sergeant that I didn't like and I was trying to bust him; it goes to show you how much of an amateur I was. To make a long story short, I lost it all, but shortly after that game we left to go to the British airfield.*

D-Day was supposed to be June 4, 1944. Because of inclement weather it was delayed 24 hours and we took off on the fifth about 10 o'clock at night. Now, 10 o'clock at night was daylight because England was on Double Summer time, so it was still daylight. When taking off I had probably 125 pounds of equipment on my body. I couldn't believe what I had... a teller mine, 100 pounds of ammunition, hand grenades, my reserve chute, all those sort of things. We had to be helped to get into the airplane. While we were going over, I was saying one rosary after another. This was the beginning of the dawn for me at least in terms of realizing what was going to happen or could happen in war. I might die. I made sure I was covering all my tracks by saying all these rosaries. I remember one of the guys next to me asking to borrow the rosary and I said, "No, you can't because I am using it." When we crossed into Normandy, our plane started shaking, rattling, and rolling. I had no idea what was going on.

What was happening was, we were coming under antiaircraft attack. I didn't realize this. The other guys did, especially the old timers. They knew what was going on. I happened to look out a window and I saw, what I thought, fire coming out of one of the engines on our C-47. I said to the guy next to me, "Look at that fire. Is that something to worry about?"

He said, "Fire? That's ack-ack."

The light went on in my head. They are firing at me, the Germans are firing at me! Well, soon after that we got the call to "Stand and hook up." We were hooking up and we were checking the equipment of the guy in front of us when all of a sudden we went [head over heals] and we hit the deck. What had happened was our C-47 had been hit by ack-ack and the pilot veered off course and it went, sort of rolled on its side. We couldn't get back on our feet fast enough to get out of there. What I didn't know at the time was that we were jumping at a much lower altitude than we normally would have jumped and at a rate of speed much too great. When my chute opened I said, "1,000, 2,000, 3,000," and the chute opened. I spun once and went up in the air and the next thing I knew I came down flat on my back in a tree. This landing will have a lot to do with my baseball career. We jumped at probably six or seven hundred feet, which is really low. A few more feet and I wouldn't have made it. My back was killing me!

I cut myself out of my parachute. I threw away the anti-tank grenade. I threw away my gas mask. I threw away anything I didn't need and I started looking for somebody...anybody. There was nobody to be found. I didn't realize it at the time, but a German fired at me. He fired his machine gun. AT ME! I took my M-1 rifle, turned, and pointed into the direction where I thought the fire was coming from and I pulled the trigger. "CLICK" I realized then that I failed to put ammunition in my M-1 rifle, that's how advanced an infantryman I was at that point in time. I scrambled to get to a hedgerow, to find cover. I then realized how I was totally unprepared for combat.

I walked around and around and around until daybreak...we'd jumped off about one o'clock in the morning. I didn't see anybody for the next seven hours. I heard some gunfire. I heard the battleships, the shells they were sending over sounded like trains, not shells. I was never at that point and time so frightened of anything in my life. I felt like a scared kid in the dark, walking around Normandy all by myself. I would stop and rest in one of the hedgerows and get up and start walking again. I don't know where I walked. I don't know how I even survived. One moment would be like a walk in the park on a Sunday afternoon, quiet and very peaceful, then all of a sudden all hell would break loose. There would be artillery fire, and machine gun fire and so forth, but I was nowhere near it. It wasn't until quarter to eight in the morning or eight o'clock, when Lieutenant Tallerday found me. Lieutenant Tallerday was the executive officer of my company. He had about seven or eight different paratroopers from all different regiments, even some from the Screaming Eagles of the 101st. I was never so happy to see somebody in my life.

He was going to take us back to our objective, which was the La Fiere Bridge outside of Ste.-Mere-Eglise, Normandy. As we started back along the road toward the bridge, and we got closer and closer, Tallerday said, "You guys stay here." While we were waiting, I saw this GI sitting in a firing position nearby with his rifle....I approached him from the rear, and I started talking to him. There was no answer. I got closer, closer and closer, I kneeled down and looked into his face, and he had a bullet hole right between his eyebrows. What was so unusual about it, I didn't see any blood. That was the first dead person I ever saw. I ran back to where there was some comfort and security with the rest of the troops.

Dutch went on to fight in Holland, and somehow survive the Battle of the Bulge. But baseball was always in his heart.

'Hey, Kid, You've Got Talent. Come to Shibe Park!'

Baseball? Let me tell you, it kept me alive. I thought about it all the time, even in combat. I was going to play when I got home. I believed in myself. Because of the Army, I had more confidence than I ever had. I was going to make it. Failure was not an option in the service and it wasn't going to be on the ball field either. I am Airborne; we never fail.

When I was discharged, I went to San Francisco, where my mother was now living and immediately started playing college ball at San Francisco State. I noticed that I was having trouble swinging through the ball and that my foot speed had slowed down. I had a hell of a time. I had not played ball in three years, but I made the varsity for SFSU. I was playing first base, and I was not hitting well, and the coach pulled me a number of times. I got furious with that. I had never been pulled or taken out of a game. Never! That was difficult to accept. Just as difficult was my new wife and her endless requests to take her back to Philly.

I left college and we went back east and I started playing in one of the top sandlot leagues in Philadelphia. Sandlot was like a semipro team usually owned by a business. We played a few minor league teams.

Somehow I got my batting eye back. For a long period of time, I was batting well over .400, getting a lot of doubles, line drives over third base or shortstop. I got a call from Bob Carpenter, the owner of the Philadelphia Phillies, offering a tryout at Shibe Park. Here it was; my big chance. The Phils and the Brooklyn Dodgers were playing a few hours later. I tried out at first base. God, I was 10 feet tall when I walked out on that field. They put me through an infield/outfield workout. Then I took hitting practice.

During a break, I had a moment to speak with Leo Durocher, manager of the Dodgers. My Lord, what a thrill! I was in the penthouse, man. I was really taking myself seriously. Then I came in off the field and the rest of the Phils got ready for the game. Nobody talked to me or told me what to do. They all went to work. So I just sat down on the bench. Wow! What a great seat I was going to have. So I guess it was near game time and there was this fiery player on the Phils, their third baseman Ben Chapman. As the lineup was being announced, he said, "Hey you rookie, get the [heck] out of here. You don't belong here." As I left the dugout, I looked back just one more time, looked at those guys wearing the Phillies uniform and looked at the Dodgers across the way and started to walk down that long black tunnel. It was to be the last time I ever set foot on a ball field.

I also knew the day of reckoning had come with baseball. I had to admit to myself I would never play again. I couldn't pick up foot speed, I couldn't swing for power, my back was causing me problems. What had happened to me in Normandy on June 6, 1944 was I had ripped the cartilage in my spine when I landed on my back in that tree. I actually had three bulging discs and a hairline fracture in one of my vertebrate. You know, I had walked across Europe, fought, and tried out for pro ball with a broken back! Sometimes I wonder what could have been. But the Good Lord had a higher purpose for me.

My Moment of Truth

My moment of truth actually evolved over a period of time. It evolved when I decided to become involved in company reunions after the war. It was a gradual sort of thing. I had no interest in going back and associating with my war-time buddies. I was working at the Frankfurt Arsenal and there was a notice on the bulletin board that anybody who had been in D-Day should contact Cornelius Ryan, who was writing a book [The Longest Day]. I wrote him a letter and told him about my experiences. Next thing I know, I got a call. He wanted to come down to Philadelphia from New York to interview me. He did and we spent two or three hours talking.

He said, "You know what, Dutch? Most people I have talked to are grandiose about all the things they did or think they did and you don't do that." I never did. I didn't take any credit for killing 50 Germans or our company's successes at Normandy. Ryan just liked the idea that I blew all that money shooting craps. I was an innocent Catholic kid, and he liked the story about my being lost. Also he liked that I shared my fears and this sort of thing. He was a very, very nice man, so he wrote about me. It changed my life.

He featured me as one of the major characters in the movie The Longest Day and that sort of loosened me up somewhat about dealing with my past. It made me famous.

The Purity of Baseball

But even today, my heart wanders back to baseball. I still love the Phillies for giving me a chance. I always will.

I believe baseball is a metaphor for America, I say that only because I see what is happening today in terms of greed, and the fight over money between the players and the owners. It seems as if today some people don't have the kind of motives and teamwork we had yesteryear. You know, back when the families owned teams. To me, all these millions and millions of dollars made today . . . it's incomprehensible.

I would have played baseball for fifty dollars a week, man. To me, baseball was my love, my first love, and I would have played baseball for nothing. If they want to give a handout, fine, I'll take it. But to me, baseball has become a big business like everything else. Whether we want to accept it or not, we got so much focus on money. Money, money, money, money. Back in the old days it mattered what kind of a person you were.

Of course there are good points about baseball today. It's not all evil. Joe Torre is a class guy. Apparently, he is making a great deal of money with the Yankees, but I think he is a class guy. I've always thought that. He's got a sister who is a Nun. He's a good Catholic boy. I've got to root for him.

And look at Curt Schilling. He is almost a throwback to my era. He sees the game for what it was. He's a real team guy. Just look at what he did in the World Series. That's courage. You have to respect that. Plus, Todd, his dad was Airborne too. Somehow I think that is where Curt gets his courage.

Also, look at the small towns with the minor league baseball teams.

They've got community spirit, they've got their fans and that's where the ballplayers, I think, still have some degree of purity about them.

Regrets?

Am I bitter? Do I regret my missed chance? Not really. I got to work and help save lives and I believe that through it all God was testing me. He's testing all of us. What will your moment of truth be?

First Pitch: June 6, 2004

I sought to make the second anniversary of my father's passing a happy one. Sitting home feeling sorry for myself was no way to honor his memory, nor would that offer any comfort to my mother.

The D-Day Museum was hosting a huge event in France for the 60th Anniversary of the Normandy Campaign. Oh how I wanted to be there, but I sought out something different, something unique. I looked for a way to tell Dutch thank you for his service to America. Dutch Schultz is a larger than life man to me, because he embodies so much of all of us; contradictions, fears, sin, redemption and human frailties and dignity of character. His honesty and compassion gives me a peace of mind I cherish.

When he told me about walking down that dark runway at Shibe Park, never to return, the look on his face was one of loss and regret.

The Detroit Tigers were in town in early spring and I went down to see my good friend Todd Maulding of the Tigers, and Mickey. I love it when we are all together. I don't think I ever laugh so hard. Mick had arranged for me to get a field pass to watch batting practice. While watching, I talked with Angels TV broadcaster Steve Physioc. Steve asked me how my book was coming along and I told him "great, but slowly." I told him about Dutch Schultz's story and he was impressed. Steve's own father was in the Marines in W.W. II and was a very courageous man. He was known as a "cave rat"—his job was to go into these Japanese underground tunnels and blow them up. I believe Steve's brother was also a member of the 82nd Airborne Division. He knew who Dutch was. Then it hit me and I asked, "Are the Angels in town on June 6?" He pulled out his schedule and indeed they were, playing the Indians.

I said, "Wouldn't it be great to have Dutch Schultz throw out the opening pitch on June 6, 2004 here at Anaheim Stadium?"

"That would be fabulous, Todd!" Steve said. "Hey! There is Tim Mead over there, the Director of Communications for the Angels. He can make it happen. Let's ask him." Tim was all for it.

Now the most important thing was seeing if Dutch was up for it. With his health issues and his oxygen tank, I thought there might be a problem. There wasn't. He was up for it. His devoted wife and best friend Gail was going to make sure this happened for her guy.

Everything fell into place. It was going to be a big deal! My sister was even going to sing the National Anthem. It was a team effort, all of us working together to honor a noble warrior. My students chipped in to pay for Dutch's hotel room at the Doubletree Inn in Anaheim. They wanted to be a part of it!

It was becoming something special. I really felt God's presence in this. It was almost spiritual. Dad would have wanted this. In some way, he was here.

June 6, 2004 arrived and my wife Sue and my children Jamie, Jason, and I rode together to Anaheim. It was going to be a difficult day for me, but we were so busy with this event, I hoped that my pain would somehow diminish, transformed into a celebration of Dutch. I arrived at the hotel to meet up with the Schultz group and there he was, Dutch Schultz wearing his 82nd Airborne uniform. He looked so heroic, so "larger than life" to me.

His presence reminded me of the magnitude of my loss for only a brief moment. In one sense, I'm sure that a first pitch is no big deal. They happen before every game. But this time it was different. The Angels had a very important war veteran throwing out the pitch celebrating the most important date in the 20th Century. The Angels are indeed a classy organization and both Tim and Steve are true professionals. They made a D-Day veteran's day. I am forever grateful.

I pushed Dutch in his wheelchair through the labyrinth of hallways until we found our ride, a waiting golf cart. Our driver drove for what seemed to be forever until we reached the tunnel in left field, and the brightness of the sky and sun made it seem we were entering heaven. For me, we were. The little golf cart made its way to home plate where my sister Susan and her husband Jeff awaited. My brother Brent was taking pictures. Directly above us in the loge section were my mom, brother Greg, and sister Peggy, all waving. I was happy to see them, but I started to panic. Where were my wife and our kids? I was furious. I couldn't find them. Of all the people I wanted to share this moment with, it was them. My wife has been the rock, and supported me through all the highs and lows. Her natural skepticism, after having our hopes raised and lowered, also inspired me to complete this mission. Jamie and Jason prayed at night, "God, please let Daddy's book happen." I searched for them, my anger building, until Mickey told me they had his seats. I looked over, and there they were.

My best friend Morgan was there as a witness, too. He had purchased his own ticket. He had to be there. This indeed was a big moment and I wanted those I loved and who really knew me to see all of this happen. It wasn't just a first pitch; it was the definition of everything Dad was all about. This moment embodied everything this journey was about. Dutch and I were coming home.

On this, the 60th Anniversary of the Allied assault on Hitler's "Fortress Europe," Arthur "Dutch" Schultz and I walked out to the pitcher's mound at Angel Stadium. It was a glorious day. Dutch held in his hand a pristine white baseball that he was to throw to our catcher, Mickey Hatcher.

The PA announcer intoned, "Ladies and gentlemen...Today marks the 60th Anniversary of the Allied Assault on Europe. D-Day! Joining us is Dutch Schultz of the 82nd Airborne Division...." I couldn't hear any more. The roar of the crowd was deafening and everyone stood. It was at this moment that my entire journey became worth the struggle. I was home, standing alongside a true hero from the generation I so revere and miss.

Dutch asked me, "Who are they standing for?"

I said, "You...you idiot!"

Dutch stood at attention and saluted all corners of the stadium and he looked over at first base longingly and quietly said, "That's where I wanted to be."

I said, "I know."

"God. . . . I hate war!" Dutch replied.

I thought . . . "I knew it!" There was the admission of what his sacrifice had cost him. Try as hard as he might to keep that from me, deep down inside he wanted to be a ball player. For this brief moment he was!

He walked the ball up to home plate rather than throwing it. His damaged back wouldn't allow it. Mick yelled out, "Underhand it to me" and Dutch said, "Only [women] underhand a baseball."

He slammed the ball into Mick's glove and the crowd cheered. Dutch was satisfied and very proud. At the time none of us realized it would be his last big outing as he became more and more ill over the next few months.

The Passing of a Legend

Dutch was dying, and his devoted and loyal wife Gail and I regrettably knew it, although we didn't say it to each other. It was late September–early October 2005. I went over to St. Mary's Hospital in nearby Apple Valley to see him. The nurses all said that when I came in, his vitals just jumped up to normal. Heck, Dutch even put in his teeth and tried to eat a little when I was there. Dutch always told me I was the son he never had. Some people might avoid such a dreary place as Dutch's hospital bed, but not me. I visited often and we talked and at times I rubbed his feet mindful of where those feet had trod. His doctor was worried about his circulation problems in his swollen feet and Dutch mentioned how much his feet were aching him. One night I noticed how quiet the room was and I chastised Dutch for not having the playoff game on between the Braves and Astros. "Well, turn the TV on," he said.

I did and sat down on the corner of the bed by the headboard since there wasn't a chair in the room and I didn't feel like standing for an hour. So Dutch scooted over. Dutch fell back asleep and I just watched the game propped up by a pillow behind my back. Then the sound of an Astros walkoff home run to win the game, and the fans' jubilation woke this aged paratrooper. Dutch then tapped my arm, looked me in the eye and said... "Pal, isn't that the greatest game ever made?"

The tone was so much like my father my eyes began to fill with tears....

Why?

I missed my dad of course and I knew how much I was going to miss Dutch. I knew what his death was going to feel like... the emptiness of a loss. As I was thinking and feeling this, Dutch intrrupted my somberness...

"You miss your old man don't ya? Well, when I see him, I'll tell him 'hi' and that he raised one hell of a son."

I was an emotional wreck by this point. What do you say to a friend you know you might not ever see again? Dutch saw my vulnerability and heartbreak and, though deathly ill, instinctively sought to comfort me. That is the way he was.... He loved giving hugs.... I bet there are many men who wish they could get just one more hug from a loved one... a person so much like their father.

It must have looked strange to the ICU nurse see a 6'7" fully grown man getting a hug from such a frail figure with arms full of I.V.s. The nurse said Dutch's vitals hadn't been this strong for so many consecutive hours but "You have to go now, sir." It was getting late... it was the last time I ever saw him.

Dutch died a few days later and his ashes were formally laid to rest in Arlington National Cemetery on December 7th 2005... Pearl Harbor Day. I was honored to be there as a guest of his family.

17

Mission Accomplished

*"The mission of this Allied force was fulfilled
at 0241 local time, May 7, 1945"—
General Dwight D. Eisenhower, Supreme Allied Commander*

When Dad and I came up with this idea back in 2002, it led to many discussions between us. Most of these talks were centered on a lesson in gratefulness. Dad reminded me it was a privilege to be an American citizen and with that came responsibility. Of course I knew that, but knowing something and feeling something are two completely different matters. When Dad died, it was a great loss for me, but I realize now I had gained something, too. Simply put, it was his time to go and I am okay with that. I was not content, though, to let our honest desire to remember and honor our two passions just recede into memory. I would fulfill my father's last mission and somehow tell this story of baseball during wartime.

Thomas Edison said before he invented the light bulb that he had found 10,000 ways not to do it. It only takes one time to find the right way. Churchill said, "Never give up, and never give in. Never surrender. Never! Never!" He did not and we are free because of it. Just because this project is hard, should I stop? Well, I almost did.

Al Lowman was the agent representing the project and me. Al died of lung cancer, and with his death I feared once again that this vision of honoring baseball's most honorable men had died as well. A few days after Al's death, I was teaching about Edison in my classroom and his quotation about failure bowled me over like a ton of bricks. I knew I'd come up with many ways NOT to do this baseball project, but I knew I shouldn't be deterred. I just needed to find the right way.

Perhaps I had this all wrong. Was the answer right in front of me? Did I just need to ask? Indeed it was. Seeing this project as a visual one worthy of a documentary, I plunged into writing and imagining something better. I looked up a quote that Ted Williams said about how he wanted a movie on him to start:

"Now I'll tell you how it's supposed to start.... It's in a fighter plane, see, flying, from the pilot's eye, over KOREA. Seoul. And it's flying, slow and sunny and then bang WHAM BOOOOMMM the biggest goddamn explosion ever on the screen, I mean BOOOOOMMM. And the screen goes dark. DARK. For maybe ten seconds there's NOTHING. NOTHING. And then when it comes back there's the ballpark and the crowd ROARING...and that's the beginning."—Ted Williams

Awesome! What a show! Why hasn't it ever been done? I thought. Somebody in the entertainment field has to "get" this scene visually. But who will listen to me? They might listen to a celebrity representing the idea, but whom? Billy Crystal? Tom Hanks? Ron Howard? Maybe. But not yet. I kept thinking.

Then a visual image hit me. It was of Curt Schilling's bloody sock during the 2004 playoffs and World Series championship victories and the press conference with him afterwards. So much was made of his "heroic" performance, people labeled him a hero. Schilling would have none of it. It was an inspiring performance and, sure, he was fine with that, but "heroic"? He wouldn't hear of it. Some reporter asked about being a hero and Curt Schilling said, "I am no hero. You want to see heroes? Go to Iraq, Afghanistan. Go visit the wounded troops at Walter Reed Medical Center. Talk to a veteran. Those are real heroes."

He gets it. Of course he would. His father was a veteran of the 101st Airborne. Curt grew up on military bases. Curt would very clearly grasp exactly what I was trying to do. He's lived it.

So I wrote to Bill Nowlin who has written so much on the Red Sox, saying that I thought we could propose a documentary hosted by Curt Schilling to ESPN, HBO Sports, or Fox News Channel. We wrote up a treatment and sent it to Curt. He loved it!

Bill and I flew out to Curt's home in Arizona to talk about the details. That was a great experience for both of us. Once Curt was on board he enlisted the help of his able publicist Katie Leighton to offer the idea to various media outlets. Katie had good contacts at Fox. It really wasn't all that long before we heard that Oliver North at Fox News had read our treatment and liked it. Producers Martin Hinton and Steven Tierney said they felt it was an awesome idea for an episode of *War Stories with Oliver North* and we all went to work to enlist players to contribute to the show. They all showed up. Many of the veterans in this book participated: Bob Feller was absolutely charming and simply larger than life; Johnny Pesky was a show stealer; both Ernie Harwell and Jerry Coleman were as inspiring as I knew they would be. Bill had contact information for Monte Irvin and Dom DiMaggio. Through the celebrity power of an Ollie North and the resources of Fox News such fine men like Morrie Martin and Yogi Berra contributed as well. We all filmed our own segments at different times. The *War Stories* staff and Oliver North flew to various places to conduct the interviews with the players and the program's historical advisors—Todd Anton and Bill Nowlin!

Could this be happening? It was all so surreal. But it was indeed happening.

Steven Tierney and Martin Hinton were very enthusiastic supporters of this show. Steven flew to L.A. and interviewed me at Dodger Stadium. What a thrill! How perfect to film it there, I thought. In between shots I kept looking out at centerfield, thinking somehow Dad was there because of the memories of years gone by in that beloved stadium. He was and still is there.

They filmed Bill's segment at his home in Boston. Bill was a natural and his fondness for Johnny Pesky and Ted Williams was evident. Bill has been on TV before. I haven't. I was so worried, but I guess it went okay. We never saw the roughs of the TV show; never saw any of the footage. Then came the air date—July 9, 2006—the Sunday before the All-Star Game. Commercials ran on the Fox News Channel all week. My sense of anxiety was only heightened with each commercial. What was it going to be like? Would the show adequately convey the deep sense of gratitude that I feel for these men? Would the show present these men in a light that would inspire viewers, maybe teach them something they didn't know? I hoped Americans watching would say, "I didn't know that about them or about the game" and remember just why it is America's greatest game. Would Morrie Martin be stopped in a restaurant by a passer-by and told "Thank you!"? Would somebody tell Bob Feller, "Thank God you didn't become a hog farmer!"? Would Americans see Monte Irvin as the pioneer in race relations he was and was intended to be?

I sure hoped so.

Surrounded by loved ones and friends, we all watched the show and indeed there it was on the screen. The emotion, the words, the visuals were all there for America to see. In my mind I kept thanking God for this finally happening and shot a silent prayer of thanks for Bill Nowlin and Curt Schilling. Without them it wouldn't have happened. It was an excellent television documentary.

Did I feel a sense of accomplishment?

Not really. This was never about me.

My satisfaction came when Yogi called America a "great country," and recounted his duty on rocket boats off of the coast of Utah Beach on June 6, 1944, and when Monte Irvin described a banner he saw on Omaha Beach shortly afterwards which read "Through these portals march America's finest soldiers" and when he said, "Freedom is not free." Watch the show, and you'll see. You'll see Bob Feller laughing when Oliver North asked him why he didn't become a hog farmer ... or why he gave Yogi such a hard time in 1946. You'll see Jerry Coleman being his usual understated self, explaining how the Marines ruined his baseball career, but also voicing his firm belief that his time in the Marines provided his greatest sense of accomplishment. How can you not get thrills hearing the melodic tone of Ernie Harwell explaining what was at stake for America in World War II or Dom DiMaggio saying if he hadn't served he would have regretted it to this day?

I had tears. Then came Morrie Martin. He landed on Omaha Beach on June 6, 1944. Martin suffered injuries later during the Battle of the Bulge which caused doctors to plan to amputate his infected leg. Fortunately, "an angel of a nurse" intervened at just the right moment. She urged him to refuse the operation, and to have them use penicillin. Morrie's leg was saved and he went on to become a major league pitcher.

The show covered the ground well, but of course I knew so many more stories and there's no way that any single hour of television could cover them all. If I had a criticism of the show, I guess it would be that it ended! I wish it would maybe have left the viewer with a stronger desire to learn even more. Hopefully, this book provides more, but it, too, inevitably only scratches the surface. The Morrie Martin segment touched me on a more personal level than I had expected. As I said, Morrie had landed on Omaha Beach on June 6, 1944. Dad was on Omaha Beach, too.

On June 23, 2006 I visited Omaha Beach for the first time.

Mission Accomplished

In 1945, Dad's war ended in the hills of a small French town called Spicheren. Pounding the German positions and flying missions over the nearby German city of Saarbrucken for weeks was dangerous and, as you have read, an emotional experience for Staff Sergeant Wallace P. Anton. But now the war was over. It was so quiet.

Dad hated seeing the ravages of war on children. It troubled him. For some reason, kids gravitated towards him. That never changed. However, Dad didn't speak French. So what did he do? He taught the kids baseball in the hills of Spicheren. They played "over the line" for chocolate rewards. Amid the background of destruction was heard the pop of a bat, the laughter of kids...then a few months later, it was time to go home. Dad left Europe to go home, embarking from none other than from Omaha Beach.

Shortly before Dad died, he asked me to take some of his ashes back to Europe: to Normandy and Spicheren to again "be with the boys." Some might think it odd that he asked to go to Normandy since he never saw combat there. I asked him why, when he made the request.

"Why Normandy, Dad? You weren't ever in combat there."

"Pal, it was from those beaches I went home and got my life back.

Those beaches were what led me to your mother and to all of you. I left it all behind there."

However, he left his blood in the hills of Spicheren and that carried more significance for me personally as I traveled to Europe with my best friend Morgan to fulfill my promise.

First I went to Omaha Beach. Finally I stepped on to the golden sand-colored beach whose stories had been in my mind and heart my entire life. I only focused on the water and the horizon. I tried to block out the countryside. I just wanted to get into the sea, and feel the water around me. Finally making it to the beach, I took off my shoes, grabbed a handful of Dad's ashes, and stepped into that water. I felt the tide of history engulf me. I walked as the waves splattered my shorts and jacket. I just kept looking at the water and there I let some of Dad go. It was from those shores he left to become the person I have always known him as, not a war hero, but my daddy. God, I missed him at that moment. Then I turned around and saw those hills and cliffs that our American boys had to have looked at some 62 years earlier as they landed on Omaha Beach amid sustained and deadly enemy fire. I didn't want to look at Normandy until I had the American perspective. It was awe-inspiring.

I thought I had expended all the emotion I could this day. But then I visited the American Cemetery at Colleville sur Mer. Words alone do not convey what is like to see over 9,000 white marble crosses standing in perfect lines. They beckoned me to come read the names. So I walked among "the boys" as Dad called them. Other than the day Dad died, this was the most overwhelming moment of my life. Looking at the first cross, I told myself, "Okay, I am going to remember this name forever. I even had a pen in my hand ready to write it down. What did the cross say?

UNKNOWN
Here lies an American Soldier known only to God

I wept. Then the chimes of the cemetery began to play ... "This Is My Country" and the National Anthem.

As if ordered by God, the overcast clouds parted and the sun shone on pristine white crosses—brilliantly, majestically, and powerfully. Indeed, freedom is not free. Someday go there and take a look and tell me that you are not humbled to be an American. Do it.

Like Father, Like Son

It was then time to go to Spicheren and mix Dad's ashes with the soil that held his blood and his memories. Dad's ashes are everywhere. My sister Peggy is our family's most sarcastic, joking one. She was calling my trip to Europe my "Ashes to Ashes Tour" as if I was in a rock band. We all got a laugh out of that one. But in all seriousness, this was the scene of my father's nightmares, his horrors. He longed to go back and confront those memories. He never got the chance.

But I was there....

As the assistant historian of my father's Division Association, "The 70th Infantry Division; The Trailblazers," I had many people in Spicheren aware of my visit because of e-mail messages. Spicheren was a part of Germany for years between 1871 and 1945. Many of the people there speak German. Germany lies only six minutes away across the Saar River. Since I speak German as well, it was fun to finally talk to my friends. Thomas and Dorothée Kirsch, youthful members of the Division Association living in Spicheren, were my guides and had planned something beyond my wildest dreams. As Dorothée drove Morgan and me up the hills of Spicheren Heights, I knew I was going to see the monument erected in honor of the Trailblazers. For years, this monument had been a fixture in my mind as this quest evolved. It was here that I was going to say "Good Bye"—*forever*. I didn't know what that was going to be like. Since I still had some of Dad's ashes from 2002 and hadn't fulfilled his request, his death didn't seem final. Now there would be some finality, some closure, at least for me.

I left the parked car and left Morgan and Dorothée behind me and walked towards that Trailblazer monument and reached out and touched it. Then I was surrounded by 25–35 people of Spicheren, and the Forbach City region, who came out to offer their respects to my Dad and, as they said, to me, too.

"Why me?" I asked.

They answered, "You are a part of your father. Just look at his picture. He is in your eyes…you are a son of a liberator. We honor you too. A promise fulfilled is important. You are to be commended for doing it. You are always welcome in France!"

French news media was there for an interview. Since we were waiting for my car to come, I had time for the interview. We did it in German. And then my ride came up the hill and my heart leapt and tears streamed down. It was not a BMW, it was not a Mercedes. It was a 1944 Jeep painted in the same W.W. II markings as my father's Jeep. This was my car for the day. Thomas was wearing the uniform of a Trailblazer. They even had the 70th divisional flag there. They proceeded with the ceremony. Something in French was said by local officials. We shared a moment of silence, and I spoke a few words and it was time to say goodbye and spread the ashes around the monument. As I did so, the citizens covered them with yellow and red rose pedals. It was beautiful. I thought I would be overcome with emotion. Funny I wasn't. I guess it was because I was surrounded by strangers. I'm not sure why. But it truly was beautiful.

Then I said my goodbyes to the people and Thomas, Dorothée, Morgan, and I jumped into the Jeep and saw my father's war. I felt Dad's arms around me embracing me that entire day. It seemed like such a long time since we held each other. For some reason I wasn't as emotional as I thought I was going to be. I didn't want the day to end, but it had to. We took a break from sightseeing and stopped by Thomas and Dorothée's home for some wine and snacks. As we sat in their back yard, Thomas played his Glenn Miller CD, and as the romantically powerful song "Moonlight Serenade" played, Thomas and Dorothée's ten year old son Jonas came out of the garage with a glove, a bat and a ball and said…

"Teach me baseball."

Like father, like son.

Bibliography

Ambrose, Stephen E. *Band of Brothers*. New York: Simon and Schuster, 1992.

———. *Citizen Soldiers: The U.S. Army from the Normandy Beaches to the Bulge to the Surrender of Germany*. New York: Simon and Schuster, 1997.

———. *D-Day: June 6th, 1944 The Climatic Battle of World War II*. New York: Simon and Schuster, 1994.

———. *The Supreme Commander: The War Years of Dwight D. Eisenhower*. New York: Doubleday, 1970.

———. *To America: Personal reflections of an Historian*. New York: Simon and Schuster, 2002.

———. *The Victors: Eisenhower and His Boys: The Men of World War II*. New York: Simon and Schuster, 1998.

Anton, Todd. *Distant Thunder: The 70th Infantry Division Artillery in World War II*. Victorville, California: 70th Infantry Division Assn., 2000.

Bloomfield, Gary L. *Duty, Honor, Victory: America's Athletes in World War II*. Guildford Connecticut: Lyons Press, 2003.

Bradley, James with Ron Powers. Flags of Our Fathers. New York: Bantam Books, 2000.

Brokaw, Tom. *The Greatest Generation*. New York: Random House, 1998.

Clausewitz, Carl von. *On War*. New Jersey: Princeton University Press, 1984.

Coleman, Ken and Dan Valenti. *Talking on Air: A Broadcaster's Life in Sports*. Champaign, Illinois: Sports Publishing Inc., 2000.

DiMaggio, Dom with Bill Gilbert. *Real Grass Real Heroes*. New York: Kingston Publishing Corp., 1990.

Finoli, David. *For the Good of the Country: World War II Baseball in the Major and Minor Leagues*. Jefferson, North Carolina: McFarland & Company, 2002.

Gilbert, Bill. *They Also Served Baseball and the Home Front, 1941–1945.* New York: Crown Publishing Group.

Mauldin, Bill. *Up Front.* New York: Henry Holt Company, 1945.

Nowlin, Bill and Jim Prime. *Ted Williams: The Pursuit of Perfection.* Champaign, Illinois: Sports Publishing L.L.C., 2002.

———. *The Kid: Ted Williams in San Diego.* Cambridge, Massachusettes: Rounder Books, 2005.

Keegan, Tom. *Ernie Harwell: My 60 Years in Baseball.* Chicago: Triumph Books, 2002.

Osgood, Charles. *Kilroy Was Here: The Best American Humor of World War II.* New York: Hyperion, 2001.

Ryan, Cornelus. *A Bridge Too Far.* New York: Simon and Schuster, 1974.

———. *The Longest Day: June 6, 1944.* New York: Simon and Schuster, 1959.

Williams, Ted with John Underwood. *My Turn at Bat: The Story of my Life.* New York: Simon and Schuster, 1969.

Wolter, Tim. *POW Baseball in World War II: The National Pastime Behind Barbed Wire.* Jefferson, North Carolina: McFarland & Company, 2002.

Index

Photo Credits

All photos courtesy of the author except where noted.

Front Cover
Cover photo of Jerry Coleman—courtesy of Jerry Coleman
Background photo—courtesy of National World War II Museum
    New Orleans

Back Cover
Photo on left of Lt. Bert Shepard—courtesy of Bill Swank
Photo on right of Lt. W.P. Anton in Korea—Author's collection
Baseballs—Author's collection